# ISAIAH

◆

ISAIAH

# ISAIAH

◆

**H. A. IRONSIDE**

Revised Edition

Introductory Notes by
**Arno C. Gaebelein**

**LOIZEAUX**
Neptune, New Jersey

First Edition, 1952
Revised Edition, 2000

ISAIAH
© 2000 by Loizeaux Brothers, Inc.

A Publication of Loizeaux Brothers, Inc.,
*A Nonprofit Organization Devoted to the Lord's Work
and to the Spread of His Truth*

Introductory Notes taken from
*Gaebelein's Concise Commentary on the Whole Bible*
© 1970, 1985 by Loizeaux Brothers, Inc.

Library of Congress Cataloging-in-Publication Data

Ironside, H. A. (Henry Allan), 1876-1951.
Isaiah/H.A. Ironside; introductory notes by Arno C. Gaebelein.–Rev. ed.
p. cm.
Rev. ed. of: Expository notes on the prophet Isaiah.
ISBN 0-87213-433-4 (pbk.: alk. paper)
1. Bible. O.T. Isaiah–Commentaries. I. Ironside, H. A. (Henry Allan),
1876-1951.
Expository notes on the prophet Isaiah. II. Gaebelein, Arno Clemens,
1861-1945–III. Title.

BS1515.3 .I76 2000
224'.1077–dc21

99-059334

Printed in the United States of America
10  9  8  7  6  5  4  3  2  1

# CONTENTS

# INTRODUCTORY NOTES

## BY ARNO C. GAEBELEIN

### *The Author and His Times*

The opening verse of this great book gives us information concerning the prophet Isaiah and the period covered by his official ministry: "The vision of Isaiah the son of Amoz, which he saw concerning Judah and Jerusalem in the days of Uzziah, Jotham, Ahaz, and Hezekiah, kings of Judah."

Of Isaiah's personal history we know but little. Jewish tradition claims that he was related to King Uzziah. That the prophet must have come from a prominent family may be gathered from the fact that he had ready access into the presence of Ahaz and Hezekiah, and probably also the other kings of Judah. That Isaiah was married we learn from his book. He had two sons who bore prophetic names. One was named *Shear-jashub* ("a remnant shall return"), prophetically indicating that God would leave a remnant of His people. The name of the other was *Maher-shalal-Hashbaz* ("hasting to the spoil, hurrying to the prey"), which was prophetic of the threatening invasion by Assyria.

Nothing else is said of Isaiah's personal history in the book that bears his name, nor do we find anything about his death. There is a trustworthy tradition that because he reproved the vices and idolatries rampant during the reign of the wicked king Manasseh, Isaiah suffered martyrdom by being "sawn asunder," and if this is true, Hebrews 11:37 applies to him. Josephus wrote of the cruel persecutions under the reign of Manasseh in the following words: "He barbarously slew all the righteous men that were among the Hebrews;

nor would he spare the prophets, for he every day slew some of them, till Jerusalem was overflowed with blood."

Isaiah must have lived to a very old age, for it is quite certain that he exercised his God-given office for seventy years during the eighth century before Christ. The prophet's home was in Jerusalem, the capital of the southern kingdom of Judah, and from there he witnessed the calamity that befell the northern kingdom of Israel. The glory had departed from both Israel and Judah, but because of Israel's gross idolatries God's righteous judgment fell on them first, and the ten northern tribes were carried into captivity by the Assyrians.

Isaiah began his ministry under the reign of the good king Uzziah and had his remarkable vision, which is recorded in chapter 6, in the year Uzziah died. Uzziah's son Jotham, who reigned in his stead, did not trouble himself about the corruption and idol worship rampant in his nation. It was during his tenure that the dissolution of the great Assyrian monarchy took place. Jotham was succeeded by the ungodly Ahaz, whose reign was marked by disaster. His son Hezekiah, who proved to be the very opposite of his wicked father, was one of the most godly of the kings who occupied the throne of David. A large portion of the prophecies of Isaiah up to chapter 39 are occupied with events that took place during the reigns of these kings and can only be rightly understood in the light of the history of Judah during that period.

### The Message of Isaiah

Isaiah's name means "Jehovah saves" or "Jehovah is salvation," and he has well been called the evangelical prophet. In the New Testament there are more direct quotations from, as well as allusions to his book than any other prophetic book. The early church held Isaiah in high esteem, and all the great men of God down through the centuries have acknowledged the importance of his book and its message. First Peter 1:11 describes the contents of the writings of the prophets as "the sufferings of Christ, and the glory that should follow" and this is more true of Isaiah than of any of the other prophetic books except the Psalms.

Isaiah's message reveals the Redeemer and King of Israel, and he refers to Him by the title, the "Holy One of Israel," twenty-five times. The prophet announced His virgin birth; revealed many of His titles; described Him in His lowliness, His tenderness, and His miracles; and presented Him as the servant of Jehovah. Above all else, he depicted Him as the sin bearer in his wonderful fifty-third chapter. Isaiah also pictured in prophetic vision the kingdom that is yet to come with the return of our Savior-Lord in glory, and predicted future blessings for Israel, Jerusalem, and the nations.

Isaiah was but the mouthpiece of Jehovah; he wrote under the guidance and direction of the Holy Spirit as He moved him and put words into his pen. Though wide in scope, the book of Isaiah is an organic whole. It can be divided into two main sections: chapters 1–35, which contain the earlier prophecies; and chapters 40–66, which contain the later prophecies. Between these two sections is a historical parenthesis as it were (chapters 36–39). In the earlier prophecies judgments on Jerusalem, Judah, and other nations are announced. While blessings of the future are also given, they take a secondary place. In the later prophecies we likewise read of judgments, but the major portion of those chapters reveals the glories and blessings of the future.

In the earlier prophecies, the Assyrian invasion is announced and at the same time a forecast is given of an invasion from the north in the time of the end. In the later prophecies the Assyrian is no longer mentioned. The Babylonian captivity announced in chapter 39 is seen by the prophet as past and he predicts the return of some of the captives to Judah. Beyond that, he foretells the return of a remnant from the greater dispersion and the final glory of the kingdom with the coming of the King.

# OUTLINE
## OF THE BOOK OF ISAIAH

I. ISAIAH'S EARLY PROPHETIC MINISTRY (1:1–35:10)
   A. Vision concerning Judah (1:1–5:30)
   B. Call for Service (6:1-13)
   C. Messianic Prophecies (7:1–12:6)
   D. Burdens regarding Israel's Enemies (13:1–23:18)
   E. Judgment on the Earth (24:1-23)
   F. Songs of Salvation (25:1–27:13)
   G. Six Woes (28:1–33:24)
   H. The Lord's Vengeance (34:1–35:10)

II. HISTORICAL INTERLUDE (36:1–39:8)

III. ISAIAH'S LATER PROPHETIC MINISTRY (40:1–66:24)
   A. God's Controversies with Israel (40:1–57:21)
      1. Over Their Worship of Idols (40:1–48:22)
      2. Over Their Treatment of Messiah (49:1–57:21)
   B. Visions of Coming Glory (58:1–66:24)

# FOREWORD
## TO THE FIRST EDITION

(WRITTEN BY MRS. H. A. IRONSIDE)

In December 1949 Dr. Ironside gave lectures on the book of Isaiah at Dallas Theological Seminary. One of the students, Ray C. Stedman, made wire recordings of the classroom lectures.

Mr. Stedman also did a great deal of secretarial work for Dr. Ironside during his stay at the seminary. He was so efficient and helpful that my husband asked him if he would be willing to travel with us during the summer and help with the writing of his exposition of the book of Isaiah, which had long been delayed on account of his failing sight.

Mr. Stedman joined us in June 1950 after his graduation from the seminary and for two months served as chauffeur, secretary, and companion. As a "brother beloved" he was so helpful in all the varied activities of the itinerant ministry that we came to love him as a son. Without his help and cooperation the publication of Dr. Ironside's *Isaiah* would have been impossible.

Traveling constantly, Dr. Ironside carried with him a reference library consisting of W. E. Vine's *Isaiah—Prophecies, Promises, and Warnings;* F. C. Jennings' *Isaiah;* a one-volume Bible encyclopedia; and J. N. Darby's *New Translation of the Holy Scriptures.*

As Dr. Ironside was unable to read at all during this time, except with the aid of a powerful magnifying glass, his method of working under this handicap may be of interest. Mr. Stedman wrote:

> In general our procedure was as follows: I would read to him the portion chosen for comment, out of the Authorized Version—a portion which had previously been read to him and

13

over which he had been meditating. He would take a moment or two to gather his thoughts and then would begin dictating, seldom pausing for rephrasing or changes. I would then read the next section and he would dictate on that until an entire chapter had been covered. After that I would read through the next chapter, usually from Darby's "New Translation" and also the corresponding portion from Jennings and Vine. This would form the basis for his meditation in preparation for the next day's dictation.

Occasionally we would discuss interesting sections of the chapters together and he would ask me to look up certain words in a one-volume Bible encyclopedia he carried. I was always amazed at the way he kept his comments from simply being a "rehash" of Vine and Jennings, but always managed to bring out some interesting sidelight which the others had overlooked.

When Mr. Stedman left us to go to the pastorate of the Peninsula Bible Fellowship at Palo Alto, California, the first thirty-five chapters of Isaiah were completed and typed.

After the operation on Dr. Ironside's eyes in September 1950, which entirely restored his sight, he edited the manuscript and left it with Loizeaux Brothers before our departure for New Zealand. Chapters 35–39 were written by Dr. Ironside in his characteristic scrawl during December 1950 and I copied them in longhand, for I was his only secretary on the trip.

When he went to be with the Lord from Rotorna, New Zealand, on January 15, 1951, he had only completed chapter 39. As to chapters 40–66, Ray Stedman wrote:

I had taken them on wire recordings at the time of his lectures in Dallas. Unfortunately, I did not have enough wire to take the whole series. I did record the early chapters, too, but had to wipe them off and use that same wire for the later chapters, which I saved. Upon the request of one of the students, I copied off on Soundscriber discs the entire series from chapter 40 on. It was these discs which were sent Loizeaux Brothers for transcription....It certainly was the hand of the Lord that I should have retained the lectures beginning with the very one where Dr. Ironside left off and that they should be on Soundscriber discs, ready for immediate transcription. The wire originals are a precious heritage to me, and have already proven of wide blessing wherever they have been played.

Chapters 40–66, after having been transcribed from the Soundscriber discs, have been edited by Miss Emily Farmer, who edited in the past most of Dr. Ironside's manuscripts when his works were being prepared for publication. We are most grateful for her careful and efficient work as unto the Lord. (She edited *Isaiah* while she was confined to bed.)

It has been a joy to each of us to have a part in the publication of this book. May God continue to bless the written ministry of "H.A.I.," who, being dead, yet speaketh.

ANN HIGHTOWER IRONSIDE

# AUTHOR'S INTRODUCTION

The book of Isaiah is a portion of God's Holy Word in which spiritually minded believers find much to exercise their hearts and encourage their glad anticipation of the coming day when Immanuel will take His great power and reign.

Longer than any other prophetic book, Isaiah contains the fullest Messianic predictions to be found in the Old Testament, testifying in no uncertain way to "the sufferings of Christ, and the glory that should follow" (1 Peter 1:11).

Like all other books of the Bible, Isaiah has suffered much at the hands of unbelieving and haughty critics who have done their best to undermine the faith of the simple in the integrity and unity of the Bible. But for those who have faith, all doubts are settled by the Lord Jesus, who when here on earth placed the seal of His divine approval on the prophecy in its entirety. After the ascension of the Savior, the apostles drew from this book again and again in their ministry, all by the direct guidance of the Holy Spirit, thus giving the prophecy a place of unquestionable authority as the very word of Jehovah.

According to Jewish tradition, Isaiah was a man of wealth, rank, and learning. He is supposed to be the one referred to in Hebrews 11:37 as having been "sawn asunder" by the enraged rejecters of his prophetic ministry. If this be so, the execution occurred at the close of a long and honored life, for his public service extended over at least half a century. As he told us in his opening verse, he prophesied "in the days of Uzziah, Jotham, Ahaz, and Hezekiah." In all likelihood he did not appear in the prophetic office until the last year of Uzziah's long reign (Isaiah 6:1).

Chapter 6 records his divine commission, and it is questionable that he had written the previous chapters before he had the vision "in the year that King Uzziah died"—not necessarily after Uzziah died, but in the same year as that solemn event. We know Isaiah continued to proclaim the word of the Lord after the fourteenth year of Hezekiah's reign, for it was then that the prophet was commissioned to make known to the stricken monarch that fifteen years were to be added to his life.

Isaiah was therefore contemporary with Hosea and possibly for a very brief season with Amos. However, it is more likely that the herdsman-prophet had passed off the scene before Isaiah began to make known the mind of God. Micah also held the prophetic office during the reigns of the last three kings mentioned. So Isaiah would have been the chief among a goodly little company to whom the secrets of the Lord were revealed in a day when formalism and hypocrisy largely prevailed.

That there was but one Isaiah, not two, is evident from the testimony given by the inspired writer of the Gospel of Luke. He told us that on the occasion of the Lord's first public visit to the synagogue at Nazareth "there was delivered unto him the book of the prophet Esaias [Isaiah]" and from it He preached His gospel of "deliverance to the captives" and "the acceptable year of the Lord" (Luke 4:17-19). Thus the Lord cited the glorious predictions of Isaiah 61:1-2 as inspired Scripture written by Isaiah, not as the writing of an unknown poet of the Maccabean or later period.

The book of Isaiah as it stands bears every evidence of having been preserved in its divinely arranged order. Only unbelieving ignorance coupled with amazing egotism could lead anyone to want to rearrange it and dissect it in the manner of "modern" critics such as George Adam Smith. His *Isaiah* in The Expositor's Bible Series is the most commonly known specimen of virtual denial of inspiration. Smith's book is a biased attempt to destroy the true prophetic character of the Messianic portions of this magnificent prophecy.

Unbelief finds difficulties where faith bows with adoring reverence. As I write not for skeptics, but for those who truly know the Christ whose sufferings and glories Isaiah foretold, I will pay but slight attention to the objections of those unbelieving natural men, albeit distinguished in the world of letters and in the Christless religious circles of the day.

Many professing Christians pay little or no attention to the prophetic word, but in neglecting that which forms so large a part of the Holy Scriptures, they wrong their own souls and dishonor Him who gave His Word for our edification and comfort. The real value of prophecy is that it occupies us with a person, not merely with events. That person is our Lord Jesus Christ, who came once to suffer and is coming again to reign. Isaiah wrote of both these advents, and in a way more plain and full than that of any of the other Old Testament seers.

Prophecy is not simply the foretelling of future events; it is also the *forth-telling* of the mind of God for the moment. When both the priesthood and the monarchy had failed completely in Israel and Judah, God continued to minister to His people through the prophets. These were men to whom special insight was given into holy things, and who were sent by God to call an erring people to repentance. It was the responsibility of the prophets not only to inform the people of the coming glories of Messiah's day, but also to impress upon them the necessity of preparing the way of the Lord. The people could prepare the way by turning from sin to righteousness, and by turning from their idolatrous vanities to the living God, who had so wonderfully manifested His power on their behalf throughout Israel's history.

There are many things in the writings of Isaiah that are perhaps beyond our present comprehension, even as they were beyond the comprehension of the writer himself. Like the other prophets, Isaiah wrote at the command of the Lord and searched the Scriptures then available when he testified beforehand concerning the sufferings of Christ and the glories that would follow. The portions of Isaiah that deal with the sufferings of Christ at the time of His first advent have become amazingly clear in the light of the New Testament Gospels. The portions that have to do with the glories that will follow at His second advent, while linked with all prophecy concerning that glorious advent, will never be fully understood until the day of fulfillment arrives. Even though at times we may seem to see through a glass darkly as we study this book, we may be assured of real blessing as we weigh carefully before God that which He commissioned Isaiah to proclaim.

Those who are interested in the curious things of Scripture have noticed that the book of Isaiah in one sense comprises a miniature Bible. The Bible consists of sixty-six books; Isaiah has sixty-six chapters. The Bible is divided into two Testaments, Old and New; Isaiah is divided into two parts, the first having to do largely with Israel's past condition and the promise of Messiah's coming, and the second dealing particularly with their future deliverance. The Old Testament has thirty-nine books; the first part of Isaiah has thirty-nine chapters. The New Testament has twenty-seven books; the second part of Isaiah has twenty-seven chapters. This of course is a mere coincidence because it was not the Spirit of God, but human editors who divided the book in this way. Nevertheless it is interesting and quite suggestive when we realize that Isaiah deals in a very definite way with that which is the outstanding theme of all the Scriptures: God's salvation as revealed in His blessed Son.

The first part of Isaiah can be divided into two sections, the first consisting of chapters 1–35 and the second consisting of chapters 36–39. If, for the purpose of structural analysis, we make each of these sections a separate part, we can think of the prophecy as being divided into three parts: (1) chapters 1–35; (2) chapters 36-39; (3) chapters 40–66.

The first of these three parts is an orderly, connected series of messages evidently uttered by Isaiah before the illness of Hezekiah. The messages minister chiefly to the consciences of Israel and Judah. The people are warned of suffering under God's hand of judgment, and they are promised blessing in connection with Messiah's coming.

The second part, though of a prophetical and typical character, is historical, showing how all blessing for Judah is bound up with a Son of David who will go down to death but be raised up by omnipotent power. Isaiah 36–39 is almost identical to 2 Kings 18:13–20:19 and the main points of 2 Chronicles 32. Isaiah himself doubtless was the recorder of the portion of the book of Kings written during his ministry, and by divine direction he introduced the passage specified into the book bearing his name.

The third part of Isaiah concludes the prophecy by setting forth the utter failure of the first man and the arrival of the Second, the Lord from Heaven. Israel, shown to be unfaithful in every particular as a servant of God, is set aside so that the true Servant, the Elect of Jehovah, may be manifested.

Prophecy does not go beyond this earth; its scope is only "as long as the sun and moon endure" (Psalm 72:5). But we know from later revelation that the eternal Son of the Father will be the One in whom all the fullness of the godhead will be displayed forever. Through the true Servant, all God's counsels will stand and God's glory will be established.

With these preliminary thoughts before us, let us turn to the consideration of the book itself, assured that we will find it, like all other Scriptures, profitable for teaching, reproof, correction, and instruction in righteousness (2 Timothy 3:16).

# THE CALL TO HEAR

*Isaiah 1:1-6*

Abruptly the voice of the Lord broke in upon the ears of men who prided themselves on their religiousness and trusted in their formal observance of the legal ritual: "Hear, O heavens, and give ear, O earth: for the Lord hath spoken, I have nourished and brought up children, and they have rebelled against me." There is something sublime in the very simplicity of this challenge to obedience. Heaven and earth, ever subject to His will, were called to witness the base ingratitude of Jehovah's people. The objects of His solicitous care from their childhood in Egypt, they had never as a nation given Him the loving obedience that was His due. Individual faithfulness there was; but nationally, as later in the case of the church viewed as a collective body, failure had come in almost at the very beginning and there had never been recovery.

"The ox knoweth his owner, and the ass his master's crib" because of his care for them, but Israel did not know their Master. May we not well challenge our hearts as to how far *we* really know our Owner? To what extent do we sanctify Christ as Lord? Other lords have had dominion over us, but He is our Owner now. Only by Him will we now make mention of the ineffable name. The kingdom of God for us is that of the Son of His love. To the crucified One we owe unswerving allegiance.

Our Master's crib is the Word of God, a part of which we now have before us. Do we really *know* it? Does hunger ever drive us to it? Or are we often found foolishly sniffing the desert air, following the wind like the wild ass? Have we turned our backs on God's well-filled storehouse, vainly seeking a satisfactory portion in the world we have professed to repudiate? These are solemn questions, not to be evaded or ignored. They are to be faced in the presence of the Lord lest a day come when of us too He will have to say, "Ah sinful nation, a people laden with iniquity, a seed of evildoers, children that are corrupters: they have forsaken the Lord, they have provoked the Holy One of Israel unto anger, they are gone away backward."

There is no breach of relationship suggested here. Judah was still owned by God, but her moral state demanded discipline. Yet she had despised that discipline until it seemed useless to chasten her further. The sore seemed too deep to be healed; the whole head was sick and the heart faint. Everywhere the evidences of inward corruption were obvious. There was no soundness in Judah. Their hearts had not turned to God so that He who had smitten might bind them up in His grace and longsuffering.

### Isaiah 1:7-20

Prophetically, Isaiah beheld the sad result of all this coldhearted indifference to the message he brought. The country was soon to be desolate and the fair cities of Judah were to be destroyed by conflagration. Strangers would dwell in their land and only a feeble remnant would be left—like a workman's hut in a vineyard or a keeper's lodge in a cucumber field. The prophet spoke in the present tense of things not yet seen, for faith's eye can see all that God has declared as though it has already been fulfilled.

Isaiah prophesied, "Except the Lord of hosts had left unto us a very small remnant, we should have been as Sodom, and we should have been like unto Gomorrah." Those significant words were quoted by the apostle Paul in Romans 9:29. Only that remnant could be acknowledged by God, but because of it, He would not utterly cast off His people. We will observe that throughout the balance of the book of Isaiah, the remnant is given the place of the nation.

The rest of the people were already rejected as "children in whom is no pleasure." In Isaiah 1:10-20 it is this evil majority who were addressed by God, but He did not acknowledge any relationship with them. Comparing them to Sodom and Gomorrah, He called them to repentance. Rulers and people alike were evil and in their unholy state they had no right to approach Him. For such unregenerate people to offer sacrifices was to mock and insult His holiness. God found no delight in their offerings, nor could He complacently behold them treading His courts.

What a scathing rebuke of anyone who professes to draw near to God by sacramental observances while not born of His Spirit and while not broken before Him! Ritualism is an offense; religious exercises are filthy in His sight if the participants have not recognized their guilt and their need of the atonement whereby iniquity may be purged. From all Judah's solemn feasts and sacred seasons, Jehovah turned away in disgust. He said He would hide His face and close His ears to their prayers, for the proof of their defiled condition was in their hands.

What was needed? The application of the Word of God to heart and conscience. Such obedience would be evidence of genuine faith and would result in purged ways and clean lives. "Wash you, make you clean," He cried. "Put away the evil of your doings from before mine eyes; cease to do evil; Learn to do well; seek judgment, relieve the oppressed, judge the fatherless, plead for the widow. Come now, and let us reason together, saith the Lord."

Observe the order here. There is no promise of gospel blessing until the Word of God be bowed to. Grace is not contingent on works, nor is salvation dependent on human effort or advancement in righteousness, but God has no blessing in either time or eternity for the man who persists in sin and refuses to judge himself in the light of His revealed Word. Where faith is truly present, there will be contrition for sin, and amendment of conduct will follow inevitably.

It is to the self-judged therefore that the glorious Word comes in power: "Come now, and let us reason together, saith the Lord: though your sins be as scarlet, they shall be as white as snow; though they be red like crimson, they shall be as wool." No more blessed proclamation of full amnesty is found in the Bible. In this verse is the offer of full judicial cleansing for every repentant soul, no matter how grievous his record may have been. Well may Isaiah be called the evangelical prophet. A wondrous gospel pervades all his pages, though warnings of judgment are constant.

Once cleansed and forgiven, the delivered soul is called to tread the path of obedience and subjection to the One who has justified him from all things. Dispensationally, justification had to await the revelation of the glorious gospel announced in New Testament times, but every soul in every age who heard the Word in faith was cleared of every charge.

The obedience and reward here indicated were of a decidedly legal character, befitting the age of law: "If ye be willing and obedient, ye shall eat the good of the land." In this age of grace there is a land unknown to sight, but seen and enjoyed by faith; through the Spirit's gracious ministry, each subject soul eats the good fruits of that land in abundance.

On the other hand, when the Word of life and blessing is refused, and in place of contrition and brokenness a rebellious spirit is displayed, the sword must devour the gainsayer. In Isaiah the sword is that of a human enemy; in the New Testament the instrument of destruction is more clearly identified as the sword of divine judgment.

Isaiah 1:7-20 is a deeply instructive passage; every reader should weigh it carefully in the light of eternity, "for the mouth of the Lord hath spoken it." As Ecclesiastes 12:14 says, "God shall bring every work into judgment, with every secret thing, whether it be good, or whether it be evil."

### Isaiah 1:21-31

This passage has in view Jerusalem, once "the faithful city," but now corrupt and adulterous. Isaiah saw the city as the exemplification of all the evils that afflicted the land, and in dirge-like measure he bewailed its fallen state. But the Spirit of grace still distinguished a remnant, so the prophet sang of both mercy and judgment.

The city in whose devotedness Jehovah had once found such delight, the city that had once borne the name of the holy, had become a harlot, following after other lovers who could not save. Once full of discretion and the home of righteousness, Jerusalem had become a lodging place for murderers. Her silver (which spoke of atonement—see Exodus 30:11-16) had been replaced by the dross of complacent self-sufficiency. Her wine of joy had been diluted with the foul water of earth's broken cisterns. The leaders of the people, who should have set an example of subjection to the Word of God, were now rebellious bribe-lovers. Righteous judgment was forgotten in the wake of the base desire for gain.

Because of all this, the Lord Himself would awake to judgment and would pour out His vengeance on those who, though posing as His friends, were in reality at enmity with Him. But unmixed judgment it could not be, for the rebels in Judah were His covenant people still and He would correct in measure. His discipline would have the effect of removing the unjust and unholy. After purging the nation from its dross, sin, and all that was base and unpleasing to God, He would restore their judges and counselors. Then, "redeemed with judgment," Zion would once more be called "the city of righteousness, the faithful city." Other Scripture passages show us that this will be their final blessing after the long years of dispersion and the bitterness of the last great tribulation have come to an end.

Isaiah foresaw that the suffering would continue until the unrepentant transgressors and willful sinners were utterly destroyed. Those that remained—a weak but faithful remnant—would loathe themselves for their past sins and be ashamed of the many false gods who had allured them as a nation away from the God of their fathers. We see this spirit beautifully exemplified in Ezra 9, Nehemiah 9, and Daniel 9 (three ninth chapters in three "remnant" books), where faithful men confess their people's sin as their own sin, but from it turn with abhorrence to seek the Lord with all their hearts.

Isaiah warned that all who did not repent would be consumed together by the fierce anger of Jehovah. They would be like a withered oak, a waterless garden, and tow that would burn when the Lord applied a spark.

Isaiah 1:21-31 was not written for the Jew alone. The passage was also written for our admonition in this age. The failure of the professing church has been even greater than that of Jerusalem because we have sinned against greater light. Soon the Holy and the True, disgusted with such corruption, will vomit out of His mouth all that is unreal and opposed to His Word. But He stands knocking at the door, and whenever there is reality and a heart devoted to Himself, He will come in and dine there in hallowed, blest communion, though the doom of guilty Christendom is so near (Revelation 3:20).

# ISAIAH 2
# ZION'S FUTURE GLORY

I saiah 2–5 is a connected discourse, a soul-stirring message addressed to Judah and Jerusalem at a time unspecified. The parable of the vineyard in chapter 5 is a lovely yet solemn epitome of it all and is really the prophet's text. That which precedes the parable is introductory and that which follows is a fitting conclusion, pronouncing the woes of the Lord upon the vine that only brought forth wild grapes.

## Isaiah 2:1-5

Isaiah 2:2-4 is almost identical to Micah 4:1-3. There is no need to suppose plagiarism or a scribe's blunder in transferring the words of one prophet to the book of another. Rather the similarity is a blessed evidence that the same Spirit inspired both speakers or writers. The double testimony is added assurance that the thing spoken cannot fail.

These verses tell in language too plain to be misunderstood that in the last days God will restore His ancient people Israel to their land and make Jerusalem His throne-city, from which His laws will go forth to the ends of the earth. Isaiah foresaw "that the mountain of the Lord's house shall be established in the top of the mountains, and shall be exalted above the hills." Mountains are a common prophetic symbol signifying governments and throne-cities, and the mountain in Isaiah 2:2 is the city of Jerusalem.

Jerusalem will be "the city of the great King" (Psalm 48:2) and "all nations shall flow unto it." This will be fulfilled literally in the coming age after God's present work of grace has come to an end. He is now, as James pointed out in Acts 15:14, visiting the Gentiles "to take out of them a people for his name." But when this special work is completed, He will "build again the tabernacle of David" (Acts 15:16) and through restored Israel bless all the nations.

Then will be the time spoken of by Isaiah, when "many people shall go and say, Come ye, and let us go up to the mountain of the Lord, to the house of the God of Jacob; and he will teach us of his ways, and we will walk in his paths: for out of Zion shall go forth the law, and the word of the Lord from Jerusalem." In that day of His power He will rule all the nations with equity and put down every opposing thing.

It is not in this dispensation that Israel will thus be saved and, through them, the nations brought under Immanuel's sway. Therefore those who expect to see all wars ended and righteousness everywhere established in this age are doomed to bitter disappointment. It is not now while the King is sitting as the earth's rejected One upon His Father's throne that the nations "shall beat their swords into plowshares, and their spears into pruninghooks." But when He returns to this world and takes the throne of His father David, then "nation shall not lift up sword against nation, neither shall they learn war any more."

It was in view of this glorious fulfillment of Israel's Messianic hopes that the exhortation of verse 5 was delivered: "O house of Jacob, come ye, and let us walk in the light of the Lord." The house of Jacob, so long blinded because of their rejection of Christ when He came the first time, will then have their eyes opened to see the light that has been hidden from them.

### Isaiah 2:6-22

It is very evident that the verses we have just been considering (2:1-5) are parenthetical, for there is no apparent connection between 2:1-5 and 2:6. But if read immediately after 1:31, 2:6 fits perfectly.

Wealth and luxury will not avail to avert the wretchedness that is to be the portion of all who forsake the Lord and turn aside to false gods. Such gods are powerless to deliver those who put their trust in them.

In 2:10-22 the prophet spoke of the day of the Lord, when God will arise in His might and indignation to deal with wickedness and corruption wherever they are found. As in the judgment of the sixth seal, men will seek to hide themselves "in the dens and in the rocks of the mountains" (Revelation 6:15). But their hope of escaping the fierce anger of the Lord will be in vain, for "the lofty looks of man shall be humbled, and the haughtiness of men shall be bowed down, and the Lord alone shall be exalted in that day."

The day of the Lord is in contrast to the day of man, which is this present evil age when God is permitting men to take their own way, try out their own plans, and be independent of His authority. In the coming day of the Lord, high and low, rich and poor, learned and ignorant, all alike will be "brought low" before the God they have defied or forgotten.

That judgment will be like a tremendous storm or forest fire sweeping over the mountains of Lebanon, devouring the great cedars and oaks as well as the lesser trees, then reaching down the mountain slopes and consuming farmhouses and villages, and even spreading across the plains to the shipping ports, where all the ships of Tarshish and all objects of art would be destroyed. Judgment will come, for God has decreed that "the loftiness of man shall be bowed down, and the haughtiness of men shall be made low: and the Lord alone shall be exalted in that day." All that men have put in the place of God will be abolished. In their terror men will "go into the holes of the rocks, and into the caves of the earth," hoping to find shelter from the wrath of an offended God.

Casting away all in which they have futilely trusted, men will find themselves bereft of all confidence. They will seek refuge in vain in the most inaccessible places as they endeavor to flee from the majestic glory of Jehovah "when he ariseth to shake terribly the earth." Such will be the end of man's boasted civilization, the end of his effort to make this world a place of rest and security while ignoring the claims of Him who created all things for His own glory.

And so the passage closes with a solemn admonition: "Cease ye from man, whose breath is in his nostrils: for wherein is he to be accounted of?"

# ISAIAH 3

# JUDAH'S FALLEN CONDITION

*Isaiah 3:1-15*

Isaiah 3 continues along the same line as Isaiah 2 and makes it very definitely clear that it is Jerusalem and Judah which God has in view above all others when He speaks of coming desolation and unsparing judgment. The covenant people and the one-time holy city had strayed so far from the path of obedience that God Himself prepared them for the vengeance decreed by weakening their means of defense. "Children" were their princes and "babes" ruled over them. Their leaders, in other words, were like infants unable to control themselves, much less guide others aright. So disorder and confusion prevailed in place of orderly government. When God is dethroned, anarchy always results.

In their desperation, men were ready to follow anyone who might seem to be able to point out a way of escape from the present misery and might promise to bring order out of the chaotic conditions prevailing. But those to whom men turned for guidance were in utter bewilderment themselves and so refused to take the responsibility of seeking to rectify the abuses that were affecting the nation so adversely.

The root cause of all the trouble is indicated in 3:8: "Jerusalem is ruined, and Judah is fallen: because their tongue and their doings are against the Lord, to provoke the eyes of his glory." The people had brought down judgment on their own heads and therefore solemn woes were pronounced against them: two in Isaiah 3 (3:9,11) and six in Isaiah 5 (5:8,11,18,20,21,22).

In 3:9 we read, "Woe unto their soul! for they have rewarded evil unto themselves," and in 3:11, "Woe unto the wicked! it shall be ill with him: for the reward of his hands shall be given him." As for the righteous remnant, God will care for them and protect them in the day of storm and stress.

Alas, the great majority of the people were oblivious to their danger and were content to go on with children as their oppressors and women ruling over them. Such weak and powerless leadership could not lift them above the existing confusion.

The psalmist had prayed, "Enter not into judgment with thy servant: for in thy sight shall no man living be justified" (Psalm 143:2), but now there was no one to plead for the guilty leaders in Judah. Instead the Lord Himself stood up to plead against them and to judge them. Because of the way they had misled His people and abused their confidence, He would hold them accountable for all their waywardness.

### Isaiah 3:16-26

The vain women who had given themselves to folly were also sternly rebuked. In their pride and empty-headedness, their one great concern had been personal adornment. They sought to add to their beauty by using every device known to women of fashion, but God was about to smite them with sore diseases that would so disfigure them that they would be loathed by their former admirers.

If it seems strange to us that God took note of all the ornaments and apparel that the women relied on to make themselves attractive, we need to remember that in the New Testament careful instruction is given to women regarding their "adorning" (1 Peter 3:3-4). It is to be not "that outward adorning of plaiting the hair, and of wearing of gold, or of putting on of apparel," but the adorning of the heart with "the ornament of a meek and quiet spirit." Christian women would do well to pay close attention to that which the Bible says is becoming to women professing godliness. Pride and vanity—in men or women—are hateful to God and in due time must be dealt with by Him in judgment if there is no repentance.

# ISAIAH 4

# WHEN THE LORD RETURNS TO ZION

Isaiah 4, though very brief, depicts conditions that were to prevail not only in the days following the threatened Babylonian captivity, but also in the dark days of the great tribulation, for Isaiah looked far beyond his own age to days yet to come. Often in times of prolonged warfare, women far outnumber the men, and Isaiah prophesied that "in that day seven women shall take hold of one man" and seek to claim him as their husband in order to take away their reproach. Such polygamous solutions to the problem of the shortage of men were suggested by some people following both world wars.

Isaiah also foresaw that when times were darkened, deliverance would come through the Branch of the Lord, the promised Messiah of Israel, the loveliest of the sons of men. Those left in Zion and remaining in Jerusalem would be the special objects of His favor and would be set apart to the Lord. He would wash away their filth in His own blood and cleanse their hearts with "the spirit of burning" in accordance with the promises made through many other prophets.

Then mount Zion and Jerusalem would become a center of blessing to the whole earth. The glory of the Lord that once was seen over the sanctuary would be as a cloudy pillar over all the homes of the redeemed city. The pillar would be for defense as well as glory. "And there shall be a tabernacle for a shadow in the daytime from the heat, and for a place of refuge, and for a covert from storm and from rain." Thus like Israel in the wilderness so long ago, the restored nation would be under Jehovah's gracious care when He had cleansed them from their iniquities and turned their hearts back to Himself.

# THE PARABLE OF THE VINEYARD

I saiah 5 completes the prophet's address that began in chapter 2. As noted before, the parable of the vineyard is the epitome of that message.

### *Isaiah 5:1-7*

In the parable God rehearsed His ways with Israel and emphasized their lack of response to His love and patience. This "song of the vineyard" links intimately with our Lord's parable concerning the same subject, which He presented to the scribes and Pharisees shortly before His arrest and crucifixion.

We might well refer to Isaiah 5:1-7 as the vineyard poem because the words of the prophet's song are graphic and touching. God of course was the real speaker. When He said, "My wellbeloved hath a vineyard in a very fruitful hill," He was speaking of His own blessed Son, who is the Messiah of Israel as well as the Savior of the world.

The vineyard represents Israel as God viewed them at the beginning of their Palestinian history. Having brought them out of Egypt, He planted them in the land of promise and there cared for them and protected them from the ravages of their enemies. He "fenced [His vineyard], and gathered out the stones thereof, and planted it with the choicest vine, and built a tower in the midst of it, and also made a winepress therein." But the vineyard produced no fruit suitable to His holy desires. "He looked that it should bring forth grapes, and it brought forth wild grapes." Instead of bearing fruit for God,

Israel brought forth that which grieved His heart and dishonored His holy name.

And so, addressing Himself directly to the inhabitants of Jerusalem and the men of Judah, He asked, "Judge, I pray you, betwixt me and my vineyard. What could have been done more to my vineyard, that I have not done in it? wherefore, when I looked that it should bring forth grapes, brought it forth wild grapes?" After all the care He had lavished upon Israel—His loving provision for their needs, His gracious forgiveness extended to them over and over again when they failed—how could it be possible that there would be no suitable fruit for Him? Why should they produce only that which was worthless and useless? Their fruit was unsatisfactory because their hearts had departed from the living God.

After giving His people one opportunity after another to repent and judge themselves in His sight, He finally decided to give them up. He said, "I will tell you what I will do to my vineyard: I will take away the hedge thereof, and it shall be eaten up; and break down the wall thereof, and it shall be trodden down: And I will lay it waste: it shall not be pruned, nor digged; but there shall come up briers and thorns: I will also command the clouds that they rain no rain upon it."

That we are not mistaken in the interpretation of the parable is clear from 5:7, where we are definitely told, "The vineyard of the Lord of hosts is the house of Israel, and the men of Judah his pleasant plant: and he looked for judgment, but behold oppression; for righteousness, but behold a cry." This is confirmed in Psalm 80–81 and also in Hosea 10:1.

### Isaiah 5:8-25

Here we have the six woes to which reference has already been made. In 5:8 the Lord pronounced a woe upon them "that join house to house, that lay field to field, till there be no place, that they may be placed alone in the midst of the earth!" In other words, He pronounced judgment on those who selfishly seek to accumulate houses and lands for themselves, showing no consideration for the poor and the needy. Such selfish people will eventually be desolate and

their holdings destroyed; their fields will fail to bear crops, and their
hope of gain will be disappointed.

In 5:11 the Lord pronounced a woe upon those who give themselves over to voluptuousness and sensual pleasure, who "rise up
early in the morning, that they may follow strong drink; that continue until night, till wine inflame them!" Reading on through 5:17
we learn that they seek to delight themselves with beautiful music
and other worldly pleasures, "but they regard not the work of the
Lord, neither consider the operation of his hands." Because of this
they will go into captivity. They have acted as those who are without knowledge; and the leaders among them, who should have been
honorable men, have proven themselves to be fools. So "hell hath
enlarged herself." That is, the unseen world has "opened her mouth
without measure" and they and all that they have delighted in will
go down into the pit. "The mean man shall be brought down, and
the mighty man shall be humbled, and the eyes of the lofty shall be
humbled: But the Lord of hosts [whom they have despised] shall be
exalted in judgment." God, the infinitely holy One, "shall be sanc-
tified in righteousness" when He visits with judgment those who
have grievously offended.

The third woe (5:18) is upon those who "draw iniquity with cords
of vanity, and sin as it were with a cart rope." They openly defy the
God of Israel and brazenly insist on taking their own way in opposition to His Holy Word. They ridicule the message of His prophet
and spurn His commands.

The fourth woe (5:20) is upon those who fail to distinguish between good and evil, righteousness and unrighteousness. They "put
darkness for light, and light for darkness"; they "put bitter for sweet,
and sweet for bitter!" In other words, they make no distinction between that which honors God and that which dishonors Him. Like
Laodicea in a later day, they are neither cold nor hot; they are utterly indifferent to divine truth.

The fifth woe (5:21) is upon those who are "wise in their own
eyes, and prudent in their own sight!" Pride, so natural to the human heart, is hateful to God, and if persisted in will eventually bring
destruction. As Proverbs 16:18 puts it, "Pride goeth before destruction, and an haughty spirit before a fall."

The sixth woe (5:22-23) is for those who, inflamed by wine, lose all sense of righteousness in judgment. They "justify the wicked for reward, and take away the righteousness of the righteous from him!"

Having pronounced the six woes, the Lord declared, "Therefore as the fire devoureth the stubble, and the flame consumeth the chaff, so their root shall be as rottenness, and their blossom shall go up as dust: because they have cast away the law of the Lord of hosts, and despised the word of the Holy One of Israel. Therefore is the anger of the Lord kindled against his people, and he hath stretched forth his hand against them, and hath smitten them: and the hills did tremble."

In spite of warnings, the people persisted in their iniquity, their hearts unmoved by all God's dealings with them; therefore more severe judgments were yet to come.

## *Isaiah 5:26-30*

The Lord had summoned the nations of the East to overrun the land of Israel. Already the northern kingdom of Israel had felt the power of Assyria and had been carried away. Soon the southern kingdom of Judah would be destroyed by the might of Babylon. No effort on Judah's part would enable them to turn back the power of the enemy when the appointed hour had come for the destruction so long predicted. Like a roaring lioness with a litter of young lions, the eastern nations would rush upon their prey and carry it away triumphantly. In that hour of distress, the people of Judah would cry to the Lord in vain, for "darkness and sorrow" were destined to be their portion. The light would be darkened in the heavens above them.

# THE PROPHET'S CLEANSING AND COMMISSION

Here Isaiah goes back over the years and tells us how he was brought into the knowledge of cleansing from sin and how he heard and responded to the call of God to be His messenger to a rebellious and gainsaying people.

It is always interesting to hear a personal and intimate account of the revelation of God to a human soul. In Isaiah 6 the prophet tells us the secret of his wonderful power and how he was equipped for service. He takes us into the sanctuary, shows us how the Lord was revealed to him, and lets us know the circumstances of his call to the prophetic office. This was the real starting point of his effective ministry.

We know from 1:1 that Isaiah began to witness for God in the days of King Uzziah. Since the experience recorded in Isaiah 6 took place in the year Uzziah died, it may be that that experience was subsequent to the prophetic testimony recorded in chapters 1–5. But, as suggested before, there seems to be no proof of this. Isaiah may have begun his ministry during the last year of Uzziah's life and it may be that in chapter 6 he told us of his original call to the prophetic office.

Yet, many servants of God have preached to others before having a clear, definite experience with the Lord for themselves. John Wesley is a case in point. He told us in his journal that while in Georgia he learned that he who had come to America to convert the Indians had never been converted himself. In later years he doubted whether he had diagnosed his own case correctly, but he certainly preached to others for several years before he had that heartwarming experience in London when he definitely knew that he was born of God. D. L. Moody is another who began to preach before having a clear understanding of salvation by grace and the enduement of the Holy Spirit.

So while it seems unlikely, there is the possibility that the stirring prophecy of chapters 1–5 was proclaimed before Isaiah received the revelation recorded in chapter 6. However, it seems more probable that after he had written the preceding chapters, he then decided to tell the story of his own meeting with God and his divine commission as God's messenger to the people of his day.

### Isaiah 6:1-7

This revelation of the holiness of God and the corruption of his own heart was not, as some would say, Isaiah's "second blessing." It was rather a part of God's dealings with him in order that he might be prepared—by encountering the reality of God for himself—to give out the Word to others.

Isaiah told us, "In the year that king Uzziah died I saw also the Lord sitting upon a throne, high and lifted up, and his train filled the temple." That word "also" is significant. Was it a sight of God that brought the leprosy out on Uzziah's forehead? The same God revealed Himself to Isaiah while he was attending a service in the temple at Jerusalem; however, it was not in judgment, but in grace that He showed Himself as the infinitely holy One.

Others may have thronged the temple courts at this time, but only Isaiah saw the glorious vision. In an ecstatic state he became blind to all about him; his awakened intelligence was fully occupied with the glory that had been revealed to him.

Above the throne he saw the seraphim, an order of angels apparently, each with six wings. We may drop the *s* from the word "seraphims" as the *im* is the Hebrew plural. These glorious beings seem to be messengers of grace, as distinguished from the cherubim, who speak rather of righteousness and judgment.

The seraphim cried one to another, "Holy, holy, holy, is the Lord of hosts: the whole earth is full of his glory." Their words are an ascription of praise and adoration to the triune God, whose glory is displayed in all creation. As the song of worship resounded, the very posts of the doors were moved and the temple was filled with the fragrant smoke of burning incense. Strange that inanimate pillars should be moved while the hearts of men remained obdurate and motionless! But there was one man who did respond—and in a very definite way.

Isaiah cried, "Woe is me! for I am undone; because I am a man of unclean lips, and I dwell in the midst of a people of unclean lips." The effect of beholding God is to make one realize one's own unworthiness. Isaiah realized the corruption of his own heart when he saw himself in the light of Jehovah's infinite holiness. Such is the case whenever man is brought consciously into the presence of God. When Job saw the Lord, he cried, "I abhor myself, and repent in dust and ashes" (Job 42:6). When Simon Peter recognized in Jesus the Creator of the fish of the sea, he fell at His feet and cried, "Depart from me; for I am a sinful man, O Lord" (Luke 5:8). Likewise when our prophet saw himself in the light of the holiness of God, he at once acknowledged his own sinfulness. Moreover he recognized the fact that he was surrounded by men who, like himself, were "of unclean lips," for "out of the abundance of the heart the mouth speaketh" (Matthew 12:34).

Isaiah wrote that after his confession, "then flew one of the seraphim unto me, having a live coal in his hand." The creature had taken the live coal "with the tongs from off the altar." It was the altar of sacrifice, which prefigured the cross. That live coal symbolized the fire of judgment that had burned itself out on the offering. The seraphim, representatives of the grace of God to needy men, flew swiftly to tell of His saving favor based on the atoning sacrifice. With two of their wings the seraphim hid their faces as they worshipped the infinitely holy One. With two they covered their beautiful feet, and with two they hurried to do loving service.

As previously mentioned, the cherubim seem to speak of judgment. (The "living creatures" of Ezekiel 1 are identified as the "cherubim" in Ezekiel 10). They are said to have four wings. May not the six wings of the seraphim then tell us how "mercy rejoiceth against judgment" (James 2:13)?

As the coal touched his lips, Isaiah heard the comforting words, "Thine iniquity is taken away, and thy sin purged." The divinely-sent messenger proclaimed to Isaiah the good news of redemption and purification from sin through Him whose one offering was pictured in the sacrifice of the altar.

I would re-emphasize the fact that the coal was taken from the altar of burnt offering, not from the golden altar, where only incense was burned. That live coal represented the fire, ever burning, that was never to go out (Leviticus 6:13). It constantly foreshadowed the work of the cross. Through that sacrifice alone could iniquity be purged and sin be put away (Hebrews 9:13-14).

### Isaiah 6:8-13

Following the assurance of forgiveness and cleansing came the call for service. Isaiah heard the voice of the Lord crying, "Whom shall I send, and who will go for us?" In response Isaiah exclaimed, "Here am I; send me."

Who will go? It has pleased God to commit the declaration of His truth to men rather than to angels. He is still calling for consecrated men and women to carry the offer of salvation and the warning of judgment to a lost world. Such messengers must know for themselves the cleansing power of the blood of Christ if they are to give effective testimony to those who are still in their sins.

The prophet was commissioned to "go, and tell this people, Hear ye indeed, but understand not; and see ye indeed, but perceive not. Make the heart of this people fat, and make their ears heavy, and shut their eyes; lest they see with their eyes, and hear with their ears, and understand with their heart, and convert, and be healed." Even though the Word seemed to have no other effect than to harden them in their sins and rebellion, Isaiah was to proclaim the message faithfully.

The servant of God is responsible to God. Having received his commission, he is to go forth in the name of the One who sends him, declaring the message committed to him. The results must be left with God. Whether men hear or whether they refuse to listen, he who has proclaimed the Word faithfully has delivered his own soul (Ezekiel 2:3-5; 3:19-21). The apostle Paul said, "We are unto God a sweet savour of Christ, in them that are saved, and in them that perish" (2 Corinthians 2:15). God is honored when His truth is preached, no matter what attitude the hearers take toward it. His Word will not return to Him void; it will accomplish the divine purpose (Isaiah 55:11).

Faced with the solemn responsibility of proclaiming an unpopular message, Isaiah cried, "Lord, how long?" (6:11) It takes special faith and obedience to continue to preach to an unheeding people who are only hardened by the Word instead of being softened by it. The Lord's answer was that the message must be proclaimed until there is no one left to hear it.

# THE VIRGIN'S SON

I saiah 7 has been the subject of endless controversy throughout the Christian centuries. However, the Holy Spirit makes this portion of Scripture clear to those who are ready to receive His testimony because of the way it is used in connection with the birth of our blessed Lord.

### Isaiah 7:1-9

During the reign of King Ahaz (the grandson of Uzziah) war broke out between Judah and Israel. Pekah, the son of King Remaliah of Israel, entered into a confederacy with King Rezin of Syria; and they went together to besiege Jerusalem. Though the siege lasted for some time, they were unable to subjugate the holy city.

When Ahaz learned of the confederacy against him, his heart and the heart of his people were moved with fear, for Ahaz had walked in the ways of the kings of Israel rather than in those of the house of David. He had therefore little or no reason to expect divine help against his foes. But God's heart was inclined to help the people of Judah, for the time had not yet come to deliver them up to their enemies. There had been quite a measure of return to the Lord during the days of Jotham, the father of Ahaz.

God heard the prayers of His almost distracted people and sent the prophet Isaiah to meet Ahaz and give him a word of encouragement. Isaiah took with him his son Shear-jashub, whose name meant "the remnant shall return." All of Isaiah's children seem to have been named prophetically in order that they might be signs to the people of Judah.

The message that Isaiah brought to Ahaz was one of trust and comfort: "Take heed, and be quiet; fear not, neither be fainthearted."

In the sight of God the kings who had united their forces against Ahaz were like two smoking firebrands soon to be extinguished. Their wickedness and ungodliness were such that the Lord was about to deal with them in judgment and therefore would not permit them to overcome Judah or subdue Jerusalem. It was in vain that they took counsel together against Ahaz and his people and sought to make a breach in the defenses of Jerusalem.

Regarding the scheme of Pekah and Rezin, the Lord God declared, "It shall not stand, neither shall it come to pass....Within threescore and five years shall Ephraim [Israel] be broken, that it be not a people." Syria would be unable to help them against the king of Assyria, who in God's own time was to carry the northern kingdom into captivity.

## Isaiah 7:10-16

At the time when Isaiah was sent to encourage Ahaz, God confirmed through the prophet the gospel message that had been given in the garden of Eden. There God had declared that the Seed of the woman would bruise the serpent's head. *The Seed of the woman* is a most significant expression because it refers to the virgin birth of the Messiah. All others born into the world are definitely of the seed of the man, but the great Deliverer was to come only through the woman.

Isaiah told Ahaz to ask the Lord for a sign that would confirm the word the prophet had spoken. Ahaz refused, saying, "I will not ask, neither will I tempt the Lord." His words sounded pious enough, but actually they came from an unbelieving heart; he was afraid to ask for a sign lest it should not come to pass. The pretended humility of Ahaz was hateful to God. Isaiah declared, "Hear ye now, O house of David; Is it a small thing for you to weary men, but will ye weary my God also?" He who is all-powerful might have given any sign that could have been asked.

Isaiah went on to say, "Therefore the Lord himself shall give you a sign [and of such a character that men would think it was impossible for it to come to pass]; "Behold, a virgin shall conceive, and bear a son, and shall call his name Immanuel." *Immanuel,* as we

know, means "God with us." The virgin's Son was to be God manifested in the flesh. (Fuller details are given in Isaiah 9.)

Only unbelief could cause anyone to try to nullify the force of
this passage by reading "a young woman" in place of "a virgin,"
and by saying that the young woman was the wife of the prophet
and the son was their son. It is perfectly true that the word rendered
"virgin" might also be rendered "maiden," but every maiden is pre-
sumably a virgin—if not, something is radically wrong. So the prophecy here clearly and definitely declared that an unmarried virgin
would become a mother and the child would be named "God with
us." I am not saying, as Rome does, that the virgin Mary is the
mother of God. She became the mother of the humanity of our Lord
Jesus Christ, but He who was born of her was God manifested in
the flesh.

This sign would come to pass, but it was not to be fulfilled during the days of Ahaz. The fulfillment would come some time afterward, for the prophet immediately added, "Butter and honey shall
he eat, that he may know to refuse the evil, and choose the good.
For before the child shall know to refuse the evil, and choose the
good, the land that thou abhorrest shall be forsaken of both her
kings." Before this child would come on the scene and grow to
maturity, not only the king of Israel but also the king of Judah would
have ceased to reign; the land would have been left without a son of
David sitting on the throne of Judah, or any representative sitting
on the throne of Israel.

The expression "butter and honey shall he eat" is very striking,
for it indicates the true humanity of the child to be born of the virgin. Although He was to be supernaturally conceived, he would
have a real physical body, which would be sustained by proper food.
Butter (curds) is the quintessence of animal food, and honey the
quintessence of vegetable food. With such fare therefore the holy
Child was to be nourished that He might grow from infancy to manhood in a normal way. When we turn to the New Testament records,
we do not read of some remarkably precocious child whose early
activities were different from those of other little ones. Luke 2:52
says that He "increased in wisdom and stature, and in favour with

God and man." Feeding on the food provided, He grew from childhood to youth and from youth to manhood.

In the Apocryphal gospels many curious and weird legends are connected with the boy Jesus. From the very first He is pictured as acting in a supernatural way, even at His birth taking three steps forward to the amazement of those attending His mother. It is said that when playing with other boys He would work strange miracles that amazed them; on the other hand, if they failed to appreciate Him, He would visit judgment upon them. But this is not the Christ of God; the person thus portrayed is a creature of man's unholy imagination.

As a babe, as a growing child, as a youth, and as a man, the humanity of our Lord was exactly like that of other people, except that He did not sin. He was made in all things like His brethren (Hebrews 2:17) that He might properly represent us before God as our kinsman-redeemer.

### Isaiah 7:17-25

To Ahaz and his people and his father's house, God would bring distress and trouble by means of the king of Assyria's coming into the land. In fact Judah was to be the bone of contention between two great powers: Assyria on the east and Egypt on the west. As Judah contemplated the increasing might of Assyria, they turned desperately to Egypt, hoping to find in that people an ally who would help protect them from the eastern power. But Judah learned in the end that Egypt was a broken reed. Instead of becoming helpful she would herself turn against them.

As a result of the conflict that would ensue, the day was not far distant when famine and pestilence would sweep through the land. The great cities of Judah would fall. Out in the country, those who remained would exist on the produce of the soil; but even this would be available in limited quantities, for thorns and briers would soon cover large districts where industries, plantations, and vineyards had once flourished. Nevertheless God would still intervene to protect the poor of the flock and those who waited on Him; in response to their toil the land would once more bear fruit instead of thorns and briers, and oxen and sheep would again be raised in sufficient numbers to meet the needs of the people.

To some it might seem strange that the prophecy of the virgin's Son would be given in such an unexpected place, but we need to remember that God always had Christ before Him, and that every king of Judah was the anointed of the Lord in his time. Our word *Messiah* simply means "the anointed" and therefore each of these kings was supposed to prefigure God's own blessed Son, who was to come into the world as the Son of David. In the fullness of time God would present His Son to the chosen nation as the anointed One in whom alone deliverance was to be found. Many of these kings failed utterly to typify the Lord. Their behavior showed that they were far removed in spirit from what God had in mind for them. Ahaz had shown himself forgetful of the law of the Lord, and so in the hour of his distress he did not have the courage to count on God or to expect help from Him. How natural then that under the circumstances God should speak of another King, a Son of David, who would be born into the world supernaturally, and who in His own time would show who was the blessed and only Potentate, the King of kings, and the Lord of lords.

# MAHER-SHALAL-HASHBAZ

## Isaiah 8:1-4

We have already met Isaiah's son Shear-jashub and noted the meaning of his name: "the remnant shall return." Now we are introduced to Maher-shalal-hashbaz, another of the prophet's sons. His name, which was given as a sign to Judah, means "in making speed to the spoil he hastens the prey."

Some critics have insisted that Maher-shalal-hashbaz was the son of the maiden referred to in Isaiah 7 and that she was the prophet's wife. But there is no possibility of identifying Immanuel (7:14) with Maher-shalal-hashbaz. The significance of the name *Immanuel* was that God would dwell among men in the person of His Son (and this is confirmed in Isaiah 9), but the young lad with the long outlandish name was so called in view of something altogether different.

The name *Maher-shalal-hashbaz* was given and recorded in the temple before the child was born. Its significance was this: Damascus, the Syrian capital that had been at enmity with Judah and confederate with Israel, was about to be spoiled by the Assyrians; and at the same time Israel was to fall prey to that great and mighty power. These events would transpire before the child was grown.

## Isaiah 8:5-8

The allied peoples of Syria and Israel (the northern kingdom), refusing to recognize the value of association with Judah, had spurned the peaceful waters of Shiloah. They had joined forces under Rezin (king of Syria) and Remaliah's son Pekah (the upstart king of Israel) in order to destroy Judah. Therefore the Lord was bringing against them the armies of the king of Assyria. The Assyrians would flow over Syria and Israel like a great river and would even reach into Judah, thus overspreading Immanuel's land— the land promised by covenant to Abraham and his seed, which seed is Christ.

As Christians we delight to use the expression *Immanuel's land* in a spiritual sense, and we are justified in doing this. But in 8:8 the words "thy land, O Immanuel" actually refer to the land of Palestine. It was the land Jehovah had claimed as His own when He had declared, "The land shall not be sold for ever: for the land is mine" (Leviticus 25:23).

### Isaiah 8:9-15

To ward off this danger from his land, Ahaz sought an alliance with Egypt, but no such association would avail to avert the threatened judgment.

Instinctively in times of stress and danger men think of confederacies as the best means of preserving the traditions and conditions that they hold dear. It was so in Judah; it is so in Christendom today. Individuals and churches join various leagues that their organizers hope will prove to be bulwarks against the onrushing tide of evil. But again and again it has been demonstrated that all such federations tend to deteriorate as time goes by. Afterward the children of those who formed these associations revert to the evils against which their fathers protested.

The only real recourse in a day of evil is to cleave to the Lord. No matter what happens, He remains unchanged and unchangeable. So the prophet exhorted the people, "Sanctify the Lord of hosts himself; and let him be your fear, and let him be your dread."

When the Lord is given His rightful place, He will be as a sanctuary to those who put their trust in Him. But to those who reject Him, He will be "a stone of stumbling" and "a rock of offense," as He was when He appeared in human form to both the houses of Israel. These words were applied to our blessed Lord in the New

Testament (1 Peter 2:8). When He, the long-looked-for Messiah
came in lowly grace, the nation stumbled over Him and so was broken and scattered, as predicted in Isaiah 8:15.

## Isaiah 8:16-22

God's Word is a dependable resource for His obedient people.
To those who are willing to be taught of God, the Word becomes
increasingly precious as the days grow darker. Hence Paul, after
predicting the coming apostasy in the Ephesian church, said to the
elders, "I commend you to God, and to the word of his grace" (Acts
20:32). In the same vein Isaiah, speaking on God's behalf, exclaimed,
"Bind up the testimony, seal the law among my disciples."

In 8:17 we hear the voice of him who takes the place of dependence on God: "I will wait upon the Lord, that hideth his face from
the house of Jacob, and I will look for him." The Lord may seem to
be indifferent to the trials His people are passing through, but actually He is not. His face may be hidden, but His heart is always aware
of them.

Isaiah and his family were called to be a testimony to all Israel.
"Behold," he said, "I and the children whom the Lord hath given
me are for signs and for wonders in Israel from the Lord of hosts,
which dwelleth in mount Zion" (8:18). Part of this verse is quoted
in Hebrews 2:13, where it is applied to the Lord Jesus and those
who receive life through believing in His name.

Isaiah 8:19-22 gives us a solemn warning against what is now
known as spiritualism and against any form of necromancy. When
we are urged to seek light and help from spirit-mediums, we should
say, "Should not a people seek unto their God?" The living should
not ask the dead for help. All attempts to get into contact with the
spirits of the dead are forbidden in Scripture. (See Deuteronomy
18:9-12 and Leviticus 20:27.) It is a grievous offense in the eyes of
God for anyone to turn from His revealed Word to those who profess to have power to summon the spirits of the departed. Either the
mediums are charlatans, deceiving those who go to them, or they
are possessed by impersonating demons, misleading all who follow
them.

God's sure Word abides. Those who speak contrary to it are in darkness themselves and there is no morning for them. When the day dawns for the eternal blessing of the redeemed, there will be outer darkness for those who have spurned the light of truth, only to be misled by falsehood. Such individuals will be exposed at last for what they really are: blind leaders of the blind. They will look in vain for help when those who have obeyed the Word of God find light and blessing. Spiritualism is a Satanic cult that can only disappoint those who follow the will-o'-the-wisp of its direction. They will at last be driven into the darkness.

# ISAIAH 9

# THE PROMISED DELIVERER

A s we study Isaiah 9 we will notice how definitely it links with the promise given to Ahaz in chapter 7, for we will read once more of the One who is the fulfillment of all God's ways with men. This One is the man of God's counsel who came in grace to reveal the Father and to establish everlasting righteousness.

## Isaiah 9:1-5

The opening verses of Isaiah 9 continue the prophecy of darkness begun in chapter 8. There would be dimness in the future, but Isaiah foresaw that when darkness was spreading over the land of Palestine and men were groping for the light, Christ would come in infinite grace to be the Light of the world. He would come "by the way of the sea, beyond Jordan, in Galilee of the nations."

Isaiah seemed to see Him moving about among men, declaring the counsel of God, and showing His grace toward those that walked in darkness. Writing prophetically, he stated, "They that dwell in the land of the shadow of death, upon them hath the light shined." Isaiah wrote as if he could look down through the ages and see the Lord Jesus, full of grace and truth, making known the wonders of God's redeeming love to those who heard Him gladly and found Him to be the Light of life.

Isaiah 9:1-2 is the passage quoted in Matthew 4:15-16. The differences in rendering are due to the fact that in the New Testament the quotation is taken from the Septuagint instead of the Hebrew.

In Isaiah 9:3 the prophet passed over Christ's rejection and the long years to follow during which the people of Israel themselves would be rejected. For the moment he looked ahead to the day when the nation would once more be recognized by God as being in a covenant relationship with Himself. Note that it is Israel that is in question in this verse and not the Gentiles. It seems evident that in the King James version the translation is faulty in that the word "not" should have been omitted. Really the prophet was saying, "Thou hast multiplied the nation, and increased the joy." Most spiritually-minded scholars agree with this rendering, for the passage looks forward to the future blessing of the favored nation when they will be restored to the Lord and to their land. By then they will have recognized Jesus as their Messiah, as the One whom their fathers rejected but in whom all blessing is to be found.

Isaiah 9:4-5 contemplates the conditions that would prevail in the world through the long centuries of the dispersion of Israel. Although these verses had a local application to the destruction of the Assyrian army, which was besieging Jerusalem, there will be a complete fulfillment when Christ returns to deliver the people from all their enemies.

Undoubtedly when the prophet wrote, "Every battle of the warrior is with confused noise, and garments rolled in blood," he was describing the sad conditions destined to be the portion of the nations until Christ comes again to bring peace. This agrees with the words of our Lord Jesus as recorded in Matthew 24:6-7: "Ye shall hear of wars and rumours of wars: see that ye be not troubled: for all these things must come to pass, but the end is not yet. For nation shall rise against nation, and kingdom against kingdom: and there shall be famines, and pestilences, and earthquakes, in divers places." Such conditions have prevailed through the centuries since Christ was rejected. He who was once offered to the world as the Prince of Peace was rejected by both Israel and the Gentile nations. Therefore He said before He left this earth, "Suppose ye that I am come to give peace on earth? I tell you, Nay; but rather division" (Luke 12:51).

### Isaiah 9:6-7

This passage is one of the most complete prophecies concerning our Lord to be found in the Old Testament. Isaiah began this prophecy with two expressions that reveal the humanity and the deity of our Savior: "Unto us a child is born, unto us a son is given." The "child...born" refers to His humanity. As we have already seen, He was to come into the world as the virgin's Son. As such He was a true Man—spirit, soul, and body. The "son...given" refers to the Savior's deity. He was born of Mary, but without a human father. The eternal Son of the Father, Christ came from the glory that He had with the Father throughout all the past eternity. The Son was given in grace for our redemption. He linked His deity with our humanity (except for its sins) and thus was God and man in one blessed adorable person.

The Son is destined to exercise supreme rule over all the universe. As Isaiah said, "The government shall be upon his shoulder." It has often been noticed that the government of the entire world will rest on His shoulder (singular), but when the Good Shepherd finds a lost sheep, He puts it on His shoulders (plural; see Luke 15:5). Surely there is a beautiful suggestion in this plural of the security of those who have put their trust in Him.

"His name," Isaiah prophesied, "shall be called Wonderful, Counsellor..." Under the name "Wonderful" He appeared to the parents of Samson (Judges 13:18, revised version; King James version has "secret"). It may be that we should link together the two words "Wonderful" and "Counsellor," but if we separate them, we may see in the first word a suggestion of the mystery of His sonship. This mystery no man can fathom, as He told us in Matthew 11:27 and as we learn from Revelation 19:12. Only the Father understands "the mystery of godliness" (1 Timothy 3:16). It is beyond human comprehension. Nevertheless as we read the divinely inspired records of Christ's lowly birth, sinless life, vicarious death, and glorious resurrection, we find our hearts exclaiming again and again, "He is wonderful!" He stands supreme, above all the sons of men. He is the blessed, adorable Son of God, yet His heart is "touched with the feeling of our infirmities" (Hebrews 4:15). His grace is made evident in a thousand ways; His lovingkindness reaches down to the utterly lost and depraved. His name is "Wonderful" because He Himself is wonderful and the work He accomplished is wonderful.

He is called "Counsellor" because He comes to us as the revealer of the Father's will. That is what is implied in His divine title, *the Word.* It is by the Word that God has made known His mind. The Lord Jesus, who was with the Father from the beginning (that is, when everything that ever had a beginning began), came into this world to make God known. So in Him the Father has spoken out all that is in His heart. Christ's words make known to us the path of life and show us the only safe way for a pilgrim people to travel through a world of sin. As the eternal Word He is the revealer of the mind and heart of God. The Son came to earth not only to show us the way to the Father, but also to empower us to walk in a manner well-pleasing to the One who has redeemed us.

Notice that the Son is also called "The mighty God." Some people seek to tone this down in order to make Him less than the words imply, but He is also called "God" in Romans 9:5 and 1 John 5:20. Even when here on earth, He was just as truly God as He was man, and as truly man as He was God. He could not have made atonement for sin otherwise. He had to be who He was in order to do what He did.

Isaiah continued, "His name shall be called...The everlasting Father." A better rendering would be "the Father of eternity" or "the Father of the coming age." The Son is not to be confused with the Father, though He and the Father are one (John 10:30). But the Son is the One in whom all the ages meet and therefore He is rightfully designated, "the Father of the ages" or "the Father of eternity."

He was presented to the world and heralded by angels as "The Prince of Peace" (see Luke 2:14). But because of His rejection there can be no lasting peace for Israel or the other nations until He comes again. Then He will speak peace to all peoples (Isaiah 32:1-18). In the meantime, "having made peace through the blood of his cross" (Colossians 1:20), all who put their trust in Him have peace with God. As we learn to commit to God in prayer all that would naturally trouble or distress us, peace fills our hearts and controls our lives.

Isaiah 9:7 refers to the covenant God made with David that his Son would sit on his throne and reign in righteousness forever. This has not yet been fulfilled. When the forerunner of our Lord was born, his father Zacharias declared that God had "raised up an horn of salvation for us in the house of his servant David" (Luke 1:69). Such prophetic declarations make clear that David's throne was to be established forever, and that he would never be without an heir to sit on that throne. Our Lord, on His mother's side, was from the line of David and because of her marriage to Joseph, who was heir to the throne, the throne-rights passed to Jesus.

But He has not yet taken His seat on the throne of David; this awaits His second coming. At that time, as He declared through His servant John, "To him that overcometh will I grant to sit with me in my throne, even as I also overcame, and am set down with my Father in his throne (Revelation 3:21). Now He is sitting at "the right hand of the Majesty on high" on the throne of deity (Hebrews 1:3). Soon He will return in glory, take His own throne, which is really the throne of David, and reign in righteousness over all the earth. Isaiah 9:7 will be fulfilled literally, for "the zeal of the Lord of hosts will perform this."

### Isaiah 9:8-12

After 9:7 the prophet turned back to local conditions. Inhabitants of the northern kingdom were vaunting themselves, saying that in spite of the calamities that were befalling them, they would rise above them and once more become a strong and secure people. But the Lord declared that He would raise up adversaries from among the Syrians, who had been their allies, and the Philistines, who were the ancient enemies of His people, and that these adversaries would "devour Israel with open mouth." The Lord's anger was "not turned away" from Israel and His hand was "stretched out" in judgment because of their sins. There had been no return to Him even when affliction had come.

## Isaiah 9:13-17

In the Epistle to the Hebrews we are told that "no chastening for the present seemeth to be joyous, but grievous: nevertheless afterward it yieldeth the peaceable fruit of righteousness unto them which are exercised thereby." But on Israel's part there had been no exercise because of the chastening hand of God upon them. Rather there was resentful pride. They dared to boast and to resist God and His servants who came to instruct them in His truth. The leaders of Israel were terribly guilty in that instead of urging those who were subject to them to repent, they had misled them and caused them to err. Israel was on the brink of destruction because of their unrepentant condition. The Lord could not find His joy in them; His compassion was not free to flow out toward them. Their continual waywardness called for further judgment.

## Isaiah 9:18-21

Men may think lightly of sin and pay little or no attention to the solemn warnings that God gives concerning its evil effects, but if they persist in rebellion against God, they will find that "wickedness burneth as the fire" and that those who refuse to turn to God in repentance will have to endure the judgment that they have brought on themselves. God's holy nature does not permit Him to condone iniquity, so Isaiah prophesied that "through the wrath of the Lord of hosts is the land darkened, and the people shall be as the fuel of the fire."

Famine and pestilence would be added to Israel's wretchedness and misery, yet instead of turning to Him and confessing their sin and seeking forgiveness, they would blame one another for their troubles. Manasseh would turn on Ephraim, Ephraim would turn on Manasseh, and both together would turn on Judah. All this would be the sad result of forsaking the way of the Lord.

Isaiah 9 closes with the solemn refrain repeated for the third time, "For all this his anger is not turned away, but His hand is stretched out still."

# ISAIAH 10

# THE ASSYRIAN AND HIS DOOM

I t is a well-known principle of Scripture interpretation to recognize that often prophecies have double applications or fulfillments. Many of the conditions through which Israel and the Gentile nations have already passed depict circumstances that will be faced in the future. Some of those conditions prefigure the days of the great tribulation, the time of Jacob's trouble, when divine wrath will be poured out on guilty and apostate Christendom and Judaism alike.

We see an example of a double application in Isaiah 10, which deals primarily with Judah and Assyria in the days of King Hezekiah, but also looks forward to the endtimes. Then the last great Assyrian, the haughty enemy of the Jews in the time of the end, will be destroyed in Immanuel's land before he can wreak his vengeance on the remnant nation who will be gathered back to God and to their land. Only as we keep these two fulfillments of the prophetic word in mind, can we understand this chapter correctly.

## Isaiah 10:1-4

In the opening verses we see Judah's sad internal condition calling for judgment on the part of the God whom they professed to serve, but so grievously dishonored. Another solemn woe is pronounced on those who in their pride and selfishness issued unrighteous decrees in order to legalize their oppression of the poor and enriched themselves at the expense of the fatherless.

Monopolies are not a recent expression of the selfishness of the

61

human heart. In Judah, as in civilized lands today, there were those who considered it good business to take advantage of others in adverse circumstances and to profit from the ruin of their less fortunate fellow men. All this was hateful to the God of judgment who weighs men's actions.

Any economic system that is built on a disregard of the rights of the poor will inevitably be destroyed. Then what will become of the men who have ignored the Word of the Lord and gloried in their success while trampling on their competitors and forcing them to yield to their demands or go down in ruin? "What," the prophet asked the people, "will ye do in the day of visitation, and in the desolation which shall come from far? to whom will ye flee for help? and where will ye leave your glory?"

God has decreed, "Them that honour me I will honour, and they that despise me shall be lightly esteemed" (1 Samuel 2:30). He permits men and nations to go just so far in their own willful way; then He deals with them in His indignation, sweeping away their ill-gotten wealth and causing them to bewail the luxuries that they can no longer retain. What can men say when this happens? Where can they turn to save themselves from even greater disaster?

In Judah's case the overrunning of the land by the armies of Sennacherib was the cause of much of their suffering, but it was permitted by God as chastening for their sins. Without His deliverance they were helpless to defend themselves, and so would be taken as prisoners or slain by the cruel foe.

### Isaiah 10:5-12

In this passage God addressed the Assyrian directly and in a way that shows He had far more than the invasion of Sennacherib in view. He also had in mind the final enemy in the last days. Notice that it is "when the Lord hath performed his whole work upon mount Zion and on Jerusalem" that the Assyrian will be punished. This needs to be kept in mind as the passage is read and studied.

When King Ahaz was threatened with utter ruin by the kings of Israel and Syria, he asked the king of Assyria for help, only to find out later that this covetous ruler aspired to complete ascendancy over all the lands to the west, including Judah. Indeed Sennacherib would descend on the land like a mighty torrent, until his army was destroyed by pestilence in one night as he besieged Jerusalem in the days of Hezekiah. This terrible ruthless enemy from Assyria became the type of the godless foe that in the last days will attempt to bring Palestine under its control, only to be destroyed by omnipotent power on the mountains of Israel.

As the rod of Jehovah's anger, Assyria was used, as other nations have been used before and since, to chasten the people of God because of their turning away from Him. But in the day of their repentance He destroyed the enemy that had brought disaster upon Judah.

When Isaiah wrote this passage, the haughty destroyer did not yet realize that he was just an instrument in the hand of Jehovah, the God whose name he despised. But he was to learn by bitter experience that after he had been used to punish "an hypocritical nation," he himself was doomed to utter destruction. To the Assyrian, Jerusalem was just another city to be overthrown as so many others had been overthrown; but he was to learn that the God whose temple was in that city was supreme above all the so-called gods that had been powerless to deliver pagan cities out of his hands.

Jehovah's "whole work upon mount Zion and on Jerusalem" includes the return of His people to Himself. In the days that He takes them up again as a nation, He will deal with the Assyrian and with all who have afflicted them.

### Isaiah 10:13-19

Not understanding the use that God was making of him, the Assyrian vaunted himself as though he accomplished everything and won all his victories because of his own wisdom and prudence. So he ruthlessly and heartlessly robbed and oppressed the nations, including Israel and Judah. To him all other people were, like abandoned birds' eggs, to be despoiled—and other armies were as helpless as mother birds when their nests are rifled.

Not knowing that he was only an ax in the hand of Him who hewed down the trees of the forest, the Assyrian boasted as though the power and might were all his own. He magnified himself against the One who designed to use him to chasten the nations because of their wickedness and corruption. Therefore in the reckoning day that was coming, God would deal as sternly with him as he had dealt with others. Just as he had sown hatred and cruelty, so he would reap indignation and wretchedness.

In the day of Jehovah's triumph He will vindicate the remnant in Israel who have put their trust in Him, and they will be as a flame to devour the nations that have sought their destruction. As in the days of Ahasuerus and Mordecai, the Jews will execute judgment on those who have plotted to destroy them and root them out of the earth. Fulfilled will be the Word of God with its promise that while He would punish His people in measure for their sins, He would never break His covenant with them—a covenant made first to Abraham and then confirmed to David.

### *Isaiah 10:20-23*

Although many of the nations that have afflicted Israel will be completely destroyed, Israel will not. When the judgments of God are being poured out on the earth in the dark days of the great tribulation, a remnant of the Jews will turn to the Lord in deep repentance and in living faith. These will prove the greatness of His mercy and the unfailing character of His promises. No longer relying on help from the powers that persecuted and failed them in the hour of their need (as when Ahaz turned first to Assyria and then to Egypt in his desperate plight), they will find their resource and protection in God Himself.

The prophetic Word is clear and free of all obscurity. Only unbelief can deny its definite application to a literal remnant of the sons of Jacob when they turn to the Lord in the time of their greatest trouble. Then He will come to their aid, and He will save the nation in the remnant. We need to remember that "they are not all Israel, which are of Israel" (Romans 9:6). Of Jacob's descendants, who will be as numerous "as the sand of the sea," the great majority will go into utter apostasy and be destroyed in their sins. But a remnant will return and be acknowledged by God as His people. This remnant will be the true Israel and so in the day of Jehovah's power "all Israel shall be saved" (Romans 11:26).

## Isaiah 10:24-27

In view of this declaration of the divine purpose, God called on His people to trust His Word and not to fear the Assyrian, proud and powerful though he was. Then in clear and definite terms, the prophet predicted the overthrow of the enemy who was hammering as it were at the gate of Jerusalem. God would prevent the carrying out of the Assyrian's purpose even though it might seem for a time that Judah's case was hopeless.

As far as the prophecy had to do with the Assyrian of the past, all was literally fulfilled in due time. When in the last days another mighty power comes against Palestine from the same region as that occupied by the Assyrians of old, his doom will be just as certain.

## Isaiah 10:28-34

Prophecy is history written beforehand, and here Isaiah foretold the path that the Assyrian took as he marched through Palestine, wreaking his vengeance on city after city. The prophet also foretold the Assyrian's defeat when the Lord of hosts at last intervened with His mighty power for the deliverance of those who had cried to Him in the hour of their distress. No military strategy, no weapons of war could avail to save the haughty invader when the hand of God was stretched out against him.

What a lesson for faith we have here! These prophecies, while applying directly to Judah and her foes, have precious lessons for us today. It is *not* true that God is on the side of the greatest armies, as some have said. He stands ready to uphold all who put their confidence in Him and who rely not on an arm of flesh, but on His omnipotence and unchanging love for His own.

# ISAIAH 11

# WHEN GOD'S ANOINTED TAKES OVER

## (PART ONE)

*Isaiah 11:1-5*

After the Assyrian of the endtimes is destroyed and Israel is delivered from all her enemies, there will be peace during the reign of Him who is the Rod out of Jesse's stem. Coming by virgin birth through David's line, He is the Branch out of the root of Jesse, who was the father of David. The Branch of the Lord will bring all things into subjection to God and rule with the iron rod of inflexible righteousness.

This Ruler is the One who is presented in the Apocalypse as having the seven spirits of God—that is, the Holy Spirit in the sevenfold plenitude of His power. Upon Him rests (1) the Spirit of Jehovah; (2) the Spirit of wisdom; (3) the Spirit of understanding; (4) the Spirit of counsel; (5) the Spirit of might; (6) the Spirit of knowledge; and (7) the Spirit of the fear of Jehovah, which is the Spirit of reverence. We are told in John 3:34 that the Father giveth not the Spirit "by measure" to His beloved Son.

From the moment of His birth the Lord Jesus was under the controlling power of the Holy Spirit. As man on earth He chose not to act in His own omnipotence, but as the Servant of the godhead. After His baptism in the Jordan, the Spirit was seen descending on Him as a dove. This was the anointing (of which the apostle Peter spoke) in preparation for His gracious public ministry. Never for one moment was He out of harmony with the Spirit. It was this that made it possible for Him to grow in wisdom as he grew in stature, "and in favour with God and man" (Luke 2:52).

Scripture guards carefully the truths of the perfect manhood of our Lord and His true deity. Confessedly, this mystery is great: that the eternal wisdom should have so limited Himself as a man that He grew in wisdom and knowledge from childhood to physical maturity as under the tutelage of the Father; and that the Father by the Spirit revealed His will to Jesus from day to day so that He could say, "I speak not My own words, but the words of Him that sent Me." All the works Christ wrought, He attributed to the Spirit of God who dwelt in Him in all His fullness. We see Jesus in Isaiah 11:1-5 as Jehovah's Servant, speaking and acting according to the Father's will. So our Lord's judgment was inerrant and His understanding perfect.

When in God's due time Christ takes over the reins of the government of this world, all will be equally right and just at last. David's prophetic words will be fulfilled, for there will be "a righteous Ruler over men, a Ruler in the fear of God" (literal rendering of 2 Samuel 23:3). Earth's long centuries of selfish misrule will come to an end, and Israel and the nations will enjoy the blessings of Messiah's gracious and faithful sway. All wickedness will be dealt with in unsparing judgment and the meek of the earth will be protected and enter into undisturbed blessedness.

### Isaiah 11:6-9

When Christ comes to rule, the curse will be lifted from the lower creation and the very nature of the beasts of the earth will be changed.

Those who attempt to spiritualize Isaiah 11:6-9 would say that the beasts here represent violent and savage men whose hearts will be changed by regeneration. But the prophet gave no hint of such an application of his words. He very definitely spoke of that which God will do for the animal kingdom when the curse is lifted. There is no hint that the prophet was speaking allegorically or that his language should not be interpreted literally.

It seems evident that when the Second Man, the last Adam, is set over this lower universe, ideal conditions will prevail on earth. The earth will be as it was before sin came in to mar God's fair creation. Sin's sad consequences—violence and rapine among the beasts and sickness and death among men and women—will all be undone when Christ comes, as predicted by the prophets, to be the restorer of all things. "The earth shall be full of the knowledge of the Lord, as the waters cover the sea" (see also Habakkuk 2:14).

While the millennium is not to be confused with the new heavens and the new earth, it will nevertheless be a period of wonderful blessing for those who will dwell in the world during that time. Then God will head up all things in Christ.

### *Isaiah 11:10-16*

It is when Jesus returns in glory and, as the Branch out of the root of Jesse, fulfills the promises made to David, that all these things will come to pass. Then Jacob's prophecy will have its glorious fulfillment: "Unto Him shall the gathering of the peoples be" (literal rendering of Genesis 49:10). In that day, we are told, God will magnify Jesus in the eyes of Israel, and the Gentiles too will seek Him.

God's own earthly people, scattered for so long among the Gentile nations, will be gathered back to their own land. Many people think that the promises of their restoration were fulfilled long ago when a remnant returned in the days of Zerubbabel, Ezra, and Nehemiah. But in Isaiah 11:11 we are definitely informed that "the Lord shall set his hand again the *second* time to recover the remnant of his people" (italics added). We also learn that they will return not simply from Babylon as before, but from all the lands where they have been dispersed throughout the long centuries of their sorrow and suffering. Israel and Judah, no longer divided, will be drawn to the Lord Himself—the "ensign" to be set up in that day. They will flow together to the land of their fathers, no longer as rival nations, but as one people in glad subjection to their King and their God.

The chapter closes with details about the manner of Israel and Judah's return. They will be assisted by nations that were once their enemies and aided by certain geographical changes. No doubt these changes will be effected at the time when the feet of our Lord stand again on the mount of Olives and a great earthquake with far-reaching results occurs as foretold in Zechariah 14.

## ISAIAH 12

# WHEN GOD'S ANOINTED TAKES OVER

## (PART TWO)

There will be great joy when God's Anointed takes over and the remant return to Zion. Isaiah 12 gives us the song of triumph that will rise exultantly from the hearts of the redeemed of the Lord, as in the days when the people sang on the shore of the Red Sea after all their enemies had been destroyed.

It is a blessed and precious experience when the heart is fixed on the Lord Himself and the soul realizes the gladness of reconciliation to the One against whom he has sinned. Then with joy he is able to say, "Though thou wast angry with me, thine anger is turned away, and thou comfortedst me."

It means much to know God as the One through whom deliverance has been wrought and who is Himself "salvation." Such knowledge is the end of all worry and anxiety. And so we hear the remnant saying, "I will trust, and not be afraid." Faith is the antidote to fear. As we learn to look to God in confidence, all anxiety disappears, for we know that He who saved us will stand between us and every foe. He does not leave His people to fight their battles in their own power; He is the strength of all who rest on His Word.

The self-righteous Jew, seeking to save himself by his own efforts, has long spurned the wells of salvation. But from that well the returned remnant will draw the water of life as they call on His name and bear witness before all the world to the salvation He has provided.

The exultant song in Isaiah 12 is a psalm and it ends with a call to praise and adore the God of Israel, who will dwell in the midst of His redeemed people in that day when His glory "is known in all the earth." Even now those who come to Him in faith can make this song their own as they know the reality of His saving grace.

# ISAIAH 13

# THE BURDEN OF BABYLON

## (PART ONE)

I saiah 13–23 is a distinct section of Isaiah's prophecy, dealing particularly with the nations who had caused Israel to suffer in the past. In these chapters are "burdens"—that is, prophetic messages—relating particularly to Babylon (13–14); Moab (15–16); Damascus, the capital of Syria (17); some unnamed maritime power west of Ethiopia (18); Egypt (19); Egypt and Ethiopia (20); Edom and Arabia (21); and Tyre (23). Some of these nations will appear on the scene in the last days, still manifesting their old enmity toward the chosen race. Chapter 22 refers definitely to Palestine in connection with the attacks of their enemies.

In Isaiah 13–14 the prophet predicted the future destruction that would come upon Babylon as a result of the Medo-Persian invasion of Chaldea. It may seem strange that Babylon occupies the place it does in these prophetic visions inasmuch as it was an insignificant power completely overshadowed by Assyria in Isaiah's day. But the spirit of prophecy enabled Isaiah to look ahead to the time when Babylon and Assyria would be combined in one great dominion, of which the city of Babylon would be the capital. Babylon was the power destined to carry out the judgments of God against Judah because of its rebellion and idolatry.

As you read Isaiah 13–14 you will see that behind the literal rulers of Babylon was a sinister spirit-personality named Lucifer, the "son of the morning" (14:12). That this evil angel is identical with Satan himself seems to be perfectly clear.

The prophecy regarding Babylon was to have a double fulfillment: first, Babylon's destruction by the armies of Cyrus and Cyaxares (who is probably the same as the Darius of Daniel 5); and second, the final destruction of the Assyrian of the last days. In eloquent and dramatic language Isaiah pictured the downfall of the future oppressor of the people of God.

### Isaiah 13:1-11

The picture presented goes far beyond that of the literal destruction of Babylon on the Euphrates in the days of the Medo-Persian conquest. Reflected here are the conditions that will prevail not only among the nations of central and western Asia, but among all Gentile powers in the day of the Lord's indignation. In other words, the doom that fell upon Babylon of old was an illustration of the terrible fate that awaits the godless Gentile powers who will be taken in red-handed rebellion against the Lord and His Anointed in the last days.

Note that many of the expressions used in these verses are practically identical with those in other prophecies concerning the day of the Lord and with those describing the events to follow the breaking of the sixth seal in the book of Revelation.

### Isaiah 13:12-16

If you compare this passage with Haggai 2:6-7, Hebrews 12:25-29, Zechariah 14:4-5, and other passages relating to the day of the Lord, you will learn that the kingdoms of the world will be broken to pieces, but that is not all. There will also be tremendous natural convulsions that will shake the earth and cause disorder even among the heavenly bodies. The people of the world will be in abject terror because of the judgments of the Lord.

Such a large portion of the human race will be destroyed in the conflicts and natural catastrophes of those days that a man will be more precious than gold. Fear will take hold of all the inhabitants of the earth who do not know and wait for the Lord in that day of His power.

## Isaiah 13:17-22

Here the prophet reverted to the literal destruction of Babylon that began with its siege and overthrow by the Medes and Persians. Its destruction was fully consummated some centuries later when at last that one-time proud city was leveled to the dust. Its palaces were demolished and its hanging gardens ruined. In all the centuries since, Babylon has never been able to rise again, for God has decreed, "It shall never be inhabited." It is true that from time to time small villages have been built near the site of the ancient city, but even to this day Arabians refuse to pitch their tents on the site. They think that demons prowl by night among the ruins where owls, lizards ("dragons" in 13:22), and other nocturnal creatures abound. The ruins of Babylon uncovered by archeologists show how completely the prophet's words were fulfilled.

The Babylon of the Apocalypse is a symbolic picture of the great religious-commercial organization that will become fully developed in the last days after the true church has been caught up to be with the Lord. The doom of that organization, like that of the ancient city, will soon be consummated and it too will fall, never to lift itself up again against God and His people.

# ISAIAH 14

# THE BURDEN OF BABYLON

## (PART TWO)

I saiah 14 shows that God linked Israel's restoration with Babylon's doom. Part of this divine prediction concerning the recovery of Judah was fulfilled when through a decree of the conquering Cyrus a remnant was permitted to return to Jerusalem. Likewise the future final restoration of Israel will be connected to the complete overthrow of Gentile power.

### Isaiah 14:1-2

Note the expression in 14:2, "They shall take them captives, whose captives they were." This seems to explain that much-debated passage in Ephesians 4:8: "He led captivity captive." Paul was quoting those words from Psalm 68:18. The same Hebraism is found in Judges 5:12, where the meaning is perfectly clear: Barak was to lead captive those who had held Israel captive. Similarly Christ by His triumphant resurrection has overthrown the powers of Hell and led captive Satan and his hosts who had held humanity captive for so long. The devil was utterly defeated at that time and those who had once been his victims are now delivered from his power (Hebrews 2:14). In Colossians 2:15 we are told that Christ, in rising from the dead, spoiled or made a prey of principalities and powers—that is, the hosts of evil—and therefore Satan is now a defeated foe. His judgment has not yet been carried out, but it is as certain as

God's Word is true. The believer, knowing that the devil can have
no power against those who cleave to the Word of God, is to resist
Satan and remain steadfast in the faith.

## Isaiah 14:3-8

This passage shows Israel exulting over the destruction of her
great enemy. The "king of Babylon" seems to be used in 14:4 as a
synonym for all the Gentile powers that throughout the centuries
have taken part in the persecution of God's ancient people. When
their last great enemy is destroyed, they will be able to rejoice in the
display of Jehovah's power. Just as Israel sang on the shores of the
Red Sea when they viewed the destruction of the pharaoh and his
host, so in that coming day they will be able to raise the song of
Moses and the Lamb when they see all their enemies brought to
naught.

## Isaiah 14:9-15

These verses enable us to understand how sin began in the heavens
and to comprehend something of the unseen powers that throughout the centuries have dominated the minds of evil-disposed men
who seek to thwart the purpose of God. This passage, which por-
trays the fall of Lucifer (Satan), links very closely with Ezekiel 28,
which should be carefully considered in an effort to understand
Isaiah's words fully.

These words of Isaiah cannot apply to any mere mortal man.
Lucifer (the light-bearer) is a created angel of the very highest order and is identical with the covering cherub of Ezekiel 28. Apparently he was the greatest of all the angel host and was perfect before
God until pride caused him to fall. His ambition was to take the
throne of deity for himself and become the supreme ruler of the
universe. Note his five "I wills" in 14:13-14: "*I will* ascend into
heaven, *I will* exalt my throne above the stars of God: *I will* sit also
upon the mount of the congregation, in the sides of the north: *I will*
ascend above the heights of the clouds; *I will* be like the most High"

(italics added). The assertion of the creature's will in opposition to the will of the Creator brought about his downfall, and thus an archangel became the devil!

Cast down from the place of power and favor that he had enjoyed, he became the untiring enemy of God and man, and throughout the millenniums since his expulsion, he has used every conceivable device to ruin mankind and rob God of the glory due to His name. In John 8:44 the Lord showed that Satan is an apostate, having fallen from a position once enjoyed, and we know from 1 Peter 5:8 that he ever goes about "as a roaring lion...seeking whom he may devour." The cross was the precursor of Satan's doom, but because his heart is filled with hatred against God and those whom God loves, he is determined to wreak his vengeance on mankind as much as he can before his own final judgment takes place.

We know from passages such as 2 Peter 2:4 that Lucifer was not alone in his rebellion. This is confirmed in Matthew 25:41, where our Lord spoke of "the devil and his angels," and in Revelation 12:7, where we read of the coming war in Heaven between Michael (and his angels) and the dragon (and his angels). These evil angels are "the world-rulers of this darkness" (literal rendering of Ephesians 6:12). They seek to dominate the hearts and minds of the rulers of the nations and stir them up to act in opposition to the will of God. Therefore it is not surprising to find that in the next verses of Isaiah 14 the king of Babylon seems to be confounded with Lucifer. The meaning of course is that the king was controlled or dominated by Satan.

### Isaiah 14:16-27

This passage, which describes the downfall of the king, is highly poetical. Yet it was in no uncertain terms that Isaiah depicted the utter destruction of the last great enemy of Israel in the day of the Lord. (See also Ezekiel 31:16-18.) All the glory of the warrior and the pride of world conquest will be destroyed. No one who has dared to rise up in pride and arrogance to defy the living God has ever been able to escape the inevitable result of his folly.

In the Assyrian of the last days we see the incarnation as it were of all the persecuting powers who have distressed Israel since their dispersion among the Gentiles. When the nations are gathered together for the Armageddon conflict, the Lord Himself will destroy the Assyrian and every other enemy of Christ and His truth. Israel will be completely delivered and God will be glorified in the kingdom to be set up in righteousness.

### Isaiah 14:28-32

In the last five verses of Isaiah 14 we find a separate prophecy relating to Palestine and its people. This prophecy was given in the last year of King Ahaz.

For the time being God had turned back the armies of Syria and Assyria, but greater conflicts were in store for Judah in the days of Hezekiah and at the close of the short reign of Zedekiah. First the land was overrun by the Assyrians. They had to turn back without accomplishing their purpose, but because of Judah's lack of repentance and self-judgment, the armies of Nebuchadnezzar eventually destroyed Jerusalem, slew thousands of the people, and carried many more into captivity.

This was not to be the last distress that would come upon that doomed land. Throughout the long years since the Jews' dispersion, Palestine has been a veritable battleground and Israel's sufferings have beggared all description. The day of their deliverance is yet to come and that deliverance will be through the very One whom the nation rejected when He came in lowly grace as the promised Savior and Messiah.

# THE BURDEN OF MOAB

## (PART ONE)

I n the short fifteenth chapter the prophet predicted the eventual destruction of Moab. The country bearing this name lay to the north of the land of Edom and was bounded on the west by the Dead Sea and on the east by the Arabian desert. Moab's northern boundary ordinarily was the Arnon river, but because of frequent strife with the Ammonites, the border changed from time to time; occasionally it extended miles north of this river.

The Moabites were descendants of the illegitimate son of Lot and his eldest daughter. Moab therefore might picture for us those who make a profession of being children of God, but actually have no legitimate claim to that name. In other words, Moab might represent to us the easy-going profession of Christianity made by many who fail to recognize the importance of the new birth.

Generally speaking, Moab was somewhat friendly toward Israel. But when the Israelites were first passing through Moab's borders on the way to their inheritance in the promised land, Balak was fearful of being destroyed by them and so hired Balaam, the son of Beor, to curse them. As we know, God turned the curse into a blessing.

The book of Ruth tells us of the visit of Elimelech and his family to Moab in the time of famine—and the unhappy results of that sojourn. When David was pursued by Saul, he took his parents to Moab and put them under the protection of its king (1 Samuel 22:3-4), but as the years went on, Moab (like Edom) became an enemy

of Israel. Likewise no matter how friendly those who merely profess to be religious may seem, the day always comes when they
resent what seems to them to be the assumed superiority of those
who really know the Lord. So from time to time we find in Scripture that Moab was allied with the enemies of Israel and Judah.

Isaiah depicted most graphically the day of Moab's destruction.
Those predictions had their initial fulfillment when Moab as a nation was utterly destroyed, evidently to a great extent through the
armies of Assyria and Babylonia. For centuries the Moabites' land
has been inhabited by the Arabians of the desert because "the grass
faileth, there is no green thing."

Moab's doom may be looked on as a solemn warning of the judgment that will fall on those who profess to be Christians, but are
dead toward God (see Revelation 3:2). They are content to go on
with an empty profession instead of turning to God in repentance
and finding new life in Christ.

# THE BURDEN OF MOAB

## (PART TWO)

Continuing the subject of Isaiah 15, chapter 16 begins with an earnest entreaty on the part of the Lord Himself for Moab to turn from its enmity against His people and meet their ambassadors in a spirit of friendliness.

### Isaiah 16:1-5

Moab was devoted largely to the raising of sheep and cattle, and during the reigns of David and Solomon and even later Moab paid tribute to Israel and Judah by sending them a specified number of animals from their flocks and herds every year. In Isaiah's day Moab had revolted and refused to continue to pay this tribute, and the prophet, speaking by divine inspiration, pleaded with them to send their quota of lambs to the ruler of the land of Israel. He also pleaded with Moab to cease acting vindictively toward those who, in terror of invading armies, had fled across the Jordan for refuge. By thus demonstrating friendliness to Jehovah's people, Moab might at least for the time being avert her judgment.

The prophet went on to emphasize the authority given to the prince who sat on David's throne. Isaiah could envision the coming of the Messiah, God's anointed King, who was to sit on this throne and rule the nations in righteousness.

## *Isaiah 16:6-14*

To what extent Isaiah's entreaty influenced the nation of Moab at that time, we have no way of knowing. It seems, however, that there was no response. Instead the Moabites met the pleadings of the prophet with coldness and arrogance, and therefore judgment had to take its course.

Like many another people with whom God has pleaded earnestly through His prophets, beseeching them to turn from their evil ways and submit to His authority, the leaders of Moab responded to the prophet's entreaty with defiance. Since they refused to heed the call to be subject to the God of Israel, there was no hope of recovery. Moab would be exposed to the ravages of the armies of Assyria, first under Sennacherib and then under other leaders, until Moab's national existence was brought to an end.

The language used by the prophet is stirring indeed and indicates how deeply he himself yearned for the deliverance of Moab and longed to see them yield to the commands of Jehovah.

Isaiah 16:13-14 predicts a preliminary judgment. Just when or how these words were fulfilled we do not know because of lack of familiarity with the ancient records—records which have to a great extent now been destroyed. But we may be certain that the prophecy was fulfilled and that Moab's destruction began in Isaiah's day.

# ISAIAH 17

# DAMASCUS AND EPHRAIM

Now we will consider the burden of Damascus. Closely linked with Damascus is the nation of Israel, generally known as Ephraim after the break with Judah. Because Ephraim had formed an alliance with Syria, the kingdom of which Damascus was the capital, the Ephraimites would share in the judgment that was about to fall on that proud city and on the Syrian dominion.

Damascus is sometimes said to be the oldest city in the world. This may or may not be so, but it certainly has existed through several millenniums and has passed through many wars and other distressing experiences. Yet it stands today as a great commercial center in the midst of a strikingly beautiful district. We are told that when Muhammad and his army drew near the city and looked down on it from a hilltop, the Arabian false prophet turned to his followers and said, "It is given to men to enter but one paradise. We will not go into Damascus." And he and his cohorts turned away.

### Isaiah 17:1-5

"Damascus is taken away from being a city," prophesied Isaiah, "and it shall be a ruinous heap. The cities of Aroer are forsaken." There were two cities or districts known as Aroer: one east of the Dead Sea in the land of Moab, the other near Damascus. It is evidently the latter that is in view here.

At the time when Isaiah prophesied, Sennacherib's hosts were rapidly moving toward Israel and Syria and it is of this onslaught that the first verses of chapter 17 speak. The prophet foresaw that as a result of the Assyrian attack, Damascus and all the surrounding towns and villages would fall prey to that great eastern power. Israel too would suffer at the hand of the Assyrians.

All of the prophecy in 17:1-5 has been fulfilled; yet we may look upon the entire passage as being prophetic of that which will take place in the last days when God will deal once more with both Israel and the Gentile nations.

### Isaiah 17:6-8

In the last days, as in the Old Testament, a remnant of Jacob who will seek the face of the Lord will be preserved. This remnant is distinguished in many of the books of the prophets and is clearly identified again in the New Testament. It is this godly company in whom "all Israel shall be saved" (Romans 11:26). Many have thought that Paul was implying that the entire nation would be delivered in the time of Jacob's trouble, but we need to remember that "they are not all Israel, which are of Israel" (Romans 9:6). It is in the remnant that God recognizes the true seed of Jacob. Those who turn to the Lord will be preserved in the last time of trouble as they were in the past, and through them the land will again be inhabited. Abhorring idolatry, they will find their resource in the God of their fathers. As the remnant look to Him for protection, He will undertake for them.

### Isaiah 17:9-11

Are we to take the words of 17:9-11 literally or figuratively? Possibly both. Surely they picture the folly of Israel in days gone by when although they had turned away from the Lord God of hosts, they still encouraged themselves to believe that they would prosper in their sinful condition; so they planted lovely gardens and built great cities, only to see them visited at last by divine judgment. But is there not something in these verses that perhaps has had its literal fulfillment on more than one occasion in the past and at the present time is being fulfilled again?

By the time the Ottoman Turks conquered Palestine, the forests of Lebanon had long since been cut down and the wood used for many different purposes. The trees that had once grown on the mount of Olives and mount Scopus had, according to Josephus, all been cut down by Titus and used during the siege of Jerusalem. But it is a well-known fact that during the long years of Turkish misrule the land was almost denuded of trees. During the last century of Turkish dominion the Ottoman government put a tax on all trees. The tax was so exorbitant that the inhabitants of Palestine rebelled against it and rather than pay the tax, they cut down nearly every tree on their estates.

After World War I when the mandate of Palestine was entrusted to Great Britain, one of the first programs the British government set in motion was the reforestation of the mountains of Lebanon. Thousands upon thousands of young trees were planted on those heights; and thousands of eucalyptus or blue gum trees were imported from Australia and planted in the swampier parts of the country in order to assist in draining the land. Following this, the returning Jews immediately began planting oliveyards and orchards of orange and other citrus-fruit trees, so that the entire country was literally planted with "strange slips."

It certainly began to look as though Palestine had a wonderfully prosperous era ahead of it. But all has not been according to the hope of the Jews, for troubles and disasters have fallen upon the land. Forest fires have again destroyed many of the trees of Lebanon, and what the future has in store we dare not attempt to say, except that Scripture depicts great and terrible trials such as Jacob has never known. Surely the harvest will be a day of grief and desperate sorrow. How this should move our hearts to cry to God for the salvation of Israel and to pray for the peace of Jerusalem!

### Isaiah 17:12-14

The words of 17:12-14 had a primary fulfillment in the destruction of Israel's foes, notably the Assyrians of Isaiah's day and the Chaldeans later on. Yet the predictions in these verses also coincide with what our Lord prophesied concerning the great tribulation. He said it would be preceded by the time when "nation shall rise against nation, and kingdom against kingdom: And great earthquakes shall be in divers places...the sea and the waves roaring; Men's hearts failing them for fear, and for looking after those things which are coming on the earth" (Luke 21:10-11,25-26).

As the closing hour of tribulation strikes, the nations will be gathered together against Jerusalem. The hosts of the Gentiles will come from the east, the north, and the west to engage in bloody conflict in an effort to obtain possession of Immanuel's land. Then the glorious appearing of the Lord Jesus Christ will bring the last great war to an end. The beast and the false prophet and their adherents will perish by the breath of the Lord, and the hosts of Gog and Magog and the kings of the East will be destroyed by the omnipotent power of God, acting for the deliverance of His people Israel.

# THE LAND SHADOWING WITH WINGS

I saiah 18 has given ground for many differences of opinion among Christian scholars, particularly interpreters of prophecy. Many have taken it for granted that "the land shadowing with wings" is Egypt because of the winged solar disk that was a symbol of that country's power and greatness and is seen on so many of its monuments. But it could hardly be said of Egypt that it lies "beyond the rivers of Ethiopia," for the Nile descends from Ethiopia, passes through the midst of Egypt, and empties itself into the Mediterranean sea in the north.

Some have thought that the wings refer to the United States because of the fact that on our great seal an eagle is represented with outstretched wings. Other nations have used the eagle on their ensigns and coats of arms, but not with overshadowing wings. Many other people have assumed that inasmuch as "the land shadowing with wings" is undoubtedly a great maritime power, Isaiah was referring to Great Britain, who used to glory in ruling the waves. But it does not seem possible to make the identification with either Britain or America with certainty. Perhaps "the land shadowing with wings" includes both these countries along with the other nations that will be linked together in the last great confederacy.

F. C. Jennings, in his monumental work on Isaiah, pointed out that there were two districts known as *Cush,* the Hebrew word translated "Ethiopia" in 18:1: one on the banks of the Euphrates, and the other in the area that we now call Ethiopia. The great stretch of country between these two districts was included in the land promised to Abraham and was ruled by both David and Solomon for a time. It seems evident from many prophetic Scriptures that Israel will possess all of this land in the millennial day. So it could be that "the rivers of Ethiopia" are the Euphrates and the Nile, and the land "beyond" them includes western European nations and other areas of the western hemisphere unknown to the prophets of old.

We know that ten kingdoms rising out of the ancient Roman empire are to come to the front in the last days. They will be bound together by an offensive and defensive alliance ruled by the sinister character designated as "the beast" in Revelation 13. This last confederation of the Gentile nations of the West will for a time act as the friend and ally of Israel as a nation restored to their own land. It is therefore reasonable to conclude that Isaiah was referring to these western powers in the opening part of chapter 18.

### Isaiah 18:1-2

"Woe to the land shadowing with wings," Isaiah cried. The word translated "woe" in 18:1 is the same as that rendered "Ho" in 55:1. It is a call to attention. Jehovah was summoning the great power lying "beyond the rivers of Ethiopia" to come to the aid of His people. Undoubtedly it was the people of Israel who were in view, for through the centuries they indeed have been, "a nation scattered and peeled." What other people have suffered as they have and yet maintained their unity and national existence in spite of every effort made to destroy them? They have been "terrible from their beginning," for when they went forth as directed by the Lord, the fear of them fell upon all nations that confronted them. Their power seemed unlimited, but when they became disobedient, disaster followed.

### Isaiah 18:3-6

The ships of the Gentiles will bring Israel back to their land while Jehovah, as it were, looks on but does not interfere in any special sense. The return depicted in 18:3-6, evidently not that which is spoken of elsewhere in the prophets, is based on the repentance of the nation and their recognition of Jesus as the Messiah. The "ensign" lifted up on the mountains will be the signal, for those who through the centuries have wandered among the Gentiles, to return to Palestine.

We may be seeing this prophecy being fulfilled already, for Jews are now in their land and Israel is recognized by other nations as an independent republic. We would hope that the sufferings of the Jews were over if we did not know that even greater distress awaits them in the future when the horrors of the great tribulation burst upon them in fury. Then a remnant will be distinguished from the mass and with this remnant Jehovah will be identified.

### Isaiah 18:7

The prophecy of 18:7 coincides with the actual return of the Lord when He will arise to deal in judgment with the enemies of Israel and to recognize the remnant as His people. The great trumpet will be blown and the outcasts of Israel will be summoned to return from every land of earth to their ancient patrimony. Surely we may see in all that is going on at the present time in connection with Palestine and the new nation Israel now established there, how readily all these predictions will have their complete fulfillment as soon as the church of God has been taken out of this scene and caught up to be with the Lord.

God's heart has always been inclined toward Israel. It is true that He has permitted them to pass through terrible sufferings during the long centuries of their dispersion because they did not recognize their Messiah. But the day will surely come when, their transgressions forgiven and their hearts renewed, they will be restored to God and planted again in their own land, which "the rivers have spoiled" so often.

Rivers are a well-known symbol in the prophetic Scriptures. Invading armies are often pictured as destructive overflowing rivers. Such "rivers" have passed and repassed over the land of Palestine throughout the nearly two millenniums since the rejection of Christ and the destruction of Jerusalem and the temple forty years later. Palestine has been an almost continual battleground.

Assyria, Babylonia, Persia, Greece, Egypt, Rome, and later the Turks and other powers fought over this land. Whoever won, the Jew was always the loser until, in God's due time, General (later Lord) Allenby entered Jerusalem without firing a shot and the Turkish army fled beyond the borders of the land.

God has been working providentially toward the fulfillment of His purpose for Israel. Their reliance, however, has been on their own wisdom and might, and at times the assistance of the Gentiles, rather than on God. So there have been many disappointments and there will be more before the promises of God have their complete fulfillment.

# THE BURDEN OF EGYPT

## (PART ONE)

However little we understand all the details in Isaiah 19–20, we cannot fail to recognize in these chapters the hand of God dealing with Egypt. This one-time haughty kingdom would experience retaliatory judgments because of its independent spirit and proud attitude toward the people of the Lord. In centuries gone by they had been subjected by the Egyptians to cruel bondage and often since had suffered through Egyptian violence. Even though at the time Isaiah prophesied Egypt was outwardly in alliance with Judah, she proved utterly undependable when it came to helping Ahaz and later Hezekiah stand against the onrush of the Assyrian armies.

The philosophy of history might be summed up in the words of Galatians 6:7 if "nation" is substituted for "man," and "it" for "he": Whatsoever a nation soweth, that shall it also reap. Down through the centuries the blessing of God has rested on nations that have followed after righteousness, even in measure, and His judgments have fallen when corruption and violence have taken the place of subjection to His hand.

There is not enough agreement among historians and archaeologists to enable us to speak positively as to just when the predictions contained in the first part of Isaiah 19 were fulfilled, but we may be absolutely certain that (whether or not we have monumental confirmation of them yet) they all came to pass as divinely foretold. We do know that about the time of Isaiah's prophecy, Egypt was in a state of internal strife. The pharaoh was unable to control either the populace or his armies and as a result his dynasty was eventually overthrown. A number of independent states were set up until a king arose who was able to unite them again into one empire. Remember that Egyptian records go back to the dawn of history. In the beginning the religion of Egypt was a pure monotheism. What the apostle Paul said in Romans 1 about the heathen generally was true of the Egyptians to a marked degree. When they knew God, they turned away from Him and worshiped and served the creature rather than the Creator. First they set up images made in the likeness of corruptible men, and they recognized these images as gods of the various forces of nature. Later the Egyptians deified birds like the sacred ibis, and beasts like the sacred bull and the cat of Bubastis, and then degenerated to the worship of reptiles such as the sacred crocodile and the asp. Last of all they even deified certain forms of insect life, the sacred scarab being the one with which we are most familiar.

Neither the life of a man nor the life of a nation is any better than that of the gods that are worshiped, so Egypt became debased politically, morally, and spiritually until at last that once-proud empire was destroyed. It became an inferior kingdom, not to be reckoned among the major dominions.

### Isaiah 19:1-3

In the opening verses of Isaiah 19 God is pictured as riding the divine chariot, coming down from Heaven to deal with this guilty nation. When Isaiah wrote, God's patience with Egypt had at last come to an end. He Himself would deal with their false gods by demonstrating their inability and His own omnipotence. Isaiah foresaw that the worshipers of these idols would be exposed to sufferings; terrified, they would seek in vain for help from their false deities. The heart of the people would fail and in their desperation they would turn to those who professed to deal with departed spirits, the necromancers and other charlatans who already abounded in great numbers in that land of superstition.

No longer respecting the king who ruled over them, city after city would revolt and independent rival states would be set up. This new system would not result in peace and security because of jealousy among the counties.

## Isaiah 19:4-10

History records that after years of almost constant civil war and internal strife, a cruel and tyrannical leader known as Psammetichos arose. He founded a new dynasty and succeeded in bringing about at least an outward semblance of unity. He is generally considered to be the "cruel lord" in 19:4.

However, the events prophesied in Isaiah 19 may not have followed in immediate sequence. Some have thought that the prophecy pointed to the day when Egypt would be so weakened that she would be powerless to resist the onslaught of the Arabs and later the Ottoman Turks. In that case, the "cruel lord" would refer to the succession of Ottoman rulers who subjected Egypt to the hardest servitude and taxed the people until they were reduced to the most desperate poverty.

After predicting the reign of this fierce ruler, Isaiah went on to foretell the destruction of the great commercial enterprises in which Egypt once excelled. The centuries since bear witness to the literal fulfillment of these prophecies. In some way the great fishing industry of Egypt was brought to an end and the Nile, which once abounded with fish, ceased to be productive. Egypt was at one time the center of the papyrus industry, but production stopped because the papyrus plant ("paper reeds") no longer grew in quantities on the banks of the Nile. Egyptian linens were once exported to all civilized lands and brought enormous income to the merchants of Egypt, but singularly enough and exactly according to prophecy, the production of flax came almost to an end. The industry, which once was monopolized by Egypt, was taken over by other nations and never since has Egypt been a linen-producing country to any serious extent. So Isaiah's prophetic words have been literally fulfilled.

## *Isaiah 19:11-15*

The prophecy in 19:11-15 definitely depicts a time of great business depression and political perplexity, a time when pharaoh's counselors proved themselves unable to handle the situation correctly. Their advice offered no real solution to the problems that the nation was facing. The princes of Zoan (Tanis) and of Noph (Memphis) sought in vain for a way out of the conditions that confronted them. The reason for their failure was that they refused to turn to the only One who could have helped them—that is, the God of Israel, whom they despised. Therefore a spirit of perversity took hold of them and they were like drunken men, unable to control themselves or their country.

In this prophetic depiction we are reminded of what is indicated so plainly in other parts of Scripture: that Egypt is a type of this present evil world, the godless system that once held the people of God in bondage. They were made to serve with rigor under the lashing of the lusts of the flesh.

This world has grown no better throughout all the centuries during which the gospel has been preached and the Lord has been taking out a people for His name. Rather it has become hardened in its attitude toward God and His Word. And "evil men and seducers," we are told, "shall wax worse and worse, deceiving, and being deceived" (2 Timothy 3:13). This state of things will not be changed until the now-rejected Christ returns from Heaven "in flaming fire taking vengeance on them that know not God" (2 Thessalonians 1:8). Then will His kingdom of righteousness supersede all the kingdoms that man has set up and "the Lord alone shall be exalted in that day" (Isaiah 2:11,17).

## *Isaiah 19:16-25*

The rest of Isaiah 19 is divided into five distinct sections, each beginning with the words "In that day": (1) 19:16-17; (2) 19:18; (3) 19:19-22; (4) 19:23; (5) 19:24-25. All look forward to the day of the Lord, the day of Jehovah's triumph.

There is a definite sense in which the words of the first section

(19:16-17) are even now in the course of fulfillment. We have seen Israel returning in unbelief to her own land, and one of her chief adversaries, the nation of Egypt, appears to dread the growing power of the nation once enslaved by the pharaohs. But according to these verses, the acknowledged weakness of Egypt and the recognition of God's power in permitting the resettlement of His people in their own land will prove to be the precursor of blessing. Egyptian enmity will come to an end in the day that Israel turns to God in repentance and receives the Messiah they once rejected.

Since in 19:16-17 we only see Egypt's fear that the Israelites will multiply and become stronger than they, it is difficult to take the prophecy as having to do with the times shortly following Isaiah's day. Rather than being a "terror unto Egypt" then, Judah was carried away by Babylon. For the time being Jehovah's testimony ceased to exist in the land of Palestine.

Commentators generally say that the second section (19:18) refers to the migration of many Jews to the land of Egypt following the destruction of the first temple. We know from history that the day came when many thousands of Israelites dwelt in the cities of Egypt; synagogues were erected there and the law of Moses was read and taught. However, it is also possible that 19:18 refers to a future day when the Egyptians and the Jews will become very close as both together acknowledge the one true and living God.

"The city of destruction" mentioned here is generally considered to be Heliopolis, "the city of the sun." Its Hebrew name was *Ir-ha-cheres,* which by the change of one letter became *Ir-ha-heres,* "the city of destruction." John Bunyan was wisely guided when he selected this as the name for the original home of the pilgrim named Graceless, who declared that he was born in the City of Destruction.

Many have been the conjectures as to the real meaning of the third section (19:19-22). Some people, including the Anglo-Israelites and the founder of the Jehovah's Witnesses, maintain that the altar and the pillar in 19:19 refer to the great pyramid. They suggest that this pyramid was erected by divine instruction and that the length of its passages, etc., indicate the exact period of the times of the Gentiles. This pyramid has been the basis of many theories as to the time when this age will end with the coming of the Lord Jesus, but all dates suggested have expired. The word remains true that "of that day and hour knoweth no man" (Matthew 24:36). The great pyramid is not an altar; nor is it a pillar. It is simply a gigantic tomb.

It seems evident that in the last days when Egypt turns to the Lord, the altar and the pillar of 19:19 will be set up on the border of Egypt in the form of a memorial of some kind and there worship will be offered to Jehovah; but it is useless to speculate any further when God has withheld additional information. What we know is that the Egyptians "shall cry unto the Lord because of the oppressors, and he shall send them a saviour, and a great one, and he shall deliver them." Surely this "saviour" can be none other than our blessed Lord Jesus. After Egypt has learned its lesson because of the judgments that will have been poured upon it, the Savior will heal it and bring it into lasting blessing.

The fourth section (19:23) doubtless refers to millennial days when two great Gentile powers, Egypt and Assyria, or perhaps more accurately the people who will be dwelling in those lands, will have friendly commercial relations with one another. They will also be on friendly terms with Israel, who will be recognized as the people of the Lord. (See also Isaiah 35:8-10.)

According to the fifth section (19:24-25), the one-time warring powers of Egypt, Assyria, and Israel will be brought into fullness of blessing "in that day." In this prophecy we see Jew and Gentile enjoying together the blessings of the promised kingdom when the Lord Himself takes over the government of the universe.

# THE BURDEN OF EGYPT

## (PART TWO)

Isaiah 20, continuing the prophecy regarding God's dealing with Egypt, refers to Sargon, the king of Assyria, who exercised tremendous power for a short time. Sargon was unknown to history (except for the Bible) until his name was, in our times, found on monuments. These monuments confirm Isaiah's record. However, Scripture does not need to be vindicated by the often conflicting histories of ancient times or by archaeological inscriptions. We may be sure that the Bible is God's inerrant Word and therefore always right, even though some of the ancient records might seem to be in conflict with it. But again and again it has pleased God through the spade of the archaeologist to give full confirmation of the truth of His Word, thus settling doubts and questions that unbelievers have been only too glad to raise.

Isaiah was commanded by God to become a sign to the Egyptians—a sign of the hardships that would be brought on them by the Assyrian armies. The prophet was instructed to lay aside his outer garments, take off his sandals, and walk "naked and barefoot" among the people as an indication of the circumstances the Egyptians would have to face. Observe that it was not nudity, but nakedness that was commanded; the laying aside of his long robe would give the appearance of nakedness to an oriental. Other commentators have pointed out that we are not told in 20:2 that Isaiah had to go about in this manner for three years, but that in all likelihood three days represented the three years in which the Egyptians were to suffer.

(F. C. Jennings wrote that 20:3-4 could be read, "And Jehovah said, As My Servant Isaiah goeth naked and barefoot, a *three years' sign and wonder against Egypt and against Ethiopia, so shall the king of Assyria lead away the Egyptians prisoners, etc.*")

In their desperation the Egyptians would recognize their helplessness and cry out for a deliverer. That Deliverer was yet to be revealed in the coming day of the Lord.

# ISAIAH 21

# BABYLON, DUMAH, AND ARABIA

Three burdens, or oracles, are grouped together in Isaiah 21. What they have in common that is of interest to us is that each country mentioned became prominent, in its turn, as an oppressor or enemy of Israel and Judah. Verses 1-10 relate to Babylon. Verses 11-12 relate to Dumah, a synonym for Edom. Verses 13-17 relate to Arabia.

### Isaiah 21:1-10

Here the prophet looked far into the future, for in his lifetime Babylon could scarcely have been recognized as even a potential enemy to the people of God.

After Hezekiah's healing, messengers came from the apparently friendly king of Babylon to bring their felicitations to the Jewish king and to inquire about the miracle of the shadow on Ahaz' sundial going back ten degrees (Isaiah 38–39). Hezekiah received this embassage without hesitation or suspicion, but Isaiah later informed him that the day would come when all that they had seen would be carried away to their distant land. God had already made it clear to His servant that Babylon was pre-eminently the enemy they had to fear.

In the vision in 21:1-10, however, Isaiah foresaw the doom of this great enemy. He shared the vision in a most graphic manner that fits perfectly with what actually took place in the day of Babylon's overthrow.

It might seem strange to describe the great and prosperous city of

Babylon as "the desert of the sea," but God speaks of the things that are not as though they are. Isaiah was looking forward prophetically to the hour when that great political, religious, and commercial center would be utterly destroyed and become but a part of the waste desert lands through which the Euphrates flowed.

In the Old Testament the city of Babylon was the original home of idolatry. It was because of its opposition to God that it was at last entirely destroyed, as already predicted in Isaiah 13 and as prophesied in Jeremiah 50–51. Literal Babylon is to remain a waste forever; it is never to be rebuilt.

But that city was a type of a great religious, political, and commercial system that has been slowly rising for many centuries and is to come to the fullness of its power after the true church has been caught up to be with the Lord. We read of this Babylon in Revelation 17–18. It is a significant fact that when the angel was about to show John a vision of this mystical Babylon, he took him out into a wilderness, for wherever Babylonish principles prevail, all true spirituality disappears, and parched, arid wastes abound. So we need not be surprised at the designation of the vision in Isaiah as "the burden of the desert of the sea."

Isaiah foresaw in literal Babylon the treacherous enemy of everything divine, yet it was the unconscious instrument in the hands of God for the chastisement of His rebellious people—the flail with which they were to be threshed in order to separate the chaff from the wheat. When God's purpose had thus been accomplished, Babylon itself was to be judged. That judgment was to be so terrible that the prophet's whole being was stirred with deepest concern as the Spirit of God revealed to him the fearfulness of the overwhelming disaster that was to bring that pretentious city to an inglorious end.

God even declared the names of the countries whose mighty armies would be used to destroy Babylon: "Go up, O Elam: besiege, O Media." Elam was Persia, and Media was to be confederate with it. Prophecy was fulfilled when together they took the chief cities of Chaldea, Ecbatana and Borsippa, and finally Babylon itself as told in Daniel 5.

It gave Isaiah no pleasure to be able to predict the awful suffering to which Israel's enemies were to be exposed. His tender heart grieved deeply over the desolation and destruction that their idolatry and corruption were to bring down on them.

Isaiah spoke almost as if he were an eyewitness of the scene of revelry that was to take place on Belshazzar's last night. Then in a few lucid words the prophet pictured the scene of terror that would follow the influx of the troops of the allies who would enter Babylon.

According to Herodotus the troops entered through the dry bed of the Euphrates after Cyrus had turned away the water of that river miles above the city. Some modern historians reject this story, but whether Herodotus was right or not, in some way the Medes and the Persians overcame every obstacle to the taking of the city. They thronged its streets, slaying old and young, while the princes of Babylon, utterly unprepared for such an assault, tried to rally the defenders of the city. But it was too late. Daniel 5:30-31 tells us, "In that night was Belshazzar the king of the Chaldeans slain. And Darius the Median took the kingdom."

In Isaiah 21 the prophet took the place of a watchman and beheld with prophetic eye the chariots of the triumphant conquerors. He heard the cry, so similar to the one in the New Testament: "Babylon is fallen, is fallen; and all the graven images of her gods he hath broken unto the ground." And so at last this great fountainhead of idolatry was to be destroyed. As Isaiah solemnly asserted that the vision was given by God, he realized that Babylon's destruction would mean the deliverance of Israel, whom he referred to as "the corn of my floor."

### Isaiah 21:11-12

The burden of Dumah has a message that applies to any time before the final judgments of God fall on the earth.

*Dumah* means "silence" and the Hebrew word is almost exactly the same as our English word "dumb." Here *Dumah* is used as a synonym for the land of Edom, which is also called Seir. This was Esau's inheritance. A rugged mountainous region, it was inhabited by a nation of men of the Esau type: virile men of the open air, delighting in war and the chase. Esau himself, their progenitor, was revered as a great hunter and a fearless fighter. Many predictions of Edom's coming doom had been uttered by Jewish prophets, but those predictions had been completely ignored by the Edomites. The Edomites were so closely related to Israel that they might have been expected to be allies, but the opposite was the case.

The picture that Isaiah 21:11-12 seems to present here is that of two watchmen on opposite sides of a chasm. We may suppose that on one side is a city of the Judean wilderness and on the other, an Edomite stronghold. Watchmen pace back and forth on the walls of these cities. They are near enough to each other to hear each other's voices. The voice from Dumah calls out in skeptical tones, "Watchman, what of the night?" In other words, "How much of the night has gone?" He seems to mean, "How near is it to the time when Israel's glory will be revealed, as their prophets have been predicting?"

The answer comes back, "The morning cometh." This statement is the declaration of faith that takes God at His word and dares to believe that Israel will be brought into fullness of blessing. But the Judean watchman adds, "And also the night." The day of Israel's glory will be the night of Edom's doom. And then comes the serious entreaty: "If ye will enquire, enquire ye: return, come." It is the voice of God, speaking through His servant, calling Edom, which represents the insensate men of a godless world. God pleads with them to make diligent inquiry as to what the Lord has actually revealed and to return from their sin and rebellion to Him who still says, "Come." He waits to receive all who accept His invitation.

### Isaiah 21:13-17

The burden of Arabia contains much that we may not be able to explain clearly because of our limited knowledge of what actually took place in connection with the cities of the sons of Ishmael. Whether or not we are able to follow each detail here recorded, it is evident that Arabia was to suffer at the hand of the Assyrians in a very definite manner. For a while at least, the pride of the Ishmaelite tribes was to be humbled and their cities spoiled. Yet there is no hint of their eventual destruction, as in the case of the Edomites, for Arabia is still to be blessed in the coming day. Throughout all the centuries God has preserved these descendants of Abraham's son born after the flesh, whereas the sons of him who was born after the promise have been scattered all over the world because of their iniquities.

# THE VALLEY OF VISION

The prophet now turned his attention away from the burdens of other nations in order to deliver a message from the Lord to the people of Jerusalem. The city was in danger of being destroyed by the Assyrian armies of Sennacherib and his allies from Elam and Kir. Elam, or Persia, had for centuries been an enemy of Assyria, but at this time it had become a tributary of Assyria. As such, Elam had sent an army to cooperate with Sennacherib in an attempt to conquer the land of Judah.

### Isaiah 22:1-11

In the opening verses Isaiah exposed the true state of those who were professedly the people of God but had forgotten Him and turned aside from obedience to His Word.

Like many other passages in Isaiah, the words in 22:1-8 evidently will have a second fulfillment in the last days. Then Palestine will be exposed to the great eastern powers that will be seeking to dispossess the Jew and take over their land. However, the primary application of this prophecy was to those in Hezekiah's day who dreaded the approach of Sennacherib's armies, but tried to stifle their fears with mirth and frivolity instead of turning to the Lord and seeking the deliverance that He alone could give.

The condition of the Lord's people caused the prophet intense anguish of heart. As he looked down, as it were, on the city that two centuries later would be destroyed by the Babylonians, he wept over it. Likewise our blessed Lord at a later day looked down from the

mount of Olives on the glorious temple that Herod had built, and
bewailed the fact that Jerusalem had not acknowledged Him and so
must be doomed to destruction. In Isaiah's time defeat was deferred
because of the faithfulness of King Hezekiah and later King Josiah;
nevertheless the prophet recognized the fact that the holy city was
eventually to become the prey of the cruel and covetous Gentile
nations.

In 22:9-11 Isaiah spoke of the preparations that Hezekiah made
to enable the city to resist the threatened siege. His precautions demonstrated his wisdom and foresight, but those measures alone would
not have saved the city. It was divine intervention that destroyed
the Assyrian army and delivered Jerusalem.

### Isaiah 22:12-14

While Hezekiah sincerely turned to the Lord, the masses did not.
Even the grave danger to which the people were exposed failed to
bring them consciously into the presence of God. Neither did their
peril lead them to self-judgment so that they might be in a position
to seek His face and count on His mercy. The people seemed to
have no true realization of either their danger or their lamentably
low spiritual condition. When they should have been humbling themselves before the Lord, waiting on Him with fasting and prayer and
other evidences of repentance, they were feasting and rejoicing, living as though life was only intended for merriment and frivolity.
Their motto seemed to be, "Let us eat and drink; for to morrow we
shall die."

The apostle Paul quoted these words in 1 Corinthians 15:32 when
he was demonstrating the folly of those who, while professing to be
saved through faith in Christ, denied the resurrection. Without the
resurrection, Christians are absolutely hopeless. If we have nothing
to look forward to in eternity, why should we give up the pleasures
of the world for Christ's name's sake? Why should we not adopt
the philosophy of the epicurean poets Aratus and Cleanthes, who
expressed exactly the same sentiment as the careless, materialistic
Jews of Isaiah's day did?

"Let us eat and drink; for to morrow we shall die"—to every

thoughtful person this statement expresses the height of folly. It is a tremendously serious thing to be alive in a world like this and to know that an eternity of either happiness or misery lies beyond. Surely every sensible man should recognize the fact that life is not given to be frittered away in pleasure-seeking, but to be used sensibly and in the fear of God, with eternity's values in view.

### Isaiah 22:15-25

The last part of the chapter is of an altogether different character. The passage directs our attention to two men, both of whom held positions of trust in Hezekiah's government: Shebna and Eliakim. We will read of them again in Isaiah 36–37.

Shebna was what we might call Hezekiah's premier and chancellor of the exchequer or, to use a term more common in our land, his secretary of the treasury. But Shebna was evidently selfish, greedy, crafty, and ambitious. He used his office for personal enrichment and self-glorification.

Shebna had arranged for his own mausoleum to be built or cut out in the limestone rock where the kings of Judah were buried. He wanted a grand tomb because he thought it would perpetuate his memory in years to come. But God, who sees not as man sees, discerned the worthlessness of his character and was about to deal with him in judgment. Shebna was to be removed from his office and carried into captivity. He would die in a distant land; who then would occupy the sepulcher he had prepared for himself?

Many think of this man as a type of the antichrist of the last days and it may be that this interpretation is correct. At any rate, the character of the man of sin is akin to that of Shebna, and in each case judgment was to be followed by recognition of another who would fulfill God's purpose. After judgment fell on Shebna, he was succeeded by Eliakim, who is a type of our Lord Jesus Christ. When the antichrist has been destroyed, Christ will take over the reins of the government of this world.

Eliakim was a trustworthy man, a true statesman, and a loyal servant of Hezekiah. Not a mere politician, Eliakim was motivated by sincere love for his country and characterized by the fear of God.

Since he was to take the office vacated by Shebna, the key of David would be committed to him—that is, the key to the royal treasury, which he was given authority to open and close as he saw fit.

In 22:22 Eliakim is clearly seen as a type of our blessed Lord, for when Christ addressed the church in Philadelphia, He used the same expressions that Isaiah had used in reference to Eliakim. The Lord said in Revelation 3:7, "These things saith he that is holy, he that is true, he that hath the key of David, he that openeth, and no man shutteth; and shutteth, and no man openeth." To those who look up to the Lord as their divinely-given guide and protector, He opens the treasure house of divine truth, revealing to them the precious things that God has stored away in His Word.

Eliakim was to be as a nail fastened in a sure place. The reference is to the wooden peg driven into the supporting post of a tent. On this peg were hung vessels used in camp life and the garments of those dwelling in the tent. So on Eliakim would be hung the means of refreshment and comfort that God had provided for His people; they would be able to depend on him.

We may see in this figurative language an illustration of the security of those who have put their trust in Christ for salvation. He is indeed a nail fastened in a sure place, and on Him may be hung various vessels, from little cups to large flagons. Their safekeeping consists not in their own ability to cling to the nail, but in the fact that they are hung on that nail. They will remain secure as long as the nail stays in its place, and it will, for our blessed Lord never fails. The old creation fell in Adam, but the new creation stands in Christ, upon whom all the glory of the house of God is suspended.

Isaiah 22:25 evidently refers again to Shebna. It could not possibly refer to Eliakim, for if it did, it would be contradicting what had just been declared concerning him. The expression "in that day" definitely refers to the day when Shebna would be set to one side and Eliakim would take his office. Thank God, the day is not far distant when all that is of Satan will be annulled and destroyed and only that which is of God will remain. Then our Lord Jesus will take over the authority conferred on Him by the Father and all things will be subjected to His will and sustained by Him.

# THE BURDEN OF TYRE

T he burden of Tyre is the last of the special prophecies in Isaiah 13–23 relating to nations and cities that had caused Israel to suffer. Three of these (Egypt, Babylon, and Tyre) may be looked at as very definite types of this present evil world, which Christ died to deliver us from.

Egypt speaks of the world as we first knew it in our natural state: a scene of darkness, bondage, and death. That nation's pharaohs were recognized by the mass of the people not only as kings, but also as gods, and divine honors were paid to them; thus the pharaohs may well be symbolic of Satan, the prince and god of this world. Israel was delivered from Egypt by the blood of the passover lamb and the omnipotent power of God, who led them triumphantly through the dried bed of the Red Sea. Pharaoh's hosts, who plunged in after them, were destroyed, and on the farther shores of the Red Sea Israel sang praises to Him who had so wonderfully rescued them. We too, through grace, have known such deliverance. Henceforth we can say that just as Egypt was dead to Israel, and Israel was dead to Egypt, by our identification with the crucified Savior we have died to the world, and the world has died to us.

Babylon speaks of the religious world: a religion based not on divine revelation, but on the vain imaginations of men not subject to the will of God. Babylon was an idolatrous city and from it the worship of images spread far and wide throughout the ancient world. Today's counterpart is the sphere of worldly religion that has a form of godliness, but no power. We see this religion in its completeness in the mystery of "Babylon the great" in the book of Revelation.

This vast religious-commercial system will dominate the greater part of the world after the church has been caught up to be with the Lord, but at last the rulers of earth's kingdoms will tire of the incubus and destroy it utterly.

Tyre speaks of the world as a great commercial system where men seek to enrich themselves and their families through material pursuits. They revel in every kind of extravagance and forget about God. Such materialism pervades society today as nations reach out for commercial gain and people live on a scale of luxury unknown in previous centuries. But the time is soon coming when all the things on which men have set their hearts will be destroyed and the present world system will pass away. We may see a prediction of that day in the prophecy relating to the doom of Tyre.

### *Isaiah 23:1-5*

The prophet foresaw the complete destruction of Tyre, a great metropolis whose ships reached every known port in the world of that day. Sidon was the mother city, but she never attained the greatness of her daughter. Tyre was settled by merchants who left Sidon to build a great city by the seaside, partly on the mainland and partly on a rocky island some distance from the shore; the two parts were connected by a stone causeway. The history of Tyre reads like a thrilling romance and will repay anyone who takes the time to acquaint himself with it.

The Sidonians were Phoenicians, an active race from which sprang some of the more progressive peoples of modern times. They are credited with having invented the alphabet at a time when other nations still used pictographs in order to express themselves in writing. Our own alphabet in many respects is linked with the ancient Phoenician characters.

It must have seemed incredible at the time of Isaiah's prophecy that Tyre should ever become little more than a memory, yet his predictions were fulfilled to the letter. The Tyre of today is but a squalid reminder of the great metropolis of olden days. The doom of the city would affect nations as near as Egypt and as far away as

Tarshish because it was through the ships of Tyre that their merchandise was profitably disposed of.

### Isaiah 23:6-9

"Tarshish" seems to be a somewhat general term, certainly including Spain and possibly also Great Britain. We are told that the Tyrian merchants brought tin, lead, and other metals from Tarshish (Ezekiel 27:12), and these metals were found in the mines of Spain and Britain. In fact *Britannia,* the ancient name of that island kingdom, means "the land of tin."

On the other hand, in 1 Kings 10:22 we are told that Solomon's navy brought gold, silver, ivory, apes, and peacocks from Tarshish to Palestine. Peacocks came originally from India, so here "Tarshish" would seem to refer not only to Western Europe but also to Eastern Asia. Solomon's navy made the round trip to Tarshish once every three years. This fact suggests a lengthy sea voyage through the Mediterranean, out past the pillars of Hercules into the broad Atlantic, southward past the shores of Africa, around the cape of Good Hope, up through the Indian ocean to Hindustan, and back.

It is noteworthy that these voyages were taken in ships made in Tyre, though belonging to King Solomon. We can well understand how the great merchant princes of Tyre were looked on as "the honourable of the earth" (Isaiah 23:8), even as today men give honor to those who amass vast fortunes through commercial enterprises. Regrettably such wealthy men seldom give the glory to the God who gave them the ability to earn such vast sums. Tyre did not take God into account at all and so He decided to bring other great powers against her. He "purposed...to stain the pride of all glory," for He has decreed "that no flesh should glory in his presence" (Isaiah 23:9; 1 Corinthians 1:29).

For us as Christians today the cross of Christ speaks of the shameful death of One whom the great ones of earth rejected, but in whose death we may now see the end of all earthly glory. With the Apostle Paul we may well exclaim, "God forbid that I should glory, save in the cross of our Lord Jesus Christ" (Galatians 6:14).

### Isaiah 23:10-18

The destruction of Tyre would diminish the prestige of many of the great merchant cities that had been founded by or were in close alliance with Tyre. Tartessus in Spain was a daughter of Tyre because it was founded by Phoenicians. The same was true of Cartagena and of Carthage in North Africa. Chittim, or Cyprus, owed its economic success chiefly to the business it did with Tyre. The merchants of all of these commercial centers would "howl" when the great city that was the chief source of their prosperity fell beneath the judgment of God, whom it had ignored.

The immediate agent for the accomplishment of this prophecy of the destruction of Tyre was Nebuchadnezzar and his Chaldean armies. Babylon, originally founded by Nimrod and known as Babel, had existed for many centuries, but it had never become a great world power until it was enlarged and taken over by the Assyrians long before Nebuchadnezzar's day. Separated from Assyria, it eventually became the dominant power in the region west of the Euphrates.

Nebuchadnezzar besieged Tyre, partially destroyed it, and carried away many of its people into captivity. During the seventy years in which Israel remained in captivity, the Phoenician city was in a state of degradation and collapse, but after the death of Nebuchadnezzar and the capture of Babylon by the Medes and Persians a few years later, Tyre was largely rebuilt. It sought to establish intimate relations with various surrounding peoples in an effort to recoup its misfortunes, but it never again became the commercial city it had been. During the Persian period of world ascendancy Tyre flourished to some extent, but was at last almost completely destroyed by the armies of Alexander the Great when he overcame the Persians and conquered most of western Asia and Egypt.

Tyre has never come into prominence since and yet there is a future of blessing predicted for it. It is evident that 23:18, like so many other prophetic Scriptures, carries us beyond the present age to the establishment of the Messianic kingdom of our Lord Jesus Christ. In that day a new city will be raised up on the ruins of Tyre. That new city will be subject to Him whose right it is to reign, and will bring its glory and honor to His feet. This is predicted both here and in Psalm 45, where we see Israel once more recognized as the wife of Jehovah; "the daughter of Tyre" (45:12) is among those who rejoice in her blessing and bring their gifts to the king. "Her merchandise shall be for them that dwell before the Lord" (Isaiah 23:18).

# ISAIAH 24

# COMING DESTRUCTION AND DESOLATION

I saiah 24 presents a scene of unparalleled destruction and desolation. The chapter is closely linked with a similar passage in Jeremiah 4:23-31.

Many different interpretations have been given to the prophecy. Some suppose that it pictures the earth in its chaotic state after it fell from the glory of its original creation (see Genesis 1:2). Others, such as Mrs. Ellen G. White of the Seventh-Day Adventists' cult, say that the prophecy pictures the millennial earth. Mrs. White denies the reality of Christ's kingdom during the millennium and claims that the earth will be the bottomless pit into which Satan will be cast; he will wander about the earth, she says, until his final judgment and destruction in the lake of fire.

But a careful study of both Isaiah 24 and Jeremiah 4:23-31 leads one to conclude that both passages clearly refer primarily to the land of Palestine in the darkest period of the great tribulation yet to come. They also refer to the prophetic earth as a whole—that is, the region once occupied by the Roman empire.

In Isaiah 24 the Hebrew word *eretz* is translated "land," "world," and "earth." The scholars who produced the King James version were very fond of using synonyms, and wherever a word occurred frequently either in the Greek or Hebrew originals, they translated it into as many different terms as seemed right to them. But at least in the early part of this chapter, it is not the world as such that is in view; it is the land of Israel that the prophet sees as empty and desolate because of the terrible experiences through which the covenant people will pass in the last days.

## Isaiah 24:1-3

Palestine is often described in Scripture as a land flowing with milk and honey, but here we see it as the very opposite; it is a land parched and dry, no longer able to sustain its inhabitants. They flee in terror because of the judgments of the Lord.

Note the statement, "The Lord...turneth it upside down" (24:1). Everything that the unbelieving Israelites have trusted in will be broken to pieces. All the hopes in which they have indulged will prove to be but idle dreams because they will have returned to their own land—even as they are doing now—in unbelief, counting on their own ability and prowess to enable them to build again a great nation in the home of their forefathers.

Greater disasters than they have ever known in the past lie ahead for Israel. Not until they turn to the Lord and look on Him whom they have pierced will their hopes be realized (see Zechariah 12:10). Till then they are doomed to one terrible disappointment after another—disappointments in which all classes of the people will share.

## Isaiah 24:4-12

The reason for the desolation here depicted is plainly declared: God's law has been transgressed. The covenant wherein God pledged Himself to show His lovingkindness toward the world has been utterly disregarded by Israel. Instead of looking to Him for the mercies of each passing season, they have tried to avert disaster and procure happiness by their own efforts. They have failed to put their trust in Him who has shown unbounded mercy to a fallen race.

Isaiah said, "They have...broken the everlasting covenant" (24:5). It is a mistake to suppose that here he was referring to the covenant made at Sinai when the ten commandments were given, for nowhere is that covenant declared to be everlasting. The law was, as we know from the Epistle to the Galatians, a means of teaching man about his sinfulness and his need of a Savior.

The covenant in Isaiah 24 cannot be the one made with Abraham either. Inasmuch as God Himself is the only party to the Abrahamic covenant, it is impossible for man to break it—unless the rejection of the promised Seed is understood to be the breaking of the covenant as far as man is concerned. When Messiah came in accordance with the promises made to Abraham and confirmed to David, He was rejected and cut off, as Daniel 9:26 predicted. Certainly Israel then broke the covenant as far as it was in their power to do it. In a day yet to come—in the final week of Daniel's seventy weeks of years—they will enter into a covenant with the last head of Gentile power, thus repudiating their allegiance to their own Messiah; that covenant will be broken at the end of three-and-a-half years when the man of sin will declare himself to be the only object of worship (9:27).

Most likely Isaiah was referring to the covenant made by God as the creator and sustainer of the universe to bless the labor of men's hands and give them fruitful fields and bountiful harvests as they trust in Him. This covenant was established with Noah, under whom God set up human government, of which we read nothing in the Scriptures that deal with antediluvian days. The nations that would be set up after the flood were to be subject to God as their supreme ruler, but this stipulation is the very thing that not only Israel but also the Gentile nations have failed to acknowledge. The bow in the cloud (Genesis 9:16), which was intended to be a perpetual reminder of God's goodness and man's responsibility, has become meaningless because of unbelief and willful disobedience. Therefore every effort of men to establish stable government on the earth and peace among the nations is doomed to failure.

Our Lord's own words come to mind as we read Isaiah 24:4-12. When discussing the horrors of the great tribulation and the rise of nation against nation in bloody warfare, He said, "Except those days should be shortened, there should no flesh be saved" (Matthew 24:22). Knowing as we do today the terribly destructive power of modern weapons of warfare whereby whole cities may be blotted out in a few moments of time, we need have no difficulty in accepting His words literally. Palestine will experience the ravages of warfare perhaps to a greater extent than any other country because she did not recognize her Messiah.

But when these judgments are falling on that chosen land and the contiguous territory, a remnant will be separated from the masses of the people. That remnant will return to the Lord, yield glad subjection to His holy will, acknowledge their sins, and trust His word. To them the grace of God will be revealed as He assists them, cares for them, and brings them at last from a blazing world to their desired haven to dwell in peace in their own land.

## Isaiah 24:13-15

We like to think of the expression "Glorify ye the Lord in the fires" as an indication of the faithfulness of the remnant during the time when the judgments are falling on the earth. However, it seems that the rendering of the King James version is hardly correct. Other translations read, "Glorify the Lord in the East," or "in the land of light," thus suggesting that the dark days of the tribulation are, after all, the harbinger of the coming day of blessing. Then the remnant of Israel and a great multitude of converted Gentiles will be brought to the place where they will wait expectantly for the second advent of the once-rejected Christ of God and for their entrance into fullness of blessing in the kingdom age.

## Isaiah 24:16-20

As the prophet contemplated the sufferings of his people and the desolation of the land during the time of tribulation, he cried out in the anguish of his soul. Even though Isaiah, with prophetic vision, could see the glory following the desolations, his whole being was stirred within him as he realized what his people would go through before they were brought back to God and to their land. "My leanness, my leanness," the prophet exclaimed. F. C. Jennings suggested an alternative rendering—"My misery, my misery"—but whatever the translation, it is clear that the prophet was in the greatest mental anguish as he foresaw the results of departure from God and the consequences of breaking His covenant.

As in the beginning of the chapter, Isaiah graphically described those woes of the last days. Everything that men consider stable and lasting will be shaken to pieces so that the land will seem to "reel to and fro" like a drunken man. Indeed the land may do more than *seem* to reel, for the prophecy may suggest that great earthquakes will add to the terror of those days of grief and sorrow.

## Isaiah 24:21-23

In those last days, not only will the misguided rulers of Israel and the Gentile nations be dealt with in judgment; God will also deal with the unseen principalities and powers that have sought to dominate the hearts and minds of men in authority. These unseen hosts are described in Ephesians 6:12 as the "world rulers of this darkness" (literal translation).

Those wicked spirits in the heavenlies are evidently the same as the "host of the high ones that are on high" in Isaiah 24:21. They attempt to control the minds of men in such a way as to set them in opposition to God and to enlist them in the vain endeavor to thwart His unchanging plans. Men who are their dupes and give them willing service will be shut up together with them in prison, where they will await the time when the Lord will deal with them in the final judgment.

When the Lord "ariseth to shake terribly the earth" (2:19), the signs in the heavens to which Christ referred will be followed by the appearing of the glorified Son of man. Accompanied by His heavenly saints, He will descend to take over the government of this world and to bring in the long-awaited age of righteousness.

# ISAIAH 25

# EXULTANT SONG OF THE REMNANT

With growing interest and increasing joy we move on to contemplate the exultation of the remnant of Israel who will become the nucleus of the new nation. The powers of evil that sought their complete destruction will have been dealt with by the Lord Himself at His second advent. For this remnant "the time of singing" (Song of Solomon 2:12) will at last have come. Down through the centuries the cries of misery and lamentation have been loud and long because Israel did not acknowledge the Christ when He came to earth. But when at last "they shall look upon [Him] whom they have pierced" (Zechariah 12:10) and recognize in the once-despised Galilean their own promised Messiah, their hearts will well up with praise and thanksgiving to Jehovah. Thenceforth their God will be their everlasting portion.

## Isaiah 25:1

They who have been so grievously misled in the past will come to realize that Jehovah's counsels of "faithfulness and truth" have remained unchanged—in spite of the fact that when the Lord Jesus appeared to bring in the blessings so long awaited, they rejected Him. They fulfilled their own Scriptures in giving Him up to the death of the cross. But God made that very cross the great altar on which the true propitiatory sacrifice was offered for the sins of the world. Nor did He change His plan because they said, "We will not have this man to reign over us" (Luke 19:14).

For the time being the One whom they refused to acknowledge as King has been taken up to glory and has been seated, in fulfillment of Psalm 110:1, at God's right hand. During the long years of His personal absence from this earth, Israel has become the nation of the wandering foot, seeking rest and peace in vain because the Prince of Peace, who alone could have given them what their hearts yearned for, was to them a stranger. But in that coming day they will recognize and adore Him, and thereby experience fullness of joy.

### Isaiah 25:2-4

In 25:2-3 Isaiah clearly prophesied the destruction of all God-defying Gentile powers in the time of the end. The leaders of the Jews once declared, "We have no king but Caesar" (John 19:15), and ever since then their sufferings under the caesars have been unspeakably terrible. But at the end of the great tribulation, the time of Jacob's trouble, all the powers that have oppressed them will be destroyed and they will be freed forever from Gentile tyranny and persecution.

Doubtless 25:4 may be interpreted as applying to the entire period of Israel's scattering and distress. Although the nation as such was rejected by God when they rejected His Son, an election of grace has remained in effect during all this present age. Jews who in their anguish and misery have turned to God and found in the Holy Scriptures the revelation of His Son as their Messiah and Savior, have ever found Him to be a refuge and a comfort. Even in the midst of trial and sorrow He has enabled them to rejoice in His unfailing love.

### Isaiah 25:5-7

Coincident with the destruction of the beast and the false prophet (see Revelation 19) will be the fulfillment of the prophetic Word in regard to the return of the Lord and the establishment of His throne on mount Zion. From there the law will go forth into all the world. Men everywhere who have been spared from the judgments of that awful day will be invited to revel in the riches of God's abundant grace. He will spread His table not only for Israel, but also for Gentile converts, as indicated in Revelation 7. "In this mountain," wrote Isaiah, "shall the Lord of hosts make unto all people a feast." The prophet was referring not to some literal feast, but to the spiritual refreshment that will be offered to all in that day.

Ever since sin came into the world, men have been blinded to the eternal truths of God's Word. The people of Israel are now unable to understand their own Scriptures because of the veil that is on their hearts, and Ephesians 4:18 describes unsaved Gentiles as "having the understanding darkened...through the ignorance that is in them." But when the Lord appears in glory, this blindness will pass away from both Jews and Gentiles.

### Isaiah 25:8-9

Paul quoted from 25:8 when writing about the truth of resurrection in 1 Corinthians 15. The apostle showed that this prophecy of Isaiah will have its partial fulfillment when, at the rapture, the dead will be raised, the living will be changed, corrupted bodies will "put on incorruption," and mortal bodies will "put on immortality." For all the children of God, living and dead, death will be "swallowed up in victory."

That there will be a further fulfillment at the end of the great tribulation is evident from Revelation 20:4-6. The first resurrection will include not only the saints of this and past ages, but also those who will be put to death for refusing to worship the beast and his image during the days of the great tribulation. Together these souls will constitute the heavenly company, while the spared of Israel and of the Gentile nations will enter into the millennial kingdom here on earth.

Isaiah foresaw and we can imagine something of the exultant joy of the remnant as they look on the once-despised Jesus and see in Him the God of their fathers manifested in flesh. "Lo," they will cry, "this is our God; we have waited for him." Under His beneficent but righteous reign, their wanderings will come to an end and they will possess the land promised to Abraham and David.

## *Isaiah 25:10-12*

"Moab," the prophet added, "shall be trodden down." As already noted in connection with Isaiah 15, Moab represents the pride of those who falsely profess to be religious. Isaiah foresaw the time when they will no longer be a menace to the peace of God's people, for everything that would mar the joy of that day of blessing will be utterly destroyed. This destruction will be brought about not by human effort or man's ingenuity, but by the Lord Himself. He will "spread forth His hands"—in judgment on those who refuse to bow to His will, and in grace on those who put their trust in Him.

# ISRAEL'S DELIVERANCE

In Isaiah 26 we continue to enter into the joyous experiences of the remnant of Israel as they praise Jehovah for fulfilling His promises to deliver them and as they revel in their spiritual enrichment under Messiah's righteous rule. It should surely be a delight to us who through grace belong to the heavenly company, to reflect on what God has in store for His earthly people when in accordance with His promise to Abraham they take full possession of the land that He declared would be theirs forever.

Their deliverance will be twofold: first, from the power of their enemies who for so many centuries have oppressed them; and second, from their sins when they comprehend the true meaning of the great day of atonement and see in Christ Jesus the true sin offering. In their joy they will sing the songs of Moses and the Lamb. Those who will sing "in that day...in the land of Judah" include both those who have been slain as martyrs during the reign of the beast and the antichrist as seen in Revelation 15:2-3, and those who have been saved alive out of the time of Jacob's trouble and thus are prepared to enter into the kingdom when the Lord Himself appears.

Today we look forward to the time when, gathered around the throne in glory, we will sing the new song, but our singing will have nothing to do with the overthrow of earthly powers or our deliverance from them. With Israel it will be otherwise. As in Old Testament times they sang with Moses the song of triumph over their enemies when God delivered them out of Egypt, so in the coming day they will rejoice when every oppressor has been destroyed. Yet with the song of Moses will be the song of the Lamb—that is, the song of redemption through His precious atoning blood.

As we consider the song in Isaiah 26, we can relate to its spiritual aspects, for we have been blessed "with all spiritual blessings in heavenly places in Christ" (Ephesians 1:3). And although it is not the Christian attitude to rejoice in the destruction of evildoers, we can well sympathize with God's earthly people as we reflect on what the overthrow of their enemies is going to mean to them.

### Isaiah 26:1-2

"In that day shall this song be sung in the land of Judah; We have a strong city; salvation will God appoint for walls and bulwarks." Surely in these opening words of the song the remnant mention the "city" in a spiritual rather than in a material sense. As they look forward to the establishment of Jerusalem as a great center of blessing to the whole earth and as a fortress never again to be destroyed by their foes, they recognize that the Lord Himself is their "strong city." They rejoice in the assurance that their spiritual foes will never again be able to overcome them.

However, they are also contemplating the actual rebuilding of the literal Jerusalem when they cry, "Open ye the gates, that the righteous nation which keepeth the truth may enter in." In that day Israel "shall be all righteous" (60:21). Their iniquities will be purged, and their hearts cleansed by "the washing of water by the word" (Ephesians 5:26) according to the promise given in Ezekiel 36:25-26: "Then will I sprinkle clean water upon you, and ye shall be clean: from all your filthiness, and from all your idols, will I cleanse you. A new heart also will I give you, and a new spirit will I put within you: and I will take away the stony heart out of your flesh, and I will give you an heart of flesh." The veil having been taken away from their eyes, the remnant will be delivered from unbelief and will find an all-sufficient Savior in Jesus, their once-rejected Messiah.

### Isaiah 26:3

The song continues, "Thou wilt keep him in perfect peace, whose mind is stayed on thee: because he trusteth in thee." These words may well apply not only to the remnant in that coming day, but to every trustful believer in all dispensations. "Perfect peace," rest of heart and mind, and freedom from worry and anxiety are found only as we learn to commit all our ways to the Lord and trust Him implicitly to take care of us. As we heed the admonition of Philippians 4:6, "the peace of God, which passeth all understanding," will keep our hearts as surely as a military guard protects a fortress.

Every believer has peace *with* God through the blood of the cross, as we know from Romans 5:1: "Being justified by faith, we have peace with God through our Lord Jesus Christ." But the peace *of* God, the "perfect peace" of which Isaiah spoke, is something more. It is the quiet assurance that all is well no matter what adverse circumstances we have to face, because we realize that our Father is ordering everything for blessing. What untold comfort has come to myriads of believers through meditation on and faith in such a verse as Romans 8:28: "All things work together for good to them that love God, to them who are the called according to his purpose"!

### Isaiah 26:4-6

Faith, trust, and confidence are synonymous terms. He who confidently looks up to the Lord and commits everything to Him is lifted above all that might otherwise cause distress or anxiety. We who know God as our Father rejoice in the fact that "like as a father pitieth his children, so the Lord pitieth them that fear him" (Psalm 103:13).

To Israel God is known by the covenant name *Jehovah,* a Hebrew compound meaning literally "the ever-living" or as the New Testament puts it, "the Lord, which is, and which was, and which is to come" (Revelation 1:8). In the French translations the word *L'Eternel* is aptly used; it well expresses the true meaning of Him who declared Himself to be Jehovah, the I AM. In Isaiah 26:4 the name is, as it were, doubled: "the Lord Jehovah," or literally "Jah, Jehovah," the name *Jah* speaking again of His eternal existence, and the full name telling of His covenant relationship to His people.

It is to the Lord Jehovah that the remnant will ascribe their complete deliverance. They will praise Him because of the way in which He has dealt with their proud and cruel persecutors, the great Gentile powers that have sought their destruction.

## *Isaiah 26:7-11*

This passage contrasts the just and the unjust. Habakkuk 2:4 says that the just will live by faith. Therefore the just who Isaiah said walk in the path of "uprightness" are those in Israel who have learned to put their trust in the Lord, to endure "as seeing him who is invisible" (Hebrews 11:27).

The unjust who know no shame are those who have turned away from the living God, acted in independence of Him, and persecuted those who seek to do His will. Although He makes His sun to shine and His rain to fall on the just and unjust alike (Matthew 5:45), these evildoers fail to be moved by His goodness or be drawn to Him by His grace. They only become hardened because of the favors bestowed on them. They will have to learn the importance of righteousness the hard way when His judgments fall on them—when all the nations are made to know His wrath because of their sin and rebellion.

In that day of Jehovah's power the inhabitants of the world who are spared when the judgments fall will learn righteousness and will, with Israel, enter into the blessedness of Messiah's reign.

## *Isaiah 26:12-18*

At long last the people of Israel will learn the lesson that peace, not only from conflict, but peace in regard to the sin question, is found only in Christ, who has "made peace through the blood of his cross" (Colossians 1:20). For centuries God has in vain called on Israel to take hold of Him in faith and thus make their peace with Him, and they have not responded. But in that coming day following the anguish of the great tribulation, they will know that peace is found in a person and that person is the Lord Jesus Christ. We know the blessedness of this peace, and they will know Him who is our peace.

From time to time during Israel's dispersion and suffering under

Gentile domination there have been what seemed like birth pangs, but all expectations have ended in disappointment. Christ has not yet been born as far as their comprehension is concerned. But in that day they will be able to understand the full meaning of the prophecy in Isaiah 9:6: "Unto us a child is born, unto us a son is given." Then in their own consciousness they will recognize in Jesus the man-child who is to rule the nations with a rod of iron.

### Isaiah 26:19

This verse has been the subject of much controversy among prophetic students. Some think that it refers to the literal resurrection of the body at the return of the Lord. Others have taken the verse to refer to the national and spiritual resurrection of the remnant of Israel who, like men long dead, will come up out of their graves among the Gentiles to enter into the enjoyment of the coming kingdom.

It seems clear, however, that the reference here is not to physical resurrection. Rather, the verse is to be linked to the vision in Ezekiel 37. Ezekiel saw a valley full of dry bones. These bones came together; then flesh came upon them; and eventually breath entered into them. The meaning of the vision was made clear as the Spirit of God interpreted it: "These bones are the whole house of Israel" (37:11). In other words, the remnant of the last days—those referred to in Romans 11:26—will stand for all Israel.

Daniel 12:2 speaks, if I am not mistaken, of the same resurrection of the nation, but includes the unrighteous as well as the righteous. Today we see Israel once more a nation in the land, but we know from Scripture that the great separation between the righteous and the unrighteous is yet to take place.

### Isaiah 26:20-21

The last two verses of Isaiah 26 need not be considered as part of the song of the remnant, for they contain a special prophetic message. They tell of the provision that Jehovah will make to preserve the remnant who are to be saved out of the time of trouble and who will thus be able to sing the song we have just been considering.

Some have thought that 26:20 refers to some special hiding place where the remnant will find shelter from the beast and the antichrist—perhaps in the ruined cities of Petra. However, it seems rather that Jehovah Himself is to be their protector. He will hide them away in the "wilderness of the peoples" (Ezekiel 20:35, revised versions). My interpretation is that when the abomination of desolation is set up in the holy place, as predicted by both Daniel and our blessed Lord, the remnant will flee to far-off heathen nations who will not be fully under the actual domination of the beast and who will give shelter to these outcasts for the truth's sake.

Proverbs 18:10 says, "The name of the Lord is a strong tower: the righteous runneth into it, and is safe." Blessed are all who even now realize the truth of this word. Abiding under the shadow of the Almighty, all His people are protected from the power of the enemy.

# ISAIAH 27

# JEHOVAH'S VINEYARD RESTORED

In the song of the vineyard in Isaiah 5 we saw the Lord looking for grapes and finding only wild grapes, for wayward Israel bore no fruit for God. In Isaiah 27 we find another song of the vineyard, but it depicts entirely different conditions. All is changed and we see vines loaded with luscious grapes, thus giving satisfaction to the heart of the Owner. By showing us this picture, the Spirit of God tells us of the joy that Jehovah will find in His people when, having been restored to Himself, "Israel shall blossom and bud, and fill the face of the world with fruit" (27:6).

### Isaiah 27:1

Since the first verse has no connection with the song of the vineyard as such, it might have been better if chapters 26 and 27 had been divided after 27:1 rather than before it. The verse tells of the judgment to be meted out to "that old serpent, which is the Devil, and Satan" (Revelation 20:2). He is to be bound and cast into the bottomless pit for a thousand years when the kingdom of God is established in power and glory over all this earth, where for so long the adversary has exercised his control over the hearts and minds of men.

### Isaiah 27:2-3

The great dragon having thus been dealt with, the voice of the Lord Himself is lifted up in song as He rejoices over His delivered

127

people. He sings of wine, which in Scripture is a symbol of joy. Judges 9:13 speaks of "wine, which cheereth God and man." Psalm 104:15 speaks of "wine that maketh glad the heart of man." Because of its exhilarating effect when used in moderation, wine represents that which cheers the spirit and gladdens the heart.

When Israel returns to Jehovah in penitence and self-judgment after long years of rebellion and self-will, their lives will become fruitful with the graces of the Holy Spirit, and God will rejoice over them as a bridegroom rejoices over his bride (Isaiah 62:5). No longer will Jehovah's vineyard be let out to unfaithful husbandmen; He will watch over it Himself, protecting it from everything that would tend to destroy it or make it unfruitful. "I the Lord," He says, "will keep it night and day."

### Isaiah 27:4-6

No more will the Lord demonstrate His indignation against His people because of their waywardness. His Spirit will be quieted toward them who are called by His name. It would be folly indeed for anyone ever to rise up against Him again. To do so would be to meet immediate destruction, as when a fire consumes thorns and briers. By returning to God in contrition and confession, His people will make peace with Him whose wrath would otherwise have been poured out on them.

Isaiah 27:5 is the only place in Scripture where there is a suggestion of man making peace with God: "Let him take hold of my strength, that he may make peace with me." Note that the verse does not have to do with eternal things; it has to do with submission to the government of God in this world. When it comes to the settlement of the sin question, there is no man who by any effort of his own can make his peace with God. The glorious truth of the gospel is that Christ has "made peace through the blood of his cross" (Colossians 1:20) and that peace becomes ours the moment we put our trust in Him. Romans 5:1 declares, "Being justified by faith, we have peace with God through our Lord Jesus Christ." Ephesians 2:14 reminds us, "He is our peace." Romans 5:10 clearly states that we are "reconciled to God by the death of his Son."

As far as divine government is concerned, man is called on to submit himself to the will of God, and he must recognize the folly of rebelling against His law. Israel will be brought to this submission in the coming day; then they will no longer be a curse among the nations (Jeremiah 29:18) and the name of the Lord will no longer be blasphemed by the Gentiles because of Israel's perversity. They will be a means of blessing to the whole world, as God has intended from the beginning. Israel will be a nation of priests through whom God will make known His salvation to the ends of the earth.

### Isaiah 27:7-9

In Amos 3:2 the Lord declared concerning Israel, "You only have I known of all the families of the earth: therefore I will punish you for all your iniquities." The Lord permitted certain Gentile powers to chastise Israel and then He destroyed the very nations that had been His rod for the correction of His people. Other nations will be similarly dealt with in the day of the Lord, but Israel will be preserved and after their time of affliction has passed, they will be restored to divine favor. Then they will abhor themselves because of the idolatries and abominations to which they gave themselves in times past. Every evidence of those follies will be utterly destroyed and the Lord's name alone will be exalted in the day of Israel's recovery and repentance.

### Isaiah 27:10-11

These words may refer not only to the cities of the Gentile nations, but also to the apostate part of Israel. When God arises in His wrath to deal with man's defiance of His authority, He will not cease to exercise His vengeance until all who continue to resist Him are blotted out.

Sin of whatever character is an insanity; it is evidence of a disordered mind. In the parable of the prodigal son, our Lord told us that it was when the young man "came to himself" that he said, "I will arise and go to my father" (Luke 15:17-18). Men may think of themselves as too wise or too learned to accept the Word of God at its face value; but little do they realize that their very unbelief and arrogance only make obvious the fact that they are a people of no understanding. It was thus with Israel when they turned away from God. It is thus with all men everywhere who refuse to submit to His holy will.

### Isaiah 27:12-13

This passage refers to the second advent of the Lord Jesus, when He will come as the Son of man to set up the kingdom of God on earth. The great trumpet will be blown in order to summon the outcasts of Israel to return to Zion and be gathered unto their long-looked-for Messiah and to rejoice in His favor. (See Joel 2:15-16 and Matthew 24:31.) It is vain to say that this prophecy of Isaiah concerning the regathering of Israel had its fulfillment in the days of Ezra and Nehemiah when a remnant returned to Palestine to rebuild the city and temple at Jerusalem. The Lord has declared, as we have already seen in Isaiah 11:11, that He will gather the remnant a "second time," and it is to this future gathering that 27:12-13 refers.

# ISAIAH 28
# JUDGMENTS PAST AND FUTURE

I saiah 28 introduces a new series of prophetic messages embracing chapters 28–33. This series is characterized by six woes, reminding us of those of chapter five, but having to do particularly with Israel and the surrounding nations in the last days.

The first woe has already had a partial fulfillment in the judgment that fell on Samaria when Shalmaneser V, king of Assyria, overthrew the northern kingdom in 722 B.C. But that judgment was a precursor of a greater disaster yet to fall on the land to which Israel has now returned and which has now been recognized by the Gentile powers as an independent nation.

## Isaiah 28:1-4

Verses 1-4 are complete in themselves and give us the reason for God's dealing with Ephraim (the northern kingdom of Israel, also called Samaria) when He allowed the Assyrian to overrun the land, destroy its cities, and carry a vast number of Israelites into captivity. The passage gives a vivid description of the luxurious conditions prevailing in Samaria before the captivity. Under Jeroboam II and the later kings of Israel, the city of Samaria had become a grand and glorious metropolis. Built on a high hill, the sides of which were terraced and planted with delightful gardens and groves, Samaria was perhaps the loveliest city in all Palestine. The valley below, which reached to the great plain of Esdraelon (Jezreel), abounded in orchards, vineyards, and fruitful fields. So richly had God lavished His benefits on the people of the entire region that in their enjoyment of His gifts they utterly forgot the giver.

Copying the nations round about them, the Israelites turned to idolatry of the vilest kind. As they worshiped false gods, they also followed the ways of the heathen. Reveling in luxury, they gave themselves to drunkenness and licentiousness until as a people they became so corrupt that God Himself could no longer tolerate them. Therefore He caused the heart of the king of Assyria to look covetously on their beautiful land and he came against it with a great army.

Israel, buoyed up by self-confidence and groundless optimism, feeling secure in their own might, scorned the power of the invader. But when the test came, Israel's armies were utterly defeated and the Assyrians were triumphant. Thus Samaria becomes for us a warning concerning the folly of trusting in self rather than in the omnipotent power of God. Had Israel been living for Him and worshiping Him, they could have counted on Him to defend them against every foe. But He had long since declared, "Them that honour me I will honour, and they that despise me shall be lightly esteemed" (1 Samuel 2:30). So it was at that time, and so it ever will be in days to come.

### Isaiah 28:5-13

For a moment the Lord, through Isaiah, directed the attention of His people to the coming day of His power: "In that day shall the Lord of hosts be for a crown of glory, and for a diadem of beauty, unto the residue of his people, And for a spirit of judgment to him that sitteth in judgment, and for strength to them that turn the battle to the gate." The expression "In that day," as used in the prophetic Scriptures, almost invariably refers to the time when He will arise in judgment on His enemies and deliver the remnant who put their trust in Him.

Immediately after this glimpse of coming glory, the prophet called attention to the bewildered and confused state of the people of Judah. Although they exulted in having the temple of the Lord in their land and gloried in the fact that they remained faithful to the house of David, practically they were as far from God as their brethren of the North were.

"They also have erred through wine," wrote Isaiah. Drunkenness
is often used in Scripture to illustrate or represent the effects of
spiritual intoxication brought about by refusing obedience to the
Word of the Lord and giving heed to false teaching. God had dealt
with His people patiently, sending them men who could teach them
the way of righteousness. These teachers had endeavored to instruct
the people as one deals with little children, giving them "precept...
upon precept, precept upon precept; line upon line, line upon line;
here a little, and there a little," as they were able to bear it. Yet they
had not profited from such careful teaching. They had turned away
from the truth and like many today accepted in its place the traditions of men.

Therefore judgment long delayed would at last fall on them. They
would still be taught "precept upon precept, precept upon precept;
line upon line, line upon line," but the purpose of the instruction
would be to prepare them for the doom that awaits all those who
forsake the living God and walk in their own self-chosen paths.

In the day of the great tribulation, the time of Jacob's trouble, the
apostate part of the nation will fully experience the reality of this
judgment. But the Lord will deliver the faithful remnant who refuse
to obey the behest of the beast and the antichrist and chose instead
the path of obedience to the Word of God.

Because Judah had refused to hear this Word, God was about to
teach them the folly of departure from Himself. He would send
against them the armies of their enemies, who spoke languages with
which the Hebrews were not familiar. In that way He would teach
them through men "with stammering lips and another tongue." In
the New Testament the apostle Peter quoted this verse, but applied
it to the miraculous gift of tongues, which was given on the day of
Pentecost so that the disciples could proclaim the gospel in many
different languages. Thus through men of other tongues did God
deliver the message of grace.

We need not think for a moment that in the New Testament there
is any misapplication of the passage from Isaiah. In its primary
meaning it clearly refers to the men of the nations who were to
come against Judah and teach them in a time of disaster what they
would not learn in times of peace. But in this gospel dispensation,

the Spirit of God Himself applied the passage as indicated. God, who delights in mercy, deigned to use the gift of tongues in order to give men the gospel in the quickest possible way.

People today talk of the gift and many profess to possess it; and we are told distinctly in Scripture that we are not to forbid speaking in tongues (1 Corinthians 14:39). But is there anyone today who can preach the gospel in a language he has never learned? Should such a miraculous instance occur, surely no right-minded Christian would object. When speaking in tongues is just a matter of uttering meaningless gibberish, we may be confident that it is not the Spirit of God who is at work.

### Isaiah 28:14-15

In their immediate application, these words refer undoubtedly to the attempt of Judah to form an alliance with Assyria or Egypt in order to protect themselves against one or the other of these two powers. Judah thought that it had made binding covenants, first with the one and then with the other of these nations, and it attempted to rest content with the assurance that the southern kingdom would thus be preserved from destruction. But the people of Judah were soon to find that their optimism was ill founded.

That Isaiah 28:14-15 has an application to the future, surely no instructed student of prophecy can question. In the last days a covenant will be made between the head of the Jewish state at that time and the beast, the head of the ten-kingdom empire. The beast's empire is pictured by the ten toes on the feet of the image in Daniel 2, the ten horns on the last beast in Daniel 7, and the ten horns on the beast in Revelation 13 and 17. This covenant will be made for seven years, as we are told in Daniel 9:27, but in the midst of the "week"—that is, at the end of three and a half years—the covenant will be broken. It is this compact that is described in Isaiah 28:15 as "a covenant with death, and with hell."

This prophecy refers to the future effort of the nation of Israel, who will have returned to the land in unbelief, to ensure protection from their foes in the East and in the North. Those foes will be looking with covetous eyes on Palestine and its increasing wealth.

Israel will find, however, that by looking to man instead of to the Lord they will fail to maintain the peace and security that they hoped thus to safeguard. Only in the Messiah, whom they once rejected, can lasting blessing be found. Of this truth the following verses speak.

### Isaiah 28:16-20

We know from 1 Peter 2:6 that the Stone referred to in Isaiah 28:16 is our Lord Jesus Christ. The prophet wrote, "Thus saith the Lord God, Behold, I lay in Zion for a foundation a stone, a tried stone, a precious corner stone, a sure foundation." Christ came to Israel in lowly grace only to be rejected, but as Psalm 118:22 tells us, "The stone which the builders refused is become the head stone of the corner." All blessing for Israel and Judah, as well as for the Gentile world, is bound up with Him. To refuse God's testimony regarding His Son is to deliberately choose everlasting judgment. To receive Him means everlasting life and blessing.

How sad that Israel has been blinded for so long! Because of their failure to receive their King when He came in grace, they have had to endure incredible sufferings throughout the long centuries of their wanderings. Even after they return to their land, they will suffer greatly until at last they look on Him whom they have pierced and mourn for Him "as one mourneth for his only son" (Zechariah 12:10).

When that day of trouble comes, those who refuse allegiance to the beast and the antichrist will wait in faith for the appearance of the living Stone, which is to fall on the feet of the great image of Gentile supremacy and grind it to powder. Those who quietly wait in faith will realize the truth stated in Isaiah's prophecy that "he that believeth shall not make haste." God's plan will be fulfilled in His own time. Then righteousness and judgment will prevail and "the refuge of lies" will be utterly swept away.

The Lord's appearing will destroy "the refuge of lies" and annul the "covenant with death" and the "agreement with hell." Suitable judgment will be meted out to all those who accept the mark of the beast and the number of his name, but those who put their trust in Jehovah will be vindicated and given their place in the coming glorious kingdom of God when it is set up on earth in visible power. Until that day, those who turn away from the Lord will trust in their own plans for deliverance and will find themselves like the uncomfortable sleeper described in 28:20.

## Isaiah 28:21-22

In Old Testament times, as God led His people through the wilderness to the land of promise, He delivered them from their enemies by wielding His power and enabling His people, who were weaker than their foes, to overcome their foes. Similarly, in the coming day He will deliver the remnant of His people from all those that rise up against Him, and He will pour out His judgment on all those that despise His name.

God has no delight in judgment, for His heart goes out to all men everywhere. He desires "all men to be saved, and to come unto the knowledge of the truth" (1 Timothy 2:4). God says, "I have no pleasure in the death of the wicked; but that the wicked turn from his way and live" (Ezekiel 33:11). But if men refuse His mercy and spurn His lovingkindness, then in righteousness He must deal with them in judgment. Judgment is His "strange work," the "strange act" of Isaiah 28:21. God would far rather show mercy and save than condemn and punish. However, He respects the sanctity of the human will and if men will not turn to Him to find life, they themselves deliberately choose death whether they realize it or not.

## Isaiah 28:23-29

In 28:23-29 Isaiah drew precious and important lessons from the cultivation of herbs and grains. First the ground must be well prepared by plowing and then the soil further broken up by harrowing. After that the seed is cast in; then when the herbs or grains are ready for harvest, each one is dealt with according to its nature. Likewise God seeks to break up the hard soil of man's opposition to Himself by the plowshare of His truth and by careful instruction as to the way of life. If when the seed has been cast into the ground of a good

and honest heart it brings forth abundantly, He deals appropriately
with that one who has responded to His truth. God does not work
with everyone in the same way, just as the careful farmer does not
thresh the softer herbs in the same way that he handles harder grains.
Those who go forth in the name of the Lord to sow the seed need to
have these principles in mind so that they can deal wisely with those
whom they endeavor to help.

## ISAIAH 29

# WOE TO ARIEL

In Isaiah 29 we find the second and third of the six woes of chapters 28–33. The second woe starts in 29:1 and the third in 29:15.

### Isaiah 29:1-6

Through His servant the prophet, God pronounced "woe to Ariel, to Ariel, the city where David dwelt!" *Ariel,* a name that had not previously been mentioned by Isaiah, may be translated in two different ways: (1) in 2 Samuel 23:20 it is rendered "lionlike" or "lion of God"; (2) in Ezekiel 43:16 the first part of the word is rendered "altar." Thus *Ariel* might mean either "lion of God" or "altar of God." The reference undoubtedly is to Jerusalem, David's city.

After taking Jerusalem, David made it his capital and built his palace there on mount Zion. During the years that followed, the glory of God was displayed in that city in marvelous ways. In Solomon's day the temple of Jehovah was erected on mount Moriah in another section of the holy city. In that temple the service of God was carried on by His anointed priests, officiating as representatives of deity; they stood between God and His people to offer up their sacrifices and offerings.

But as the centuries went by, declension set in. Judah turned away from the fear of the Lord, and formality took the place of true spiritual worship. Eventually God could no longer tolerate the unfaithfulness and hypocrisy that so frequently characterized the people with whom He had entered into a covenant relationship. Isaiah foresaw that since they had completely failed to carry out their part of the covenant, Jerusalem, which had been like the lion of God, would be like a great altar-hearth. Its own population would be sacrificed through the ruthless enmity of their bitter foes.

The prophecy could not possibly be referring to Sennacherib and
his army, for when he threatened the city, God intervened to deliver
Jerusalem and destroy the Assyrian host. We must look to the future for the fulfillment of that which is predicted in Isaiah 29:1-6. In
the last days, the time of Jacob's trouble, God "will gather all nations against Jerusalem to battle" (Zechariah 14:2), and then the
judgments on Ariel will be consummated. So terrible will be the
sufferings of the people that they will cry to God as "out of the
dust," and their voices will be like the whisperings of those who
profess to communicate with the spirits of the dead. Nevertheless
the Lord will at last appear for their deliverance and for the destruction of their enemies.

### Isaiah 29:7-8

Just when it seems as though Satan will succeed in his effort
to destroy Jerusalem and blot out the nation of Israel from the
face of the earth, the Lord will go forth and fight against the
nations that are besieging Ariel. Ariel's foes will find themselves
deprived of their prey. After their "dream" of world conquest,
they will awaken to realize that they have been fighting not only
against Judah, but also against Jehovah. His power will completely annul their attempts to blot out the people whom He has
separated to Himself.

Judah's enemies will be like a hungry man who dreams that he
has a rich repast before him, but just as he is about to partake of it,
he awakens to realize his starving condition. They will be like a
thirsty man who dreams that he has an abundance of water to refresh his parched throat, but awakens to realize that his condition is
worse than before. Thus will it be with all those nations who are
taken in red-handed opposition to God and His people.

### Isaiah 29:9-12

In this passage the prophet again depicted God's reasons for giving up Judah to judgment until they turned to Him in repentance. In
spite of all the revelations of His will given to them through His

Word and confirmed by His prophets, they had turned to their own devices, walking in the imaginations of their own hearts. Like men surfeited with wine, they were inebriated with the traditions of men that make void the Word of God. Judah had failed to act on or even comprehend the messages sent to them by the Lord. His Word had become unintelligible to them not because it lacked clearness of expression or simplicity of teaching, but because they themselves were blinded by unbelief. They read the Old Testament with a veil on their hearts (2 Corinthians 3:15).

Isaiah said that if the Word of God was handed to the worldly wise, they declared that it was sealed and therefore incomprehensible. If it was presented to the illiterate, they protested that they were not educated and turned from it. May we not see in Israel's attitude to their prophetic records an illustration of the attitude of many in Christendom today toward the one great prophetic book in the New Testament? That book is The Revelation, God's final word to man before the return of His Son from Heaven. Many of our so-called Christian scholars and prominent pulpiteers declare that it is useless to attempt to study the book of Revelation. Some say it is sealed. Some say it is merely a collection of weird dreams without meaning or coherence. Others say that only the learned can understand The Revelation and therefore simple Christians cannot expect to unravel its mysteries. Yet the Lord Himself twice pronounced a blessing on those who read the book and those who keep its sayings (Revelation 1:3; 22:7).

### Isaiah 29:13-14

Isaiah prophesied that because of the people's willful blindness, God would send judicial blindness. Those who have no heart for His Word will be given over to "strong delusion" (2 Thessalonians 2:11), and they will believe the lie of the antichrist. All who do not obey the truth and take pleasure in unrighteousness will be judged.

Outwardly the Jews of Isaiah's day kept up the form of religion and professed to worship and honor the God of their fathers even when by their works they denied Him. The Lord said, "This people draw near me with their mouth, and with their lips do honour me, but have removed their heart far from me." Because of this, long-delayed judgment would be poured out. Throughout the succeeding centuries they have suffered because of their disobedience to His Word and their rejection of the Savior that He provided.

In the time of the end their unbelief will be consummated; instead of accepting the Christ of God, they will accept the false messiah, the man of sin, and thus fill up their cup of iniquity to the brim. Then God will deal with them in unsparing judgment, destroying the apostate part of the nation, but saving a remnant who will turn to Him in that hour of desperate sorrow. The remnant will become the nucleus of the new nation to be blessed under Messiah's rule when He appears in glory to set up the kingdom of God in visible form here on the earth. He will return to the very city where He was crucified and from which He ascended to Heaven. On that day His feet will stand on the mount of Olives, and He will take over His great power and reign.

### Isaiah 29:15-16

The third woe was pronounced on those who presume to be wiser than God. Isaiah wrote that their "turning of things upside down shall be esteemed as the potter's clay." The apostle Paul, guided by the Holy Spirit, used the same figure of the potter and the clay in Romans 9:20-23. It is the greatest folly for man to strive with his Maker, to attempt to find fault with God, or to put on Him the blame for the misery and wretchedness that he has brought on himself by his own unbelief and waywardness. God, we are told, "giveth not account of any of his matters" (Job 33:13). A man should humble himself before the all-wise Creator and bow in subjection to His holy will. This alone is the path of blessing for the creature.

Because of Judah's failure and that of all the nations, God has to deal in retributive justice, pouring out His wrath on those who refuse His grace. But He will never forget His covenant with Abraham or the promise He made to bring blessing to all the earth through the Seed that was to come, even our Lord Jesus Christ.

## Isaiah 29:17-24

In 29:17-21 we read once more of blessing to come upon Ariel and the land of Palestine after the judgments have been meted out. We gaze on a millennial picture of Palestine when the blight that has rested on it for so many centuries is removed. The country that was once the glory of all lands is again fruitful and populous. The redeemed of the Lord are sought out and restored from all countries of earth and brought back to their ancient patrimony, there to rejoice and flourish under Messiah's beneficent reign.

In that day the blindness that has veiled the heart of Israel for so long will be taken away. The Word of God will become clear and luminous to them and they will rejoice in the revelation that He has given. The Gentile powers under which they have suffered will no more frighten them. The "terrible one" (perhaps a direct reference to the beast), the "scorner" (possibly the man of sin himself), and all who have been associated with them in their oppression of the Jews will be consumed by God, and His people will be delivered from their power.

The words in 29:22-24 have never been fulfilled in times past, but we may be assured that nothing that God has spoken will ever come to naught. These verses tell of a time when the spared of Israel will be righteous because they will be taught of God. Instead of following the vain imagination of their own hearts, they will be brought to the place of perfect subjection to His holy will. None will need to say to another, "Know the Lord," for all from the least to the greatest will know Him (Jeremiah 31:34). At that time the fullness of blessing promised to Abraham and his seed will be showered down—and not only on the natural children of him who was called the friend of God, for all nations will be blessed with them in accordance with the promise.

# JUDAH'S FAILURE AND GOD'S FAITHFULNESS

I n Isaiah 30 we find the fourth woe of this series as once more the Spirit of prophecy directs our attention to the internal condition of Judah at the time they were threatened by Sennacherib.

### *Isaiah 30:1-5*

Fearing the Assyrian, Judah appealed for help from Egypt, that land from which they had once been delivered. This in the eyes of God was a grievous sin, indicating their lack of confidence in Him and their disregard for His help in the past. They hoped to secure help from the very power that had once enslaved them and from whose bondage they had been redeemed, first by the blood of the passover lamb and then by the omnipotent power of God who brought them triumphantly through the Red Sea. He had scattered its waters on either side and thus gathered them to Himself in the wilderness and eventually settled them in the land of promise. Their going down to Egypt for help now meant that they had forgotten God's dealings with them in the past and that they no longer dared to depend on Him for their present deliverance.

The Assyrian invasion was but one of the evidences of God's displeasure with His people because of their waywardness. Instead of turning to the One they had sinned against, confessing their iniquities, and judging themselves for their idolatry and their unreality even in connection with the temple worship, they turned to their old enemy for assistance against the invader. Doubtless to the leaders of Judah it seemed to be the path of wisdom to make a friend of Egypt, but it was a mere human expedient and therefore doomed to failure. The leaders hoped that such an alliance would strengthen them and ward off impending danger. How much wiser they would have been if they had repented toward God and sought counsel, not from worldly-minded leaders, but from God Himself, who at that time was speaking to them through Isaiah and other prophets!

May we not see in Judah's attitude a lesson for ourselves today? How apt we are in times of stress to depend on some human expedient instead of relying on the living God! It is always an evidence of declension when Christians look to the world for help rather than turning to the Lord Himself, who may be chastening them because of unjudged sin. He always stands ready to meet His people in grace. We are told that "if we confess our sins, he is faithful and just to forgive us our sins, and to cleanse us from all unrighteousness" (1 John 1:9). But we are ever prone to forget this and to try to find a way out of our difficulties by human means instead of reliance on the omnipotent God. Just as Judah involved themselves in deeper trouble by their folly in turning to Egypt, we always make conditions worse when instead of looking to God we endeavor by fleshly means to extricate ourselves from the circumstances into which our failures have plunged us.

### Isaiah 30:6-7

Egypt is depicted here as a land of ravenous beasts such as are found in African jungles: "the young and old lion, the viper and fiery flying serpent." Yet to this land Judah sent ambassadors carrying treasures with which they hoped to procure the favor of the Egyptian ruler. To Judah it seemed the only way out, and doubtless they congratulated themselves on the astuteness of their political strategy. But their attempt to strengthen their position by making a close ally of a former enemy was obnoxious to God because it involved utter forgetfulness of Himself. Although they did not realize it, they would have found their own source of strength if they had quietly waited on God—if, sitting still even though the Assyrian came closer and closer, they had remained confident that if they relied on the holy One of Israel, He would in His own due time grant complete deliverance.

It is always difficult to wait for God to intervene. In Scripture there is instance after instance of those who only brought trouble on themselves by precipitate action; they felt that something must be done in order to stave off disaster, but if they had left the matter in God's hands, He would have risen up in ample time to fulfill His own purposes of grace. We need to distinguish between waiting on God and waiting for God. It is one thing to go to Him in the hour of stress and implore His delivering power; it is another thing to rest quietly, sensing His infinite love and wisdom, until He sees that the hour has struck to act on our behalf.

## Isaiah 30:8-14

It is clear from this passage that God intended the record of Judah's failure to be a salutary lesson to their descendants. For this purpose He wanted the whole story to be written in a book that could be handed down from generation to generation. "Now go," He said to Isaiah, "write it before them in a table, and note it in a book, that it may be for the time to come for ever and ever." God knew well that as in Isaiah's time, many in centuries yet to come would refuse to hear His voice and would seek to silence His messengers. Judah had turned away from the truth and gone after false prophets because, like so many in Christendom today, they had itching ears and preferred what was pleasant and agreeable over that which called for self-judgment and repentance.

We need not suppose that the people of Judah said in so many words what is recorded in 30:10-11, but their attitude expressed what was in their hearts. Is not this just as true of vast numbers today? Outwardly they profess reverence for the Holy Scriptures and the authority of our Lord Jesus Christ, but their lives make it evident that they are without any real faith. Neither do they have any love for God's truth when it runs contrary to their own desires. They turn away from the truth and follow after that which pleases the flesh and seems to the natural or carnal mind far more satisfactory than dependence on the Word of God. Such waywardness on the part of any who profess the name of the Lord can only bring down judgment.

Although Judah did not realize it, they were like people standing beside a high wall whose foundations had been undermined and which was already bulging and about to fall on them. They were like a potter's vessel that was soon to be broken into so many pieces that not even one fragment would be large enough to be useful.

### Isaiah 30:15-17

Beautiful indeed are the words of 30:15—"In returning and rest shall ye be saved; in quietness and in confidence shall be your strength"—words that are ever true for the people of God, no matter what they are called on to suffer or endure. It is as we learn to wait on God—returning to Him in confession of past failure and resting on His assurance of present forgiveness and cleansing—that we find peace of conscience, peace of heart, and salvation from whatever has caused unrest and fear.

As we look to the living God in simple faith, ceasing from all self-effort and refusing to look to the world for the help that God alone can give, we find strength to lift us above our trials. But the people of Judah refused to receive this message. Willfully they turned away from the advice of the prophet whom God had sent to call them back to Himself. They would not heed His Word. How often has the Lord had to say to those whose unbelief grieved His heart, "I would, but you would not"!

All preparations were made to "flee upon horses" at the approach of the enemy if help did not arrive in time, for Judah knew in their hearts that their dependence on Egypt might after all prove to be in vain. "Therefore," said God, "shall ye flee." Although Judah trusted in the swiftness of their steeds to enable them to evade capture, the enemy would be swifter. The foe would overtake and destroy them.

When God brought Israel out of Egypt and led them through the wilderness, He told them that if they walked in obedience to His Word, they need never fear their enemy. In the day of battle, through the might of Jehovah, one would chase a thousand, and two would put ten thousand to flight (Leviticus 26:8; Deuteronomy 32:30). Now, however, because of their unbelief and disobedience, conditions would be reversed and a thousand of Judah would flee from one Assyrian, and all of Judah would flee from five of their ruthless enemies. What folly for men to put their confidence in flesh, only to prove, as so many have done, that "the flesh profiteth nothing" (John 6:63)!

## Isaiah 30:18-21

After having tried to reach the consciences of His people, God once again, in remembrance of His covenant, declared that when his people have been chastened because of their sins, He will bring them into blessing.

Clearly the prophecy in 30:18-21 speaks of millennial blessing. After all the centuries of suffering, Israel and Judah will return to the Lord and find in Him the forgiveness that He is always ready to bestow on the contrite and penitent heart. In that day, the day of Jehovah's power, He will bring the Jewish people into everlasting blessedness. As they look up into the face of the Messiah they once despised and rejected, and find in Him an all-sufficient Savior, the sufferings of the past will seem like a bad dream from which they have awakened.

No longer will they be led astray by the wisdom of man or by false visions. Led by the Lord Himself, they will be guided in paths of righteousness. Even when there might seem to be danger of turning away, either to the right hand or to the left, they will be directed by His own voice saying, "This is the way, walk ye in it." All their tears will be wiped away and all their sufferings will be past forever.

Surely no one can think that these words have ever been fulfilled in the past. They point forward to Israel's glorious portion in the day when their lessons have been learned and they become subject to the instruction of Him whose mandates they once refused to obey.

## *Isaiah 30:22-26*

The prophet knew that idolatry had often been Judah's ruin in times past, but he foresaw that a time will come when they will abhor themselves as they remember their folly. They had been guilty of forsaking the one true and living God for the worship of senseless images that could neither see, nor hear, nor deliver them from the dangers that beset them. In that coming day Judah will cast their idols aside and find their joy in the Lord. He will feed them with the living bread and refresh them with the water of life.

No doubt 30:23 will have a literal fulfillment, for in Messiah's day He will satisfy the poor with bread, but we are surely justified in seeing in the verse a promise of great spiritual blessing. God's Word is as food to the heart of him who meditates on it, strengthening him in the inner man that he may know the will of God and have the power to do it.

The streams of living water that flow down from the hills and the mountains may well speak to us of the river of the water of life. That water, the Holy Ghost's testimony to the risen Christ, will bring joy to the hearts of the people of God, not only in the heavenly sphere, but also in the earthly kingdom yet to be set up.

## *Isaiah 30:27-33*

The closing verses of chapter 30 speak of mingled judgment and blessing: judgment on the nations who throughout the centuries have sorely afflicted Israel; and blessing on the covenant people when they return to the Lord, and all His promises of both temporal and spiritual prosperity are fulfilled for them.

Undoubtedly the judgments spoken of refer in the first instance to those that fell on Sennacherib and his armies. But the reference surely goes far beyond that, reaching down to the last days when another great Gentile power will rise up in its God-defying might and seek to destroy Judah and take possession of Immanuel's land. In His indignation the Lord will pour out the vials of His wrath on the Assyrian of that coming day so that his destruction will be complete and eternal. Judgment will also fall on every other enemy who has threatened the peace of the covenant nation.

Isaiah 30:33 is somewhat cryptic, but with the help of other Scripture passages we can understand it. We should remember that "no prophecy of the scripture is of any private interpretation" (2 Peter 1:20). The Roman Catholic Church teaches that "private interpretation" refers to the effort of an individual to understand the Scriptures apart from the instruction of ecclesiastical authorities. But that is not what the phrase means. The point is that all the prophecies of Scripture need to be considered as one whole, for they are all given by the same Spirit and they are intimately connected to each other.

So with the help of other Scripture passages we can understand what Isaiah meant when he wrote, "Tophet is ordained of old; yea, for the king it is prepared." A better rendering would be "for the king also it is prepared." The Assyrian we know, but who is the king referred to here? In Daniel 11:36 we read of the willful king who will head up the apostate Jewish nation during the time of the great tribulation. He is clearly identical to the man of sin (the lawless one of 2 Thessalonians 2) and to the second beast of Revelation 13, who looks like a lamb but speaks like a dragon. Both will be "cast alive into a lake of fire" (Revelation 19:19-20).

Some people identify the Assyrian with the beast, and they may perhaps be correct. But to me the two seem to be distinct, the beast being the little horn of Daniel 7, and the Assyrian (the king of the North) being the little horn of Daniel 8. The doom of all these enemies of God and His people will be everlasting destruction and banishment from the presence of the Lord and the glory of His power.

Tophet was the lowest part of the valley of the son of Hinnom—that is, Gehenna—the place where the carcasses of criminals and beasts as well as the filth and refuse of the city of Jerusalem were burned. It was in Tophet that the image of Moloch was set up in the worst days of Israel's idolatry. To this vile god human sacrifices were offered, little children and young maidens being cast alive into the red-hot arms of the monstrous image that was actually a furnace. As the priests of Moloch beat their drums and chanted their idolatrous songs to drown out the cries of the burning victims, God looked down with abhorrence on the terrible iniquity. Thus Tophet became the synonym for the lowest Hell. Into that place of outer darkness will be cast the last enemies of God as the day of the Lord is ushered in and man's day comes to a close.

# ISAIAH 31

# A STINGING REBUKE

It seems that the message of chapter 30 made little or no impression on the king and the nobles of Judah. Therefore the Lord again sent His servant Isaiah to warn them against the folly of still looking to Egypt for help. His message in chapter 31 is the fifth woe, which is practically the same in character as the fourth, which we have already considered.

### Isaiah 31:1-3

With a stinging rebuke, Jehovah reproved those who in time of national danger turned to Egypt for help instead of looking to Him who had brought them forth triumphantly out of Egypt and given them His holy covenant. He had promised blessing and deliverance as long as they walked in obedience to His Word. This they failed to do, so when emergencies arose they sought help elsewhere.

Egypt, which had formerly enslaved the children of Israel, is a type of the world from which Christ delivered us by giving Himself for us on the cross. For a Christian today to turn back to that world rather than depend on the living God, is to dishonor the name of Him who has thus redeemed us to Himself.

He has promised never to fail the soul that trusts Him, but we all know how easy it is to forget this when difficulties arise that seem to put us in jeopardy. In our desperation we seek help where it is not be to found instead of turning directly to Him who has said, "I will never leave thee, nor forsake thee" (Hebrews 13:5). Whether He speaks in grace or in judgment, He will never go back on His word.

This, however, we are slow to believe. Often in our folly we fear that He may not carry out His promises of blessing, but His faithfulness abides, whether we believe it or not.

To Israel, Egypt seemed to have enough strength and power to meet the opposition of the Assyrian and prevent his taking possession of Jerusalem and the land of Judah. But Israel's hopes were vain, for only in God was true power to be found. The Egyptians knew Him not, and God did not recognize them as His direct agents at this time. For the people of Judah to put their dependence on Egypt was to make the mistake of supposing that the arm of flesh could save. By so doing they ignored the arm of the Lord that was mighty in power. The Egyptian cavalry might make a brave showing, but their horses were "flesh, and not spirit," and therefore not to be depended on in the day of battle. As John 6:63 says, "It is the spirit that quickeneth; the flesh profiteth nothing."

### Isaiah 31:4-9

Since the Assyrian armies seemed almost invulnerable, the help of Egypt appeared to be necessary. But the Lord still had His people in mind and would soon demonstrate His omnipotence in the destruction of the mighty host that would come up against Jerusalem. Undoubtedly the prophecy in 31:4-5 referred directly to the time when the army of Sennacherib would be destroyed in a night—not by weapons of war, but by the breath of Jehovah.

A greater fulfillment will take place in the future when God destroys all who come against Jerusalem in the last days. The hosts of the nations will gather together against that consecrated city and when it appears as though all hope is gone, the Lord will arise in His might and go forth to fight against them. When He is "revealed from heaven…in flaming fire taking vengeance on them that know not God" (2 Thessalonians 1:7-8), the enemies of Israel will melt away and their leaders will be dealt with in summary judgment.

In view of His promised deliverance, the Lord again called on His people to turn to Him in repentance, acknowledging their sins and putting away all their graven images and idolatrous practices.

When the people of Judah turn to the Lord and demonstrate their repentance by cleansing the land of all their evil practices, God will act on their behalf. The enemy whose power they dreaded will become subservient to them and recognize them as the Lord's chosen people. Instead of hating or despising them and seeking their ruin, the Gentile powers will acknowledge them as the favored of Jehovah and will seek their favor, as many other Scripture passages testify.

# PREPARATIONS FOR THE COMING KINGDOM

Before uttering the sixth woe, which is a proclamation of judgment on Assyria (see Isaiah 33), the prophet delivered a message of hope and comfort for the afflicted people of God.

### Isaiah 32:1-2

God comforted His people with the prophecy of a glorious Messianic kingdom to be ushered in at the second advent of our Lord Jesus Christ. "Behold," Isaiah wrote, "a king shall reign in righteousness." We have no difficulty in identifying this righteous King, for He can be none other than God's anointed One, who was rejected when He came to Israel to tell them of the kingdom then at hand. Refused by those He came to deliver, He has gone into the far country to receive for Himself a kingdom from the Father's hand and to return in due time (Luke 19:12). David foresaw His glorious reign as he exclaimed, "A righteous ruler over men; a ruler in the fear of God" (2 Samuel 23:3, literal rendering). When He returns to take over the reins of government, He will choose certain ones from among those who have been faithful to Him in the time of His rejection and make them princes and judges. "Princes shall rule in judgment."

Isaiah presented Him not only as a King but also as a Savior. Beautiful are the figures of speech used by the prophet: "A man shall be as an hiding place from the wind, and a covert from the tempest." The picture is of Christ Himself bearing the brunt of the storm of judgment in order to provide shelter for all who flee to Him for refuge. Elsewhere we see Him portrayed as the Rock of ages in whose cleft the troubled soul can find a hiding place. Isaiah continued, "A man shall be...as the shadow of a great rock in a weary land." As a rock in a desert land gives shelter from the fierce heat of the sun, He freely provides salvation for all who put their trust in Him.

### Isaiah 32:3-8

Those who find in Christ an all-sufficient Savior obtain their instruction through His Word. Thereby they grow in grace and knowledge and are kept from the path of the destroyer. No matter how simple or untaught or unaccustomed to instruction one may be when he first comes to Christ, he will find all needed knowledge and wisdom in Him who delights to open up the truth to those who seek to be subject to His Word.

On the other hand, "the churl"—that is, the crafty one who plays fast and loose with divine truth—should not expect to find spiritual illumination as he pursues his self-chosen way. In the day of Jehovah's power all such persons will no longer be acknowledged as teachers or directors of others. Their true character will be fully revealed and they will be judged accordingly. These haughty despisers will no longer be permitted to mislead, whereas those who have learned from God the way of righteousness and have found delight in walking in it will be honored by Him and given a place in His kingdom. There they will be rewarded for dispensing to others what God bestowed on them. Our Lord said, "Freely ye have received, freely give" (Matthew 10:8).

### Isaiah 32:9-12

In Isaiah 3 the Lord had sternly rebuked the daughters of Zion who lived in vanity and frivolity, despising the Lord and thinking only of self-gratification. Now again He had a message for "careless" women. Their consciences should have been active and they ought therefore to have guided others in the way of righteousness. But failing to realize that the judgments of God were soon to fall on them, and living only for the present moment, they surrounded themselves with luxury and delighted themselves in worldly pursuits of every description.

The day was soon to come when poverty would rob them of all these things that had ministered to their selfish desires, and the women at last would realize the folly of forgetting God and thinking only of carnal pleasure and self-indulgence. Isaiah warned that when the fields and vineyards were destroyed by invading armies, and other means of sustenance came to an end, they would realize too late how foolish they had been in forgetting their responsibility to glorify God.

### Isaiah 32:13-14

In this passage we find another prophecy that was not fulfilled in Isaiah's day, but looked ahead to the siege and fall of Jerusalem under Nebuchadnezzar, and even further ahead to the grievous woes of the great tribulation. *Jerusalem* means "founded in peace," but this city has suffered more from war and strife than perhaps any other single city in the history of the world. Still greater horrors are in store for it in the future, immediately before the return of the Lord to reign as King on mount Zion. Jerusalem will never know lasting peace until that day.

### Isaiah 32:15-20

Scripture not only teaches a first and second coming of our Lord Jesus Christ; it also predicts a first and second coming of the Holy Spirit. He came first at Pentecost to baptize believers into one body and empower them to carry the gospel throughout the world. Peter applied the words of Joel 2 to what took place then, but he was not indicating that Joel's prophecy was exhausted by that outpouring. He was indicating that the first coming was of the same character as the second coming will be. When Israel is brought back to God, the

Spirit will be poured out on them from on high and all the spared nations will be blessed accordingly. It is of this second coming that Isaiah 32:15-19 speaks.

What a time of blessing it will be for this poor world when war and strife have come to an end, when sickness and sorrow have fled away, when poverty and distress have disappeared, and when men will enjoy the loving favor of the Lord and find every need met in abundance. So fruitful will the earth be at that time that a garden of herbs will be "counted for a forest" and the wilderness will "blossom as the rose."

It is a great mistake to try to spiritualize all this and deny its obvious meaning. There will indeed be great spiritual blessings at that time, but linked with those blessings will be the literal fulfillment of this and other prophecies. "The peace of God, which passeth all understanding" (Philippians 4:7) will be the portion of those who enter the kingdom and enjoy the blessings of Messiah's reign, but we may be sure that the Old Testament promise that they will dwell in "a peaceable habitation" is not to be taken as figurative. There will be protection from every ill when Messiah takes over the reins of government.

Until these promises of future blessing are all fulfilled, it is the responsibility of believers to continue patiently sowing the seed of the Word of God and to trust Him to give an abundant harvest. Isaiah 32:20—"Blessed are ye that sow beside all waters"—may well be taken to heart by all of God's servants in the present dispensation. The blessing is for us today as truly as for the remnant of Israel in the time of Jacob's trouble. If we go forth weeping, bearing precious seed, we can be assured that we will come again with rejoicing, bringing our sheaves with us (Psalm 126:6).

# ISAIAH 33

# SOWING AND REAPING

We now come to the last of the series of woes found in Isaiah 28–33. This sixth woe was pronounced on the enemies of the people of God, primarily Assyria but also including the other nations that have sought to destroy Israel and Judah.

### Isaiah 33:1

In all God's ways with men the principle is shown to be true that "whatsoever a man soweth, that shall he also reap" (Galatians 6:7). This principle applies to nations as well as to individuals. The powers that unprovoked have wreaked havoc on Israel must in turn be visited with judgment after God has used them for the chastening of His people.

Thus the prophet declared, "Woe to thee that spoilest." As we look back over the pages of history, we can see how these words of Isaiah have been fulfilled many times in connection with the different nations under whom the Jews have suffered so terribly: for instance Assyria, Babylon, Egypt, and the Roman empire as well as more modern nations such as Spain, Poland, Russia, and Germany. Those who in future days rise up to oppress the covenant people will be permitted to go only as far as God in His infinite wisdom and justice deems necessary. Then the oppressors will be destroyed and Israel delivered.

### Isaiah 33:2-6

As we read on, we can hear the cry of the remnant both in the past and as it will be in the days of the beast and the antichrist: "O

Lord, be gracious unto us; we have waited for thee: be thou...our salvation also in the time of trouble." The remnant are marked for destruction, but find deliverance as they look to the God of their fathers and turn to Him in repentance. Intervening on their behalf, He stretches forth His hand of power to save and comfort, and they declare the might of Jehovah. The hearts of those who confide in the Lord are moved to worship and thanksgiving as they see by faith His kingdom established over all the earth. Faith counts on God, and looks at things that are not as though they are.

It is surely a grievous misapplication of the scope of the prophetic Scriptures to spiritualize all this and make Zion mean the church, the body of Christ. Every sober expositor recognizes the fact that the judgments predicted throughout all these chapters have fallen or are yet to fall on the Jews or on their oppressors. Surely then it is inconsistent to apply the blessings to the church of the present age. Certainly the same people who have suffered at the hands of the Gentiles because of their disobedience to the Word of God are identical, nationally, with those who will participate in the privileges of the kingdom of God when it is set up in this world. Then mount Zion will be the center of blessing for the whole earth.

### *Isaiah 33:7-12*

The covenant referred to in 33:8 doubtless was that which the Jews attempted to make with Egypt in order to strengthen themselves against the Assyrian—a covenant that was to prove absolutely valueless. But we may also see in this passage a picture of the desolation that will come in the last days when the seven-year covenant made between the beast and the head of the Jewish state will be broken, as foretold in Daniel 9, in the midst of the "week." Almost incredible sufferings will fall on the remnant who in that day refuse to worship "the abomination of desolation," as predicted by our Lord in Matthew 24:15.

The land will be laid waste because of the apostasy of the mass of the people when the day of the Lord begins. No machinations of the apostate majority will avail to turn away the judgments of the Lord. When He arises to "shake terribly the earth" (Isaiah 2:19-21),

His power will brook no attempted interference on the part of His enemies who deny His name.

### *Isaiah 33:13-17*

His judgments will surely also fall on those who honor His name with their lips, but by their works deny Him. These "sinners in Zion" profess reverence for the name of Jehovah, but reveal their unbelief by the godlessness of their lives. When God arises to deal with them, their religious pretensions will fail them and they will learn at last that the hypocrite's hope will perish. Only that which is real can survive the day of Jehovah.

The questions of verse 14 have, I think, often been misunderstood. The prophet was not speaking here of that which Scripture clearly teaches elsewhere: namely, the everlasting punishment of the finally impenitent. The "everlasting burnings" are not the fires of Hell but the holiness of God, before which no unrighteous man can stand, whatever his pretensions to piety may be. As Hebrews 12:29 says, "Our God is a consuming fire." Only those who have judged themselves in His holy presence and are seeking to walk before Him in truth and uprightness can "dwell with the devouring fire."

Isaiah 33:15 provides the only possible answer to the questions in 33:14. This answer is in full accord with Psalm 15:1-3. While in every dispensation all who are saved will owe everything for eternity to the propitiatory work of our Lord Jesus Christ, the proof that they have really been born of God and justified before His face is seen in their righteous lives and humble submission to His holy will.

To the remnant, who will be characterized by subjection to God and integrity in their dealings with their fellow men, the promises of Isaiah 33:16-17 will be made real. They will behold the King in all His beauty and glory when He returns to fulfill prophetic Scripture. They will see the land—that is, the land promised by God to Abraham's seed—far extended (rather than "far off," as 33:17 in the King James version reads). From the river of Egypt to the Euphrates, all will be the inheritance of Israel when they are restored to God (see Genesis 15:18).

## Isaiah 33:18-24

The apostle Paul quoted part of 33:18 when he was expressing the limitations of the human mind in regard to comprehending divine ministries (1 Corinthians 1:20). Who, unaided by the Spirit of God, would ever have understood His purpose of blessing the nation that would refuse His Son and call down on their own heads the awful malediction, "His blood be on us, and on our children" (Matthew 27:25)? In spite of all their waywardness, God's counsels will stand and He will bring them at last into His favor, not only for the millennial age but for eternity. No matter what they may be called on to suffer in the interim through the fierceness and hatred of the persecuting nations, they will emerge at last triumphant over all their foes. Israel will be brought into fullness of blessing when the Lord Jesus descends to vindicate every promise that God has given. No longer will those who revere His name be called on to endure reproach and suffering because of their faithfulness to Him.

Glorious is the prospect presented by Isaiah. Jerusalem, so long a city of strife and warfare, will become "a quiet habitation," for the Prince of Peace will dwell there and His law will go forth to all the world. Jerusalem, without any close seaport, has been isolated, but in that day the Lord will be to the people of the holy city "a place of broad rivers and streams." No enemy ship will ever sail in those rivers, for God will be the protector of His people; the Lord Himself will be Jerusalem's defense. Sorrow and sickness will flee away and the weakest of the children of God will be stronger than the most powerful foes of the past. Those who recognize their own lameness and insufficiency will be overcomers because of their reliance on almighty power.

While we should be careful not to take a prophecy such as 33:18-24 out of its setting and give it direct application to the church of the present age, the passage has spiritual lessons from which we may well profit. It tells us what Scripture always emphasizes: that vain is the help of man, but he who relies on the living God need fear no foe, whether human or demonic. Faith is ever the victory that overcomes the world, the flesh, and the devil.

# THE DAY OF JEHOVAH'S VENGEANCE

I saiah 34 and 35 link closely with what we have already considered. Chapter 34 sets forth the judgment that is to fall on the enemies of God and of His chosen people Israel, while chapter 35 tells of the blessing that this long-despised people will enjoy under Messiah's benevolent despotism.

### Isaiah 34:1-4

We cannot read Isaiah 34 without thinking of many other passages of Scripture that clearly tell us of the same stupendous events. For example the prophecy in 34:1-3 regarding the doom of all the nations that will come against Judah and Jerusalem in the last days, is in perfect harmony with Revelation 19:19-21. In fact these words of Isaiah might be looked on as a commentary on the vision found in the Apocalypse. They also correspond with the first part of Zechariah 14.

When all nations are gathered together against Jerusalem, Jehovah will go forth and fight against them. The feet of our blessed Lord will stand on the mount of Olives in that day when He returns to deliver His earthly people and to vindicate the promises of God made to them by all the prophets of old.

Isaiah 34:4 reminds us of the judgment under the sixth seal in Revelation 6 and also carries our minds on to the end of time when the predictions in Psalm 102:26 and Hebrews 1:11 will be fulfilled.

It seems as though Isaiah 34:4 and Revelation 6 must be taken in a poetic or symbolic sense; that is, the heavens, the sun, and the stars represent the ruling Gentile civil and ecclesiastical powers of the last days. The other two passages, on the other hand, seem to point to the passing away of present conditions in order to bring in the "new heavens and a new earth, wherein dwelleth righteousness" (2 Peter 3:13).

One need have no difficulty in regard to this double application, for the same type of thing occurs in a number of other places in Scripture. God often describes certain conditions in symbolic language that may later have a literal fulfillment. For instance our Lord told us of great earthquakes that will prevail immediately before His second advent; and in the book of Revelation we read of such earthquakes, but there, in accordance with the symbolic character of the book, they have to do with the shaking and breaking down of existing institutions, the destruction of civilization as we now know it.

### Isaiah 34:5-17

This passage deals particularly with the judgment that is to fall on Idumea. This judgment has not yet fallen, but we may be assured that Isaiah's prophecy will be fulfilled literally in the endtime.

The dukes of Edom once reigned in Idumea, and in Obadiah God declared that He would cut off the people of Edom. In the last days there will be a people in the land of Idumea whose envy and hatred of the sons of Jacob will be as great as the animosity of the Edomites was. On these Idumeans, unsparing judgment will fall.

The sword of the Lord will be drawn from its sheath and will not be returned to the scabbard until all the enemies of Israel are blotted out. This time of judgment will be the day of the Lord's recompense for all the sufferings that have fallen on Zion and the people represented by that city throughout the centuries that have gone by since they were scattered among the Gentiles.

Isaiah foresaw the desolation of the land of Edom, which apparently will continue throughout the entire millennial age as a reminder of the judgment that God meted out to a rebellious people. Edom will serve as a warning to any who, even in the day of Jehovah's power, might contemplate turning against the King reigning in Zion.

It is difficult to identify with certainty all of the beasts, birds, and reptiles Isaiah mentioned in this passage, for scholars do not agree on the exact meaning of each of the Hebrew words employed. But even though we may not understand every term used, we can grasp the meaning of the context—namely, that the land of Edom, once a flourishing kingdom, will become utterly desolate and a habitation for only wild creatures.

We know this is true because Jehovah's Word is absolutely sure. No prophecy of the Scriptures will fail to be completely fulfilled. Just as type and antitype agree in connection with the truth of our Lord's person and redemptive work, so prophecy and fulfillment will be in perfect harmony. Nothing that God has spoken will prove to be unreliable. He will never go back on His word, whether it has to do with judgment or with grace.

# MILLENNIAL BLESSING

This precious portion of Scripture concludes the first of the three main parts of the book of Isaiah. Chapter 35 is a beautiful inspired poem describing the delightful conditions that will prevail in this world after the binding of Satan (Revelation 20:1-3) and the enthronement of our Lord Jesus Christ as sovereign of the universe. Isaiah's own heart must have been thrilled as he looked forward to this time of peace and righteousness following the long years of strife and wickedness that have caused such grief and suffering throughout human history.

### *Isaiah 35:1-2*

Even creation will share in the blessings of that day of Jehovah's power: "The desert shall rejoice, and blossom as the rose." Our world has been terribly marred as a result of man's sin, but all that is still lovely, such as the grandeur of Lebanon and the beauties of Carmel and Sharon's plains, will be retained in that new era. To these will be added many additional testimonies to the Creator's joy in this world that He brought into being by the word of His power.

Every fruitful field and orchard, every lovely garden that we enjoy today is a foretaste of what in Messiah's day will be everywhere prevalent. Then the parched deserts will give place to verdant meadows. The thorns and thistles brought in by the curse will vanish; instead trees and shrubs will spring up bearing fruit to appeal to the appetite and flowers to delight the eye.

## *Isaiah 35:3-7*

The physical and spiritual blessings that will come to all mankind will transcend all of the material changes in creation. For long centuries the people of earth have yearned for deliverance from the countless ills that affect humanity. Since "hope deferred maketh the heart sick" (Proverbs 13:12), the prophet exhorted those whose faith is weak and whose hearts are fearful to lift up their eyes and look ahead to the time when God will come down to earth to end its travail and bring in new and happy conditions.

When Jesus came the first time, all the signs of the coming age were illustrated as sickness of every form fled at the sound of His voice or the touch of His hand; blind eyes were opened, deaf ears were made to hear, and the tongues of the dumb were made to sing. To some extent these signs followed the preaching of His apostles, who could say with authority to the lame and helpless, "In the name of Jesus Christ of Nazareth rise up and walk" (Acts 3:6). Their very shadows at times had healing power. All of these wonders were but foretastes of what will be common in millennial days. Venomous and baneful creatures will no longer molest mankind, for only what will minister to man's comfort and security will remain.

## *Isaiah 35:8-10*

The path into God's presence is "The way of holiness." In that day when men's hearts are turned to the Lord, He will lead them along the highway of holiness to mount Zion where His throne will be established. From there His law will go forth into all the earth, and under His beneficent and righteous reign "sorrow and sighing shall flee away" and "joy and gladness" will take their place.

We who belong to the church, the body of Christ, have our hearts fixed on the heavenly hope as we look for the coming of our Lord Jesus and our gathering together unto Him. However, we cannot but rejoice to know that God has such blessing in store for Israel, His earthly people, and for the nations of the earth who throughout history have been the prey of distressing circumstances that they were powerless to change.

It is most humbling to man's pride to realize that our advanced civilization is utterly unable to prevent war and oppression in spite of peace conferences and leagues of nations. Christ alone can put things right. His return is man's only hope for lasting peace.

# RABSHAKEH'S BLASPHEMY

Chapters 36–39 form the second of the three main parts of the book of Isaiah. These four chapters, which relate certain important incidents in the life of King Hezekiah of Judah, are a historic interlude. I intend only to glance over the history rather than explain it verse by verse as I endeavored to do with the prophecy in the first part of Isaiah.

These historic chapters are almost a duplicate of 2 Kings 18:13–21:26, and the major events in them are also covered by 2 Chronicles 32–33. In all probability it was Isaiah who wrote these portions of 2 Kings and 2 Chronicles and, under the guidance of the Holy Spirit, transferred the lengthier account to its place in his great prophetic book.

There was a special reason for including Isaiah 36–39 with the prophecy: All four chapters have to do with a king on whom all of Judah's hopes were centered. In that this son of David came to the verge of death but was raised up in order that the purpose of God might be fulfilled, he points forward to our Lord Jesus Christ, who actually went down into death and was raised up to carry out God's counsels. Thus to some degree Hezekiah foreshadows Christ.

### Isaiah 36:1-10

In the fourteenth year of Hezekiah's reign the Assyrians, under the cruel and ruthless Sennacherib, invaded Judah. After destroying or capturing various fenced cities, he sent a great army to besiege Jerusalem. This host was under the direct leadership of a general named Rabshakeh, a bold but vulgar and blustering officer who had a supreme contempt for the Jews and their religion. He took his stand at a prominent place outside the wall of Jerusalem where his voice could be easily heard by the defenders of the city, and called on the leaders to surrender before he ordered his troops to destroy them completely.

Judah refused to yield to his commands, and Eliakim, Shebna, and Joah, who were what we would call members of Hezekiah's cabinet, tried to parley with the arrogant Assyrian. Speaking on behalf of Sennacherib, Rabshakeh inquired, "What confidence is this wherein thou trustest?" Insolently he declared that if they hoped for deliverance to come through the power of their God, their expectations were doomed to disappointment. Had not Sennacherib proved himself more than a match for all the gods of the surrounding nations? And had not Hezekiah himself destroyed the altars of Jehovah and thus forfeited all claims on Him even if He did have the power to protect him? Not realizing that the destroyed altars were connected with idolatrous shrines, Rabshakeh supposed that they had been dedicated to the God of Judah.

Rabshakeh demanded unconditional surrender and a large tribute as a pledge that the Jews would abide by the proposed terms. He even went so far as to insist that it was by the direction of Jehovah that Sennacherib had come against Judah. He may in some way have become familiar with the prophecies that we have been considering; he knew of Samaria's fall, and so may have learned that their own God had declared that He would use Assyria as a rod to punish Judah for their disobedience and waywardness.

### Isaiah 36:11-22

Fearful that Rabshakeh's words might have an ill effect on the morale of the defenders of the city, the Jewish leaders asked that the Assyrian general speak to them in his own language, with which they were familiar, and not in the Hebrew tongue. This request only roused Rabshakeh to greater insolence. He used language that was disgusting and revolting as he declared that he had been sent not to speak just to the representatives of Hezekiah, but to all the people of Jerusalem. Rabshakeh continued to demand of them (1) instant obedience to the call for surrender and (2) promises of allegiance to the king of Assyria. If the people met his demands, their lives would be spared and they themselves would be transported as prisoners of war to other lands where they would be permitted to live in peace and security.

Derisively Rabshakeh referred again to the folly of trusting in God and reminded the people that the gods of Hamath, Arphad, Sepharvaim, and Samaria had been unable to cope with the might of Sennacherib. What reason had Judah to hope that the Lord would intervene on their behalf and deliver Jerusalem from threatened ruin?

To all these demands and taunts the people answered "not a word," for Hezekiah had commanded, "Answer him not." Eliakim and his companions returned to Hezekiah "with their clothes rent" in token of their grief over being unable to come to terms with the Assyrian general and reported Rabshakeh's arrogant and defiant words to their king.

# SENNACHERIB'S DEFEAT

### Isaiah 37:1-4

Isaiah 37 continues the account of certain important incidents in the life of Hezekiah. When Hezekiah heard the report of Eliakim, Shebna, and Joah (36:22), he "rent his clothes, and covered himself with sackcloth, and went into the house of the Lord." There he could pour out his heart to the God of his fathers, the God who had so often given deliverance to His people in times of great distress and adversity. Feeling the need of counsel and prayer, Hezekiah sent Eliakim, Shebna, and the elders to Isaiah, and they delivered the following message to the prophet: "Thus saith Hezekiah, This day is a day of trouble, and of rebuke, and of blasphemy: for the children are come to the birth, and there is not strength to bring forth. It may be the Lord thy God will hear the words of Rabshakeh, whom the king of Assyria his master hath sent to reproach the living God, and will reprove the words which the Lord thy God hath heard: wherefore lift up thy prayer for the remnant that is left."

Such faith could not go unrewarded. God never fails those who commit everything to Him. He has said, "Call upon me in the day of trouble: I will deliver thee, and thou shalt glorify me" (Psalm 50:15). Hezekiah was soon to prove the truth of this promise, even though his faith would first be tested severely.

### Isaiah 37:5-20

Isaiah's answer was most cheering and reassuring. He said, "Thus shall ye say unto your master, Thus saith the Lord, Be not afraid of

171

the words that thou hast heard, wherewith the servants of the king of Assyria have blasphemed me." It was not just a problem between the two opposing armies, or between Rabshakeh and Hezekiah. The Assyrian had dared to challenge the power of Jehovah. He Himself would take up the challenge and display His power and might. He would show that He was not a mere idol or an imaginary deity like the heathen gods whose inability to save their devotees from destruction had been so readily revealed. Sennacherib and his servants had dared to rush "upon the thick bosses of [the] bucklers" of the Almighty (Job 15:25-26) and were soon to prove the folly of daring to fight against the omnipotent God who created the heavens and the earth.

God declared through His prophet, "Behold, I will send a blast upon him, and he shall hear a rumour, and return to his own land; and I will cause him to fall by the sword in his own land." The rumor was a report that Tirhakah, king of Ethiopia, was on his way to fight against Assyria, whose armies were divided, part besieging Jerusalem, and part warring against Libnah. Reluctant though he was, Rabshakeh was obliged to lift the siege and withdraw to Assyria, but as his armies were retreating, he sent a last defiant message to the king of Judah: "Let not thy God, in whom thou trustest, deceive thee, saying, Jerusalem shall not be given into the hand of the king of Assyria. Behold, thou hast heard what the kings of Assyria have done to all lands by destroying them utterly; and shalt thou be delivered?" And he taunted Hezekiah again for his folly in presuming that his God would prove any more powerful than the gods of other nations.

This message was put in the form of a letter and it was delivered to Hezekiah. It was a letter of blasphemy and Hezekiah did right in not attempting to answer it himself. Instead he took it into the house of the Lord and spread it out before God. Bowing in His presence, he pleaded that Jehovah would intervene to save His people. Hezekiah frankly acknowledged that the fake gods of the other nations had no ability to save and he confessed his confidence that the living God would act on behalf of those who put their trust in Him. The conclusion of his prayer is very beautiful and heart-moving:

"Now therefore, O Lord our God, save us from his hand, that all the kingdoms of the earth may know that thou art the Lord, even thou only." Such confidence could not go unrewarded, nor such a prayer unheard.

*Isaiah 37:21-35*

The answer to Hezekiah's prayer came through another message from Isaiah, assuring the king that God had heard and was about to answer his petition. God said that "the virgin, the daughter of Zion" should despise the haughty foe whose army had at first seemed invincible.

Rabshakeh had reproached the Lord. He had blasphemed the God of Judah. In his pride and folly he had lifted himself up against the holy One of Israel. Trusting in the vastness of his army and the number of his chariots and horsemen, he had thought it would be but a small matter to conquer Jerusalem and carry its inhabitants away as captives. Therefore the word of the Lord came to him saying: "Because thy rage against me, and thy tumult, is come up into mine ears, therefore will I put my hook in thy nose, and my bridle in thy lips, and I will turn thee back by the way by which thou camest." Rabshakeh was soon to learn the difference between the senseless idols of the heathen and the One in whom Hezekiah had put his trust.

To Hezekiah the promise was given that the land which had been overrun by the enemy would bring forth "of itself" for two seasons. In the third year the people were to sow and the land would produce an abundant harvest. The remnant of Judah who would escape out of the hand of the Assyrian would once more begin to prosper and "again take root downward, and bear fruit upward: For out of Jerusalem shall go forth a remnant and they that escape out of mount Zion: the zeal of the Lord of hosts shall do this."

As for the king of Assyria, he would not be permitted to enter Jerusalem, or shoot an arrow into it, or threaten it again in any way. He was to return by the way that he had come, for the Lord had decided to defend Jerusalem for His own sake and for His servant David's sake.

## Isaiah 37:36-38

The judgment was not long deferred, for God sent a terrible plague on the camp of the Assyrians, a plague so severe that in one night 185,000 died.

Led by their defeated and crestfallen ruler, the scattered remnants of the once-great army of Sennacherib departed for their own land. Upon reaching his home city and worshiping in the house of his god, Sennacherib was attacked by two of his own sons, Adrammelech and Sharezer, who slew their dishonored father with the sword and escaped into Armenia. One of their brothers, Esarhaddon, became king in his father's stead.

Thus God vindicated His holy name and freed His people from the impending doom that seemed about to fall on them.

# HEZEKIAH'S RECOVERY

The historic interlude continues in Isaiah 38, where we read of Hezekiah's illness and recovery. We might have supposed that after such a remarkable answer to his prayer (chapter 37), Hezekiah would have been drawn so close to the Lord that he would never have doubted His love and care again, and that he would have lived constantly in the sunshine of divine approval. Unfortunately his reaction was far otherwise—and so often our reactions are like Hezekiah's. When new tests came to the king, doubts and fears again prevailed and only the grace of God could bear with His poor failing servant.

### Isaiah 38:1-3

One test came through illness. Hezekiah was "sick unto death," we are told. The prophet Isaiah was sent to say to him, "Thus saith the Lord, Set thine house in order: for thou shalt die, and not live." To the stricken king these words were evil tidings indeed, for he was still a comparatively young man, thirty-nine years old. (He had come to the throne at the age of twenty-five.) Since long life was promised to obedient Israelites, the announcement that he was to die before he was forty seemed to Hezekiah like an evidence of divine displeasure. He received the message of the prophet with real distress and pleaded for a reprieve from the sentence imposed upon him.

When reading Hezekiah's prayer in 38:3 we need to remember that the Old Testament saints, however godly they might have been, did not have the light on the afterlife that has now been given to the children of God. Our Lord Jesus Christ has "brought life and immortality to light through the gospel" (2 Timothy 1:10); He has revealed the truth about what God has prepared for those who love Him (1 Corinthians 2:9-10). Having gone down to death and come up in triumph, He has annulled "him that had the power of death," even the devil, and so delivers those "who through fear of death were all their lifetime subject to bondage" (Hebrews 2:14-15). We know now that for the believer death simply means to be "absent from the body" and "present with the Lord" (2 Corinthians 5:8) and that this is "far better" than any possible earthly experience (Philippians 1:23). But all this was unknown in the days before the advent of our Lord Jesus Christ, who declared, "If a man keep my saying, he shall never see death" (John 8:51).

Therefore when the word came to Hezekiah that he was going to die, his soul was filled with fear. He cried to God in his wretchedness, pleading the integrity of his life as a reason for his days to be prolonged.

### Isaiah 38:4-8

God, who sometimes grants our requests but sends leanness into our soul (Psalm 106:15), heard Hezekiah's cry and sent the prophet to him once more. This time Isaiah was to tell him that his prayer was heard and that God would add to his life another fifteen years. God would also continue to defend Jerusalem from the evil machinations of the Assyrian king.

To confirm the promise, a sign was given that involved a stupendous miracle. God said, "I will bring again the shadow of the degrees, which is gone down in the sun dial of Ahaz, ten degrees backward." When this actually took place—"The sun returned ten degrees, by which degrees it was gone down"—Hezekiah knew beyond all doubt that the prophet had spoken by divine authority.

This is not the place to discuss the miracle itself. Whether it was caused by some amazing event in the planetary system, or it was a miracle of refraction, we need not try to decide. The fact that the astronomers of Babylon had knowledge of it would indicate that it was something far-reaching and of grave import.

*Isaiah 38:9-20*

Upon his recovery, Hezekiah wrote of the experiences he had passed through when under the sentence of death: Bitterly he complained that he was about to be deprived of the residue of his years. Leaving the world seemed to him like being banished from the presence of the Lord. His days and nights were filled with grievous pain not only of body, but also of mind as he fearfully awaited the carrying out of the decree. He dreaded the time when God, as he put it, would "make an end" of him. He mourned "as a dove"; his eyes tired from "looking upward." Yet he knew that he was in the hands of the Lord, and his heart cried out to Him for help.

It is evident that as this spiritual exercise continued, Hezekiah's soul rested more peacefully on the truth that all must be well when one is in the care of a covenant-keeping God. "O Lord," he said, "by these things men live, and in all these things is the life of my spirit: so wilt thou recover me, and make me to live. Behold, for peace I had great bitterness: but thou hast in love to my soul delivered it from the pit of corruption: for thou hast cast all my sins behind thy back." These precious words expressed his realization, after his health returned, of the goodness and wisdom of God. Hezekiah took his healing as an evidence that God had pardoned all his sins and cast them away forever.

Hezekiah could see nothing in the grave but darkness and forgetfulness. In life the Lord could be praised, but not in Sheol. Hezekiah of course wrote of conditions as he, an unenlightened Old Testament believer, understood them. "Death can not celebrate [the Lord]," he lamented, but he closed his writing with a note of praise and thanksgiving for renewed strength and added years of life.

*Isaiah 38:21-22*

The deliverance came in a very simple way. Hezekiah had been suffering from a boil, but a poultice of figs, prescribed by Isaiah, drew out the poison and started the king on the way to recovery.

It is hardly necessary to point out that had Hezekiah died at the age of thirty-nine, Manasseh, who proved to be the most wicked king who ever sat on the throne of Judah, would never have been born, for he was only twelve years old when his father was buried (2 Chronicles 33:1). Manasseh tried to undo everything that his father had done. Hezekiah in his twenty-nine-year reign had destroyed the altars of idolatry and had swept the land clear of idols. Manasseh, on the other hand, brought in more forms of idolatry than were ever known before. He also consulted spiritists and filled the land with mediums who professed to be able to talk with the dead, even though God had forbidden such practices. Manasseh brought down the indignation of God on Judah because of the corruption and sin that characterized his reign.

Yet how wonderful is the mercy of God! When Manasseh was an old man almost facing eternity, God brought that godless king to repentance. Manasseh broke down, confessed the sins of his ungodly life, attempted to cleanse the land of its idols, and tried to bring about a reformation—but it was too late to recover the people. Manasseh's son Amon repeated the sins of his father, but in the next generation God in wondrous grace raised up another son of David, King Josiah, who honored the Lord even in his youth. Josiah was the means of bringing about a great revival in Judah.

# BABYLON'S AMBASSADORS

I saiah 39, which concludes the four-chapter historic interlude, tells of another test faced by Hezekiah—and another failure on the part of this king who was on the whole so devoted to the will of God.

Second Chronicles 32:31 says concerning Hezekiah, "In the business of the ambassadors of the princes of Babylon, who sent unto him to enquire of the wonder that was done in the land, God left him, to try him, that he might know all that was in his heart." Few of us could stand such a test. If we were left alone by God so that our hearts would be exposed and our inmost thoughts revealed, we without doubt would suffer moral or spiritual breakdown. Hezekiah failed the test because of self-confidence. He acted on his own judgment instead of turning to the Lord for guidance, and the inevitable result was harm instead of blessing.

### Isaiah 39:1-2

After the Lord so graciously granted Hezekiah's request to be raised up from the brink of the grave, "Merodach-Baladan, the son of Baladan, king of Babylon, sent letters and a present to Hezekiah: for he had heard that he had been sick, and was recovered." How would the king of Judah react to this apparently friendly overture from the prince of the great city that was the fountainhead of idolatry? When Rabshakeh sent a letter of blasphemy, Hezekiah went into the sanctuary and spread it out before the Lord. But now when letters and a present came from Babylon, Hezekiah felt no need to bring the matter before God or seek instruction from Him.

Do not we all know something of this self-confidence when the world approaches us, not in open opposition to that which we cherish most, but in an apparently cordial and patronizing manner, extending the hand of friendship instead of the armored fist of enmity? We are never in greater danger of missing the mind of God than at such a time as this. A letter that is accompanied by a present may cover up a far greater danger than a letter of blasphemy.

Evidently elated by the visit of the Babylonian envoys and their retinue, and pleased with the present, Hezekiah felt no need to ask counsel of the Lord. Without hesitation he received the embassage "and shewed them the house of his precious things, the silver, and the gold, and the spices, and the precious ointment, and all the house of his armour, and all that was found in his treasures: there was nothing in his house, nor in all his dominion, that Hezekiah shewed them not." This was exactly what the Chaldeans desired. No doubt as they looked with covetous eyes on all these things, they were pondering in their hearts how best they should proceed in order that some day they might conquer Judah and have all this vast treasure for themselves.

### Isaiah 39:3-8

Scarcely had the Babylonians gone from the presence of Hezekiah when Isaiah appeared on the scene to confront the king with two questions: "What said these men? and from whence came they unto thee?" Ingenuously Hezekiah replied, "They are come from a far country unto me, even from Babylon." Surely he could not have been ignorant of the prophecies Isaiah had spoken regarding this northeastern power that was yet to come against Judah and be used by God as a rod to punish His people for their willful neglect and disobedience.

Isaiah asked Hezekiah another question: "What have they seen in thy house?" The king answered, "All that is in mine house have they seen: there is nothing among my treasures that I have not shewed them." He had no idea of the serious import of this exhibition, for he had not realized that the princes were actually spies who had come to search out the land and to report to the king of Babylon all that they found.

Therefore the unsuspecting monarch must have been shocked when Isaiah said, "Hear the word of the Lord of hosts: Behold, the days come, that all that is in thine house, and that which thy fathers have laid up in store until this day, shall be carried to Babylon: nothing shall be left, saith the Lord. And of thy sons that shall issue from thee, which thou shalt beget, shall they take away; and they shall be eunuchs in the palace of the king of Babylon." We can imagine Hezekiah's disappointment and his deep chagrin when he heard the words of the prophet. He could only bow his head and accept them as the revelation of the judgment of God. So he replied, "Good is the word of the Lord which thou hast spoken....For there shall be peace and truth in my days."

Afterward in spite of occasional revivals in Judah, things went from bad to worse until at last "there was no remedy" for their evil condition. The prophesied judgment was fulfilled in the days of Zedekiah when Nebuchadnezzar conquered Judah and carried away their chief men as captives, including a large number who were of royal blood. The conqueror also took to Babylon the treasures Hezekiah had showed to the spies (2 Chronicles 36:16-18).

# ISAIAH 40

# GOD THE COMFORTER

We have seen that the first part of the book of Isaiah (chapters 1–35) is prophetic and that the second part (chapters 36–39) is historical and typical. Now we come to the third part (chapters 40–66), which we will also find to be prophetic in nature.

There are critics who attribute part three of Isaiah's great book to one whom they call "the second Isaiah," some unnamed prophet who wrote after the Babylonian captivity; the work of this unknown person was supposedly incorporated into the book of Isaiah by a later editor. But the New Testament definitely negates this idea of authorship and attributes chapters 40–66 to Isaiah himself (see Matthew 8:17; Luke 4:17-19), so we need not trouble ourselves about such unfounded critical theories. The matter is settled for us.

As we begin to consider Isaiah 40, I am reminded of a comment made by J. N. Darby. He aptly pointed out, "We have had rather the outward history of Israel, but now we have their moral or inward history in their place of testimony against idolatry, in their relationship with Christ and the separation of a remnant." That inward history was a complete failure, as part three of Isaiah's prophecy clearly shows.

### Isaiah 40:1-8

The chapter commences with the words, "Comfort ye, comfort ye my people, saith your God. Speak ye comfortably to Jerusalem, and cry unto her, that her warfare is accomplished, that her iniquity is pardoned."

God intended to comfort His people, but in doing so He had to bring before them very definitely their true condition in His sight, and then show His remedy. Thus parts of the message of Isaiah 40 may not sound very comforting. God, in His gracious ministry of comfort, always begins by showing us our need and our dependence on His omnipotent power. He wounds that He may heal; He kills that He may make alive. We never know God in the fullness of His power to sustain and comfort until we come to the end of our own resources.

God said to the prophet, "Comfort ye my people," and then proceeded to instruct His servant as to the content of his message. "The voice said, Cry," and Isaiah asked, "What shall I cry?" The voice answered, "All flesh is grass, and all the goodliness thereof is as the flower of the field: The grass withereth, the flower fadeth." This is always the divine order. Not until we realize our own utter nothingness and helplessness, are we in a position to avail ourselves of the comfort that the Lord waits to give us.

In the New Testament we see each person of the blessed trinity engaged in this ministry of comfort. God the Father is called "the God of all comfort" (2 Corinthians 1:3). God the Holy Spirit is spoken of four times in our Lord's last discourse to His disciples as the "Comforter" (John 14:16,26; 15:26; 16:7). One aspect of our Lord's work and ministry is "to comfort all that mourn" (Isaiah 61:2). He is also called our "advocate with the Father" (1 John 2:1) and the word translated "advocate" here is the exact same Greek word as the one translated "Comforter" in John's Gospel. How blessed it is to be in fellowship with the Father, the Son, and the Holy Spirit, so that we can receive and enjoy the comfort They delight to give!

What greater privilege can we have on earth than to enjoy the abiding presence of the "God of all comfort" as we face the perplexities and bitter disappointments that we are called on to endure? If we never knew grief or pain we would never be able to appreciate what God can be to His suffering people. When we cry to the Lord in hours of distress, He does not remove the cause of our trouble in every case, but He always gives the needed grace to bear whatever we are allowed to suffer. When in Heaven we "read the meaning of our tears" and see just what God was working out in our lives, we will praise Him for our trials and afflictions. We will see in them evidences of a Father's love and His desire to conform us to Himself.

Whenever lost men of any nation take their true place before God in repentance, confession, and acknowledgment of their iniquities, He gives the comfort of the knowledge of forgiveness of sins and salvation of the soul. However, in Isaiah 40:1-8 He was looking forward to the time when Israel's iniquities will all be put away.

God told the prophet to speak to the heart of Jerusalem and tell her that "she hath received of the Lord's hand double for all her sins." He did not mean that Israel will have been punished twice as much as her sins deserved. God would never do that. When speaking to Job, Elihu very clearly said that God "will not lay upon man more than [is] right" (Job 34:23). He will deal with each man according to his light and knowledge and the actual sins that he has committed, but He will not punish anyone more than his sins deserve.

The expression "She hath received of the Lord's hand double for all her sins" is a commercial one. When a Jew was in financial difficulty and turned his home or farm over to a creditor in order to meet his debts, the information regarding the transaction would be written on paper. One copy would be kept by the creditor and the other copy would be nailed on the doorpost so that everyone would understand that the property was transferred temporarily to another. When the debt was paid, the notice on the doorpost would be doubled, tacked up double, covered over. That indicated that the account was all settled. So God was using a commercial expression to explain that Israel's account will have been fully paid; the Lord will have pardoned her iniquity and there will be nothing more to suffer.

The people were to look forward to the goal of having their account settled and later we are told how they will reach that goal. For now, we read a prophecy that relates to the first step: the coming of John the Baptist, the one "crying in the wilderness, Prepare ye the way of the Lord, make his paths straight" (Matthew 3:3; Isaiah 40:3).

Moses told the Israelites, "A prophet shall the Lord your God raise up unto you of your brethren, like unto me; him shall ye hear in all things" (Acts 3:22). When certain of the Pharisees asked John the Baptist if he were the Messiah or the one spoken of by Moses, John said, "I am not." Then his questioners inquired, "Who art thou?" John answered, "I am the voice of one crying in the wilderness, Make straight the way of the Lord" (John 1:19-27). Thus he applied to himself the words of Isaiah 40:3.

God wanted His messenger to cry aloud, to give out His message that "all flesh is grass...but the word of our God shall stand for ever" (40:6-8). First Peter 1:24-25 quotes this passage and adds a significant comment: "This is the word which by the gospel is preached unto you." So it is the gospel message that is presented to us in Isaiah.

### *Isaiah 40:9-11*

The Word of the Lord that endures forever is the good tidings of the gospel. Thus immediately following the statement that "the word of our God shall stand for ever," Isaiah cried, "O Zion, that bringest good tidings...say...Behold your God!"

"The silent glances of Scripture" in Isaiah 40:9-11 are intimately linked with the early chapters of all four Gospels, which speak of the Lord's first advent. Matthew said plainly that the events he recorded were the fulfillment of that which was spoken by Isaiah and other prophets. For example Isaiah wrote, "The Lord God will come," and Matthew told us that the coming One is *Emmanuel*, which means "God with us" (1:22-23). Isaiah described the Lord Jesus as the tender Shepherd, and John recorded that when He actually came, He took the word spoken by Isaiah and said, "I am the good shepherd....I lay down my life for the sheep" (10:11-15).

And so in the good news that God brought to Israel through Isaiah, Christ is pictured as the Good Shepherd, carrying the lambs in his bosom and gently leading those with young. Yet this One who came so tenderly is the almighty God! He who comes to us in absolute holiness as a kind, compassionate, loving man, is the omnipotent, omnipresent, omniscient God, "the Creator of the ends of the earth" (Isaiah 40:28).

### *Isaiah 40:12-20*

In 40:12-20 God, through Isaiah, spoke in power and majesty, putting Himself in contrast with the helpless man-made idols of the heathen, to which many of the people of Israel had turned. Speaking as the Creator of the heavens, the Shepherd of Israel showed that He alone has the resources for faith to lay hold upon. So great is He that no suitable offering can be made to Him. "Lebanon is not sufficient to burn, nor the beasts thereof sufficient for a burnt offering."

Sin is so terrible an affront to a holy God that no sacrifice, however great, that man could offer would ever make amends. Even if the mountains of Lebanon became like a great altar, and all the cedars thereon were hewn down and piled up for one enormous fire, and the vast herds and flocks that grazed on the pastures of those wooded hills were sacrificed on the altar, that offering would not be sufficient to atone for one sin. Only the precious blood of Christ can make propitiation for our guilt and justify us before God.

### *Isaiah 40:21-31*

Why, we may well ask, did God describe Himself as He did in 40:21-31? The reason is that those for whom He tenderly cares are faint and weary, and He turns them to Himself as the source of power. They need simply to wait upon Him, for this divine God has an interest in everyone.

Lack of power is not what prevents God from giving immediate release from trials and tribulations. His understanding is infinite and He is working out His own plans for our blessing when He permits affliction to fall on us and continue to oppress us. Like Job, we must learn the lesson that since man cannot fathom God's plans, he should seek to submit without question to His providential dealings. When distress or suffering becomes prolonged, it is easy to think that God has forgotten or is indifferent to what we are going through. But this thought is always wrong. He is ever concerned about His people, and in His own time He will give deliverance. Until then His grace is available to sustain and strengthen our souls so that we may endure "as seeing him who is invisible" (Hebrews 11:27).

Isaiah 40:29 says, "He giveth power to the faint." This fact enabled Paul to glory in his infirmities so that the "power of Christ" might rest upon him (2 Corinthians 12:9). We too can trust the Lord to supply us with enough power to meet every test He permits us to face.

God's people may grow weary, but "they that wait upon the Lord shall renew their strength." Mere natural and physical powers will be insufficient in great mental and spiritual emergencies, but they who have learned to refer everything to God and to wait quietly on Him will be given all the strength that is needed to rise above depressing circumstances. It will enable them to mount heavenward as eagles facing the sun, to run their race with patience, and to walk with God with renewed courage and confidence, knowing that they are always the objects of His love and care.

It is one thing to wait *on* the Lord. It is quite another to wait *for* Him. As we wait *on* Him, we are changed into His likeness. As we wait *for* Him in patience, we are delivered from worry and fretfulness, for we know that God is never late and in His own time He will give the help we need.

Someone has suggested that Isaiah's words in 40:31 may apply to Christians or children of God in their different age groups. The young believers mount up with wings of hope and expectancy as eagles fly into the heights of the heavens, the middle-aged believers run with patience the race set before them (also see Hebrews 12:1), and those who have reached old age walk quietly with God as they near the portals of the eternal home of the saints.

# THE INFINITELY STRONG ONE

I n Isaiah 41 God continues to contrast His strength with man's weakness. After giving an account of His majesty He promises to strengthen His chosen people, and as we read we see Israel in their weakness depending on the infinitely strong One.

To know God and to depend on Him is to be invincible. No one can really injure a person whose confidence is in the Lord, for He will cause all that seems to be evil to work for the good of those who put their trust in Him. It is through such trust that fear, the deadly enemy of the heart, is overcome. "Fear thou not," God said, "for I am with thee: be not dismayed; for I am thy God: I will strengthen thee; yea, I will help thee; yea, I will uphold thee with the right hand of my righteousness" (41:10). In due time God will deal with those who seek to injure His people; He will mete out righteous judgment to those who trouble His saints (2 Thessalonians 1:6-7). The believer can afford to leave all in His hands and go on in quietness and confidence, through good times and bad.

Since retribution is in God's hands, the enemies of God's people will soon pass away and be forgotten, but those who do the will of God abide forever. In Isaiah 41:13 the reassuring promise is repeated: "Fear not; I will help thee." It is God Himself who has given this pledge. When faith lays hold of it, the heart can be at rest. We who have committed our lives to Him can be content, knowing that He who loved us enough to give His Son to die for us will never fail us.

When assuring Israel of His help, God addressed "the seed of Abraham my friend" (41:8). These words are referred to in James

2:23, where Abraham is called "the Friend of God." What a wonderful thing for God to say of any man! The Lord Jesus said to His disciples, "Henceforth I call you not servants; for the servant knoweth not what his lord doeth: but I have called you friends" (John 15:15).

The servant is to do what he is told. It is not for him to ask, "Why should I do this?" To a friend one unburdens his heart, as the Lord took Abraham into His confidence in regard to Sodom's judgment. God delights to open up His heart and mind to His friends. The object of the prophetic Scriptures is to open up God's truth so that His friends may understand what He is about to do.

And so we understand from Isaiah 41:15 that God will make Israel a "sharp threshing instrument having teeth." That expression points ahead to the great harvest of the last days when a remnant of Israel, who have been restored to the Lord, will be used of Him to proclaim His message and bring many to repentance and faith.

As servants of Christ we too need to be sharp threshing instruments with teeth. A great deal of preaching today has very few "teeth." We should be faithful in pointing out the wickedness of mankind and the exceeding sinfulness of sin so that men will realize where they stand before God. A sermon that lacks "teeth" is so absolutely powerless and colorless that the saved and the unsaved alike can sit and listen to the preaching and enjoy it.

The promises of Isaiah 41 are an encouraging preface to passages in which Jehovah points out the folly of turning to senseless idols that are absolutely unable to help.

# THE CHOSEN SERVANT

I n Isaiah 40 the forerunner was presented—"him that crieth in the wilderness" (40:3). Now in chapter 42 Messiah Himself is presented: "Behold my servant, whom I uphold; mine elect, in whom my soul delighteth" (42:1). His coming was prophesied to Israel so that they would know the plan of God and realize what folly it would be to turn away from the living and true God and worship idols.

### *Isaiah 42:1-4*

Isaiah 42:1-4 was definitely applied to our Lord in Matthew 12:17-21. As prophesied, Messiah did not break bruised reeds or quench smoking flax. Whenever someone showed the least evidence of a desire to turn to God, He quickened and encouraged the desire and led the person on into full assurance of faith. How different was His ministry on earth from ours! We are apt to go to one of two extremes: (1) We do not like to talk to anyone about his soul or do any personal work; we pay no attention to what people say or do—we just preach to them from the platform. (2) Or we are inclined to be very obtrusive and self-assertive and do many things that are hardly in keeping with the way Christians ought to act.

These passages from Isaiah and Matthew helped me greatly when I was a young man. I began my ministry as a Salvation Army officer and at that time The Salvation Army was a mighty power for good in this country. We used to march the streets of San Francisco in processions of over one thousand people and two or three brass bands, and we won hundreds of souls to Christ. But in our intense earnestness in those early days we were inclined perhaps to go to too great extremes and do things that possibly were not wise. Sometimes instead of impressing people for God, we gave them the impression that we were unbalanced.

Personally I was under the power of legalism to the extent that I felt guilty if I rode in a street car without immediately rising to give my testimony. As soon as the trolley left the corner where I got on, I would stand up and say, "Friends, I want to give my testimony for Jesus Christ, and I want to tell you how God saved me." The conductor would come and say, "Sit down. We didn't ask you to come in here to conduct a church service." Then I would be rather rude to him and say, "Well, I'll sit down if you say so, but you'll have to answer at the judgment-bar of God for preventing these people from hearing the gospel."

I did the same thing in railroad cars. As soon as the train pulled away from the station, I would face the other passengers and begin to give my testimony. I felt that if I didn't testify, I would be responsible for their souls, and I did not realize that I was being rude. The last time I tried to witness in this way, I had just started when a Roman Catholic priest jumped to his feet and said, "What's this? What's this? Do I have to be insulted on this train? Do I have to sit in a Protestant service? Call the conductor!" The conductor came and said to me, "Young man, you can't do this; you've no right to interfere with other people's religion when you're riding on the railroad." And so I had to sit down.

The devil either tries to keep us quiet or makes us think that we must do what is unreasonable. I was greatly bothered by this problem until Isaiah's words showed me that there was a golden mean between indifference and rudeness. What delivered me at last was Matthew 12:19, which quotes the prophet as saying that the Lord would "not strive, nor cry; neither shall any man hear his voice in the streets." I was reminded that Christ went through His service here for God in such a restful, quiet way. When people came to Him and wanted to know how to find eternal life, how to be saved, He was always ready to help them. He sought out the lost, like the woman at Sychar's well, but He never did anything boisterous or uncouth.

Jesus was truly God's "gentleman." When I first saw that expression applied to Him, I was rather startled. I came across it some years ago in London when I picked up a little volume published early in the seventeenth century. The book was an old history of the world and in the section on the reign of Caesar Augustus there was this sentence: "In his days, there was born in Bethlehem of Judea that goodly gentleman, Jesus Christ." As I meditated on that, I thought, *Why shouldn't that epithet be applied to Him?* A gentleman is a gentle man, a gracious man, and Jesus was always gentle and gracious. Even when rebuking sin sternly, He never did anything that was boisterous or made Him seem uncouth.

### *Isaiah 42:16*

Isaiah 42:16 presents the Lord as our guide. If God explained all His ways with us beforehand, we would walk not by faith, but by sight. He leads us along strange paths and through new and peculiar experiences so that we may learn how marvelously His grace can sustain, and how blessedly His wisdom can plan. It is not necessary that we should see the road ahead; it is only necessary that we trust our guide. He knows the end from the beginning and He never deviates from His purpose of blessing. When at last we reach the city of God and look back over the way we have come, we will praise Him for all His dealings with us and we will understand the reason for every trial.

# GOD'S WITNESSES TO HIS FAITHFULNESS

### *Isaiah 43:1-3*

The prophecy of the Lord's gracious care of Israel is continued in Isaiah 43. We read here of how wonderfully He shares their sorrows. He who led Israel in safety through the Red Sea and the Jordan, and walked with the three devoted Hebrew youths in the fiery furnace is still the unfailing resource of His troubled people in every hour of trial, no matter how severe the test. "O Israel," the Lord says, "Fear not: for I have redeemed thee, I have called thee by thy name; thou art mine."

Faith can count on His sustaining grace and blessed companionship in every perplexity, apparent defeat, or grave danger. Millions have tested and proven the faithfulness of His promises.

### *Isaiah 43:9-13*

God has chosen Israel to be His witnesses to His gracious care. They continue to be His witnesses whether they are obedient to Him or disobedient, whether they are in the land or out of the land, whether they are keeping the law or breaking it. They are His witnesses because God has, through Moses and the other prophets, given His testimony about how He was going to deal with His people down through the centuries; He declared what blessings would be theirs if they walked in obedience, and what curses and judgments would come upon them if they were disobedient. History shows the truth of what God declared and therefore the people of Israel are God's witnesses to the truth of His Word.

After listening to Voltaire's agnostic ideas, Frederick the Great said to one of his court chaplains, "If the Bible is true it ought to be capable of very clear and succinct witness. Generally when I ask if the Bible is true, I am handed some long scholarly volume which I have neither the time nor the patience to read. If your Bible is true, give me the proof of it in one word." The chaplain answered, "Israel." Frederick acknowledged that Israel is indeed a proof that the Bible is true, the Word of the living God.

"O Israel...ye are my witnesses, saith the Lord, *and my servant*" (italics added), so in addition to Israel, God's Servant is His witness, "the faithful and true witness" of Revelation 3:14. In Isaiah 42 we were called to behold His Servant (the Messiah) and the character of His service, and in Isaiah 43 God explained the purpose of this witness to Israel: "That ye may know and believe me, and understand that I am he: before me there was no God formed, neither shall there be after me. I, even I, am the Lord; and beside me there is no saviour."

Thus Jehovah identified His witnesses to His faithfulness. He challenged the idolaters to produce their witnesses, to give some evidence of any spirit of prophecy working in them. "Tell us what is to come," He said in effect. "Tell us things unheard of. Explain the past. Explain the origin of the world." They were unable to meet the challenge, for God alone has done all these things.

# GOD'S UNCHANGING PURPOSES OF BLESSING

### Isaiah 44:1-8

God continued the theme of blessing for Israel in a very precious and wonderful way, promising to pour His Spirit on them from on high: "I will pour water upon him that is thirsty, and floods upon the dry ground: I will pour my spirit upon thy seed, and my blessing upon thine offspring." That outpouring has not yet taken place and it is not to be confused with what happened on the day of Pentecost. Isaiah was writing of the wider fulfillment of Joel 2:28-29.

### Isaiah 44:9-20

The prophet said of the idol-makers that "they are their own witnesses" to their folly. Satirically he pictured their foolishness: A man goes out into the forest, finds a noble tree, cuts it down, takes off all the branches, and with his tools fashions the timber into the figure of a man. He gathers the chips as they fly and uses them as fuel. He cooks his food and says in effect, "This is fine! I have warmed myself at the fire and have a god to worship, all out of the same tree." Thus Isaiah's remarkable satire shows the vanity of worshiping graven images. Jeremiah 10 ridicules idolatry in much the same way.

What folly for the people of Israel, after all that God had done for them, to turn aside to dumb idols! How senseless were many of the kings in Chronicles! They actually brought back the gods of the nations they had conquered, set up shrines for them, and worshiped them, even though those gods had just been proved powerless to defend their worshipers.

Idolatry seems inherent in the heart of man. Today men do not worship idols of gold, silver, brass, and iron; but every man who turns away from God sets up some kind of idol in his heart. He either worships himself or some foolishness such as pleasure or fame.

An esteemed servant of Christ spoke aptly when he was introduced on one occasion as a self-made man. He said he regretted that he had been so labeled, though he appreciated the kindly thought, and explained, "I've noticed that self-made men always worship their own creation." He knew that if men do not know the one living and true God, they set up the great god Self, and worship him.

### *Isaiah 44:21-28*

In this passage God told Israel what He had in store for them: the Redeemer who was still to come, and the comfort He would give to those who believe His word and put their trust in Him. God foresaw the dangers and sorrows that Israel must pass through—the deep waters through which they will have to go—but He promised to be with them in all their troubles when there was real faith on their part.

In 44:28 there is an abrupt change as God spoke of one who was yet to come to be the deliverer of Israel from the power of the Chaldeans: Cyrus, king of Persia. God called him by name, though Cyrus did not know Him. Isaiah recorded this prophecy long before the Babylonian captivity and it lasted seventy years; therefore many decades elapsed between the prophecy and the appearance of Cyrus. He was foretold long before his arrival on the scene so that when he did come, Israel would know it was the hour of Jehovah's deliverance.

There really should be no break between the last verse of chapter 44 and the first verse of chapter 45. Sometimes chapter and verse divisions come in the wrong places. The division of our English Bible into chapters and verses was not a matter of inspiration; it was simply a matter of human editors' trying to be helpful by separating subjects and defining certain passages. While it is convenient to have chapters and verses, sometimes the editors used poor judgment and in such cases the divisions are misleading. We may not get the full impact of a passage that is broken up in the middle.

The break between John 7 and 8 is an example. The last words of John 7 are "And every man went unto his own house." The opening words of John 8 are "Jesus went unto the mount of Olives." The editors failed to translate one little word that should have been rendered "but," and the omission broke a sentence right in two. The translation should have read, "Every man went unto his own house, *but* Jesus went unto the mount of Olives." John was implying that He had no house. He was a homeless stranger in the world His own hands had made. When others went to their comfortable homes that night, He went to the mountainside, perhaps to the garden of Gethsemane, and spent the night there, lying on the bare ground and communing with His Father.

Similarly it is very evident that Isaiah 44:28 should not have been separated from 45:1.

# THE COMING OF CYRUS FORETOLD

### Isaiah 45:1-4

This is the passage most often cited by unbelieving critics as proof that the Isaiah who wrote chapters 1–39 could not have written chapters 40–66. But as I have already said, they are simply discounting the whole idea of inspiration. If we believe, as every Christian should, that "all scripture is given by inspiration of God" (2 Timothy 3:16) and that "the prophecy came not in old time by the will of man: but holy men of God spake as they were moved by the Holy Ghost" (2 Peter 1:21), we have no difficulty in understanding that God could foretell the rise of Cyrus and what that king would do for His people.

Elsewhere in Scripture God foretold the coming of the Lord Jesus into the world and the redemption that He would accomplish. His first coming, His second coming, and the effects of both His rejection and His final acceptance by the people of Israel—all this was predicted ahead of time. In the same way, God through Isaiah prophesied the rise of Cyrus.

Media and Persia sprang from the same stock, and Cyrus the Persian was the nephew of Cyraxares, king of Media. United under the leadership of Cyraxares and Cyrus, these kingdoms eventually conquered Chaldea. Thus Babylon became one of the chief cities of the Persian empire until the time of its complete destruction.

Secular histories such as that of Herodotus give fuller information about its conquest. Ancient records reveal that Cyraxares and Cyrus in alliance marched against Babylon, and Cyrus eventually took it by turning aside the waters of the Euphrates into another channel so that he could come in on the riverbed under "the two leaved gates" of the river. That is what Isaiah indicated in 45:1, for God foresaw all this. Cyrus was no mere legendary figure. The majestic rifled ruins of his magnificent tomb still stand at Pasargadae in Iran. The original inscription concluded with these words: "Who founded the Persian Empire and was King of Asia...Therefore grudge me not this monument."

One reason that Cyrus and the Persians befriended the people of Israel was that the Persians, like the Israelites, were monotheists. The Persians did not worship idols; in fact they abhorred them. Ormazd was the Persians' name for God, and their symbol for Him was the sun, but they did not actually worship it. They also believed in the power of darkness, which they called Ahriman. Some people think of the Persians as dualists believing in two gods, the god of light and the god of darkness, but it seems more likely that they really believed in one true and living God who had a great adversary seeking to impede the carrying out of His will. A people believing in one God would look with favor on Israel because the Jews no longer worshiped idols.

It was because of idolatry that the children of Israel had been carried as captives to Babylon, but it was there, at the source of idolatry, that the Israelites were cured of idol worship. Undoubtedly through the years Jews here and there have been idolaters because of ignorance, but the nation itself learned to hate idolatry from what they saw in Babylon. Soon after their arrival, they found out that in Babylon the punishment for refusing to worship an image was death (Daniel 3:14-15)! Israel suffered under the awful conditions of that heathen kingdom for seventy years.

To this day Jews detest idols of any description. One reason that the Roman Catholic, Greek Catholic, Greek Orthodox, and other branches of the Catholic Church have had difficulty in impressing Jewish people is that the interiors of Catholic churches remind the Jews of heathen temples. They look inside and see all kinds of icons and images, and people burning incense and candles and bowing down to statues. To the Hebrew soul, all that is abhorrent.

It is only when pure Christianity is presented in lovingkindness to a Jew that any impression is likely to be made on him. Through the centuries there have been Jews who have been converted to

Romanism, but frequently their conversions have been mere pretense to escape persecution. Outwardly they have conformed to the church of Rome, but in hiding they have carried on the synagogue worship. When a Jew experiences the new birth and becomes a true Christian, he turns away from all such idolatry.

But God's reiterated warnings and pleadings in Isaiah are not unneeded, for there will be a supreme test for Israel during the great tribulation, which is yet to come. "The son of perdition" will arise "who opposeth and exalteth himself above all that is called God, or that is worshipped; so that he as God sitteth in the temple of God, shewing himself that he is God" (2 Thessalonians 2:3-4). He will persuade men to make an image and he will have power to give life to it, so that it will both speak and cause those who will not worship it to be killed (Revelation 13:14-15). Many, fearing death, will fail the test and suffer terrible results (14:9-11). Others will be victors over the image and will glorify God's holy name (15:2-4).

God foretold the rise of King Cyrus, who was to open the way for the remnant to return to Jerusalem, but this was to be but a partial return. Some people insist that all the prophecies connected with the return of Israel have been fulfilled already and therefore we are not to look for any future fulfillment of them, but Isaiah 11:11 says, "The Lord shall set his hand again the second time to recover the remnant of his people." That is what He has already begun to do as the Jews gather as a people back in their land.

### Isaiah 45:5-8

Following the revelation in regard to King Cyrus, God again emphasized man's littleness, frailty, and lack of merit and contrasted the idols to which the people had turned with His own glory. In His controversy with idols God often emphasized His own power and majesty. "What a boaster this God of the Bible is!" said the agnostic lecturer Robert Ingersoll. "How often He talks about Himself and what He has done and can do!" But who in all the universe has a better right to boast than the God who created it? And why does He declare His own glory, majesty, and power? Why does He stress

His own wisdom, strength, and ability? He does so, so that men will realize the importance of living in touch with Him and understand the uselessness of turning to anyone else.

Verses 5-8 are very striking in light of Persian beliefs. In their sacred writings such as the Zend-Avesta, the Persians gave the primary place to Ormazd, the one true living God. They gave Ahriman a very large place as the supernatural foe of God, who is in constant conflict with Him. One was the God of light; the other was the spirit of darkness. One was the God of peace; the other was the spirit of war. One was the God of goodness; the other was the spirit of evil. In answer to this and as though addressing Cyrus, God said in effect, "I am the one true and living God. Beside Me there is no other. I create peace and I create evil. I create light and I create darkness. There is no other power that can share omnipotence with Me."

Verse 7 says, "I make peace, and create evil." What does that mean? Extreme high Calvinists insist that God has foreordained everything that takes place on the earth; He has foreordained that man should sin, so that He might have opportunity to display His redemptive grace. But that is not the issue here. God was referring to evil in the sense of calamity. In other words, if there is a thunderstorm and great damage is done, God says, "I take full responsibility for it." If everything is fair and beautiful, God says, "This is from me." If there is a great earthquake, God is behind that. And so we read, "Shall there be evil in a city, and the Lord hath not done it?" (Amos 3:6) God takes responsibility for everything that occurs, but He is not always the one who is at work; sometimes He permits others to work. For instance He permitted Satan to try Job.

But the point in Isaiah 45:7 is that there are not two great powers in the universe in conflict with each other, both of whom are God— a good God and an evil god. Rather there is one God, though there is an evil power working against Him.


### Isaiah 45:9-25

How marvelous that God made Himself known in those Old Testament times as "a just God and a Saviour"! He is a God who will deal in absolute righteousness with the sin question, yet He found a way, consistent with His own infinite holiness and the righteousness of His throne, whereby He can be the Savior of the sinner who turns to Him in repentance and faith.

Long ago in Greece the wise men Socrates and Plato argued one day about forgiveness of sin. Socrates turned to Plato and said, "It may be that God can forgive sins, but I do not see how." It is remarkable that a pagan philosopher would make such a statement, for it indicates that to a very large extent he had his eyes open to divine realities! If God is the moral Governor of the universe and a righteous Judge, how can He forgive sins? It is not in the province of a judge to forgive criminals; he is supposed to pronounce sentences on evil-doers and see that those sentences are carried out. Yet in the book of Isaiah, who lived two and a half centuries before Socrates, God declared that He is a just God *and* a Savior. How could He be both?

In the Epistle to the Romans, which was written nearly five centuries after Socrates, we are told how God can be "just, and the justifier of him which believeth in Jesus" (3:26). Isaiah 45:22 also tells us how. Actually it is a wonderful gospel passage: "Look unto me, and be ye saved, all the ends of the earth: for I am God, and there is none else." Now that God has been revealed in the Lord Jesus Christ, the words from Isaiah can be used in connection with Him, for He said, "I am the way, the truth, and the life: no man cometh unto the Father, but by me" (John 14:6). As Peter declared, "There is none other name under heaven given among men, whereby we must be saved" (Acts 4:12).

What does it mean to "look" unto Him? God has used simple terms such as "believe" and "look" to show us how easily we may come into direct contact with Him through grace. To "look" here simply means to turn our eyes to the only One who can help us, just as the dying serpent-bitten Israelites in Numbers 21:8-9 fixed their earnest gaze on the brazen serpent lifted up by Moses. We are to look to Him who bids us look. It is that divine person who makes all the difference, and Hebrews 12:2 identifies that glorious person in the phrase "looking unto Jesus." We do not look at ourselves; we know our helpless condition. Rather we turn an expectant, obedient gaze on Christ.

"Look unto me...all the ends of the earth: for I am God, and there is none else." The invitation to "look" is worldwide and the results are blessed: "Be ye saved."

# THE EVERLASTING ONE CONTRASTED WITH IDOLS

God continued to contrast Himself with idols. He pointed out that idols cannot even do anything to save themselves. When Cyrus attacked Babylon and the city fell, the idolatrous priests loaded their helpless gods on carts, wheeled them away, and set them up somewhere else. Idols who could not deliver their worshipers had to be delivered by the worshipers from absolute destruction.

God said in effect, "I am altogether different from these gods who have to be carried by their makers. I will carry you. I have carried you in the past, I am carrying you now, and I will continue to carry you, even through old age. When your hair is gray, I will be there to deliver you and to sustain you."

In Isaiah 44 God had satirized the making of gods out of the trees of the forest. Now in chapter 46 He ridiculed those who made graven images out of the various metals. He used a goldsmith as an example. The goldsmith takes metal, fashions it, sets it up, and says, "This is a god." But the god cannot do anything. It cannot walk, it cannot see, it cannot hear, and in time of danger it needs someone to protect it. What a god!

Besides the satire and irony, there are precious promises in Isaiah 46. In effect God said to Israel, "How differently I have acted toward you. How could you ever turn aside to such senselessness as idolatry when you know how wonderfully I have cared for you through the centuries. Look back over the past and see what I have done. And I promise to care for you just as wonderfully in the future."

# THE DOWNFALL OF BABYLON

### Isaiah 47:1-11

As previously noted, Babylon was the fountainhead of idolatry. According to the best records, idolatry began there (see *The Two Babylons* by Alexander Hislop for details and proofs). Babylon is said to have bewitched the nations by her sorceries and her enchantments. Nation after nation followed her in the practice of idolatry. Called "the lady of kingdoms," her wealth and culture surpassed those of any nation around her.

But God, looking far ahead to the time when Cyrus and his army would come against her, said, "Thou shalt no more be called, The lady of kingdoms." The day was coming when Babylon would be stripped and laid bare; all her treasures would be destroyed and everything would be taken away from her. Then God would prove that her idols had absolutely no power and that His word comes true.

### Isaiah 47:12-15

God spoke of Babylon's folly in putting confidence in "the astrologers, the stargazers, the monthly prognosticators." Whenever people turn away from the one true and living God and refuse the Word of God, they are always ready to turn to other things. Down through the centuries, when great leaders have given up confidence in God and His Word, they have readily become prey to all sorts of charlatans. Even the infamous Hitler had a special astrologer whom he consulted about lucky and unlucky days and suitable times to attack other nations; the astrologer then consulted the map of the stars to see what was indicated. Such reliance on astrology began in Babylon centuries ago.

We must not confuse astrologers and astronomers. Astronomy is an exact science; astrology is a fraud. Yet how many people give heed to it! Many newspapers print horoscopes on a regular basis and people are foolish enough to believe them. It seems incredible, but some of the biggest traders in the New York Stock Exchange never make an important deal without first consulting an astrologer. Men still turn away from the Word of the living God to fables that are worse than follies.

One day years ago while I was in Los Angeles, I was all worn out from preaching in so many meetings and needed to relax a little on a Saturday, so I took a trolley down to Long Beach. I had hardly taken my seat when along came a Bulgarian gypsy wearing a red dress, spangles across her brow, and long black braids. She sat right down beside me and took my hand. Then she said, "Gentleman... gentleman...you cross my palm with silver...twenty-five cents...I tell you past, present, future. I am seventh daughter of a seventh daughter. I born with a veil on. I can tell all mysteries."

I grabbed her hand and said, "Well, it isn't really necessary... because I've had that all told already."

"But oh!" she said, "I am expert...I know very exact...past, present, future."

"Yes, but I got it from an expert—I have it here in a little book." And with my other hand I pulled out my New Testament, turned to Ephesians 2, and said, "Here I've got my past, present, and future. Here's the past: 'You hath he quickened, who were dead in trespasses and sins; Wherein in time past ye walked according to the course of this world, according to...the spirit that now worketh in the children of disobedience.'"

"Oh, what is that, a Bible? I got the wrong man. I got the wrong man. Let go."

"No," I said, "I won't let go. I didn't ask you to come down here and take hold of me. Now that I've got you, you're going to stay here. Now I'll give you the rest of it. Here is my present: 'But God, who is rich in mercy, for his great love wherewith he loved us,

Even when we were dead in sins, hath quickened us together with Christ....By grace are ye saved through faith; and that not of yourselves: it is the gift of God.' That's my present."

"That's all right. That's all right. I've got enough. Goodbye."

I said, "Wait a minute. I haven't given you it all yet. Now here's my future: 'That in the ages to come he might shew the exceeding riches of his grace in his kindness toward us through Christ Jesus.'"

"Yes, gentleman...I've got enough." And she gave such a pull that she got away. Down the car she went saying, "I got the wrong man....I got the wrong man."

Another day a passenger in a train was reading his Bible when a dapper-looking gentleman came along, looked at it, and said, "Oh, reading the Bible? Do you believe the Bible? I didn't think that any educated people believed in the Bible anymore. You look like a cultured man and I'm surprised that you're reading it. I believe the day will soon come when people will not believe in the Bible any more than they believe in the ghosts and witches that our forefathers thought were real."

"My friend," remarked the Bible-reading gentleman, "when people reach the place where they do not believe in the Bible any more, they believe in witches and ghosts again."

He was right. Many have turned away from the Word of God to spiritism, theosophy, and other occult systems that profess to have to do with the dead. That is Babylonianism persisting through the centuries. God has judged it all and He puts it all to one side as it were. "Why do men need this?" He asks in effect. "Here am I, infinite in wisdom, power, and might, and ready to reveal Myself in grace to the man who seeks My face."

# ISAIAH 48

# GOD'S CONTROVERSY WITH ISRAEL

This chapter covers God's dealings with the children of Israel. No other nation has suffered as they have, yet they remain nationally intact to this day and will remain so to the very end. When at last they have passed through all their afflictions, they will understand the meaning of 48:10: "Behold, I have refined thee, but not with silver; I have chosen thee in the furnace of affliction." God will refine Israel by their troubles and tribulations so that eventually they will bring glory to Him; they will be "a royal diadem" on His brow throughout the generations to come (62:3).

Just as God took care of Israel in the past, He will take care of them in days to come. Those who turn to Him in repentance, those who receive the Savior He has provided, will be fully blessed. However, "there is no peace, saith the Lord [Jehovah], unto the wicked" (48:22). Jehovah was speaking to His people whose peace might have been "as a river" if they had been obedient (48:18). But they had turned to idols for succor and help and their idols had failed them utterly. Jehovah stands in vivid contrast to those powerless images.

Chapter 48 ends the first section of part three of Isaiah. Part three (chapters 40–66) consists of three sections: (1) Isaiah 40–48, which presents Jehovah's controversy with Israel over their idolatry; (2) Isaiah 49–57, which presents Jehovah's controversy with Israel over their treatment of the Messiah; and (3) Isaiah 58–66, which presents visions of the coming glory.

The first section ends, "There is no peace, saith [Jehovah], unto the wicked" (48:22). Here Isaiah used the name "Jehovah," for He was speaking to His people. The second section ends, "There is no peace, saith my God, to the wicked" (57:21). Here it is "my God," for all who are of a contrite and humble heart are included in the promise of 57:19: "Peace, peace to him that is far off, and to him that is near." The promise and the warning in chapter 57 are for all hearers, whether of Israel or not.

Note how apt these section endings are. The section dealing with idolatry ends with the thought that there is no peace for the person who substitutes anything else for the one true and living God. The section dealing with rejection of the Messiah ends with the thought that there is no peace for the individual who rejects the Savior whom God has provided. In both instances "there is no peace...to the wicked."

# THE MESSIAH DESPISED

Now we come to a very precious and important portion of the book of Isaiah. While the apostle Peter spoke of "exceeding great and precious promises" (2 Peter 1:4), everything in God's Word is precious, even though at first sight it might not seem so. And everything in the Bible is important, for "all scripture is given by inspiration of God, and is profitable" (2 Timothy 3:16). But certain passages of God's Word speak to us more loudly perhaps than others. The section we are now beginning to consider has a very loud voice for those of us who know and love the Lord Jesus Christ, because it brings Him personally before us in such a clear and definite way.

## *Isaiah 49:1-6*

Isaiah 49 presents Israel as Jehovah's servant, but Israel as a nation failed terribly in that role. So while it is Israel who says, "The Lord hath called me from the womb...and said unto me, Thou art my servant," it is really the Lord Jesus Christ Himself who takes the place of Israel, the true Israel. The servant here is no longer the nation as such, though the nation does speak in these opening verses; the servant is the Lord Jesus taking the place of the nation.

Other Scripture passages support this interpretation. In Hosea 11:1 God said, "When Israel was a child, then I loved him, and called my son out of Egypt." God was speaking of bringing the nation out of Egypt. Yet that prophecy was applied to the Lord Jesus Christ, who as a little baby was carried down to Egypt and later brought back to the land of His birth "that it might be fulfilled which was spoken of the Lord by the prophet, saying, Out of Egypt have I called my son" (Matthew 2:15). So while the son in Hosea was Israel, it was the Lord Jesus, the true Israel, who was actually on the mind of God.

We often use language in that way, substituting an individual for a whole people. Louis XIV, that proud French monarch, exclaimed on one occasion, "France must rule the world, and I am France." Napoleon Bonaparte said, "The State must be supreme, and I am the State." If uninspired men use language in that way, how much more has Christ the right to say, "I am Israel, the true Israel." The very name *Israel* means "a prince with God" and it was Christ who was revealed as the true Prince, the Servant of Jehovah, when Israel both as a nation and individually had utterly failed.

Isaiah 49:4-6 has a remarkable prophecy of Christ's rejection by Israel and the calling of the Gentiles. Messiah says, "I have laboured in vain, I have spent my strength for nought." As far as Israel was concerned, His work seemed to be a failure on earth. "He came unto his own, and his own received him not" (John 1:11). But He leaves His rejection with Jehovah and declares, "Though Israel be not gathered, yet shall I be glorious in the eyes of the Lord." Jehovah then says to Messiah, "It is a light thing that thou shouldest be my servant to raise up the tribes of Jacob, and to restore the preserved of Israel: I will also give thee for a light to the Gentiles, that thou mayest be my salvation unto the end of the earth." Through Messiah's rejection by Israel, a greater work would be accomplished. The message would go out to the Gentile world.

### Isaiah 49:7

The Old Testament prophets do not bring the present age clearly before us. They are like a man who is looking at two mountain peaks, one some distance beyond and higher than the other; he is unable to see the valley between the peaks. Thus the prophets testified of the sufferings of Christ at His first coming and they testified of the glories that would follow the second coming, but they did not give us any clear teaching about what would go on in between.

We know now from the New Testament that God had us in His heart from all eternity. He planned to call out from the Jews and Gentiles a people who would be the bride of His Son, so that when the Lord Jesus returned to reign in power and glory, He would not return alone. He would have a bride with Him who would sit with Him on His throne.

Isaiah gave no definite instruction regarding the present day, but it is very evident that his prophecy does cover the present age as well as the millennium. It will have its fulfillment in millennial days when all the kingdoms of this world will become the kingdom of our God and of His Christ.

In 49:7 Jehovah spoke to the One "whom man despiseth, to him whom the nation abhorreth," a strong expression, but not too strong for describing the feelings of Israel toward the Lord Jesus Christ. The Talmud and other Jewish writings refer to Him in terms such as the "leper" and the "hanged one," for the nation of Israel loathed Him. The Jews could not understand who He was. "Had they known," said Paul, "they would not have crucified the Lord of glory" (1 Corinthians 2:8).

God will glorify that One whom their nation abhorred. The kings and princes of the earth will recognize Him and bow down before Him. In a remarkable sense that has been true even during the present age, though unforeseen by the prophets. As the gospel spread from land to land in the early centuries, whole nations were brought to profess, at least, subjection to the Lord Jesus, and many kings proclaimed themselves His subjects. At the time I am writing, the rulers of nations such as Great Britain, Holland, and Scandinavia are professed Christians. That does not necessarily mean that they are born again, but they acknowledge, outwardly at least, the authority of the Lord Jesus Christ.

Many leaders in the United States have taken the same stand. Franklin D. Roosevelt was a warden of an Episcopal church. President Truman, after his first press conference, asked for prayer; he professed the Christian faith and in that sense he recognized the authority of the Lord Jesus Christ.

Queen Victoria was very definite in her confession of faith. When a heathen African prince came to Great Britain and was presented to her, he inquired, "Your Majesty, to what do you attribute the great prosperity of the British empire?" She handed him a Bible and said simply, "This Book." He carried that Book back to his people so that he could tell them that the prosperity of the British empire was based on the Bible.

Toward the end of her life Queen Victoria once publicly stated, "I am a firm believer in the second coming of the Lord Jesus Christ. And I have sometimes thought that He has permitted me to reign so long that perhaps I will never lay down my crown until I lay it down at His feet when He comes again." It was a lovely expression of subjection to the Lord. Queen Victoria evidently knew Christ as her Savior.

She was accustomed to go every summer to Balmoral Castle in Scotland, and she became acquainted with the Highland women living in the little cottages in the surrounding hills. Victoria visited them all and went from one to another to chat with them. Of course they were delighted that the queen would take such notice of them. One year as she was preparing to return to London, she went to bid one old cottager goodbye. The old lady said, "Well, Your Majesty, I may never see you on earth again. May I ask Your gracious Majesty a question?"

She said, "Yes. As many as you like."

"Well," she said, "will Your Majesty meet me in Heaven?"

The queen replied, "Yes, through the all-availing blood of Jesus."

That was a good testimony from the ruler of a mighty empire. The kings truly have bowed down before the Lord Jesus Christ. The nation of Israel rejected Him, but God has made His name glorious throughout the world. Isaiah 49:7 of course looks ahead to its complete fulfillment in millennial days when all the kings of the earth will bring their riches and glory into the new Jerusalem.

### Isaiah 49:8-11

This passage clearly was in the minds of New Testament writers. Paul for example was obviously referring to Isaiah 49:8 when he wrote 2 Corinthians 6:2. The apostle quoted the prophecy—"Thus saith the Lord, In an acceptable time have I heard thee"—then added, "Behold, now is the accepted time; behold, now is the day of salvation." So God applied Isaiah 49:8 to the present time during which the gospel of the grace of God is going out into all the world.

Then Isaiah 49:9-11 carries us on to the time of the great awakening that is pictured in Revelation 7. All over the world men will recognize the Lord Jesus Christ. John, after giving us the vision of the 144,000 sealed ones of Israel, wrote, "I beheld, and, lo, a great multitude, which no man could number, of all nations, and kindreds, and people, and tongues, stood before the throne, and before the Lamb, clothed with white robes, and palms in their hands" (7:9).

Many commentators say that these people in white robes are the martyred saints who will have been slain under the rule of the beast and the false prophet and that in John's vision these saints were in Heaven. But it seems very evident to me that this interpretation is an utter mistake. I believe that the great multitude consists of those who will form the nucleus of the coming glorious kingdom of the Lord Jesus Christ here on the earth.

My view is based on the dialogue in Revelation 7:13-14. One of the elders turned to John and said, "What are these which are arrayed in white robes? and whence came they?"

John said, "Sir, thou knowest."

The elder replied, "These are they which came out of great tribulation." There are two definite articles in the Greek, so the literal translation reads, "*the* tribulation *the* great one." The elder continued, "And have washed their robes, and made them white in the blood of the Lamb." So the great blood-washed multitude in the vision had not ascended into Heaven; they had come up out of the great tribulation. They had gone through that period of trial and been preserved by God.

Revelation 7:16-17 says of them: "They shall hunger no more, neither thirst any more; neither shall the sun light on them, nor any heat. For the Lamb which is in the midst of the throne shall feed them, and shall lead them unto living fountains of waters: and God shall wipe away all tears from their eyes." The kindred passage in Isaiah says: "They shall feed in the ways, and their pastures shall be in all high places. They shall not hunger nor thirst; neither shall the heat nor sun smite them: for he that hath mercy on them shall lead them, even by the springs of water shall he guide them."

The two passages refer to exactly the same group, an earthly group who will be saved for the glorious millennial kingdom of our Lord Jesus Christ. Primarily they are the remnant of Israel, and associated with them is a great company from among the Gentiles who will have acknowledged the authority of the Lord Jesus Christ. The once-rejected Messiah will be their Savior and their Lord.

So in Isaiah 49 the Spirit of God was saying, as it were, to the Lord Jesus Christ, "It is true the nation did not recognize You, that You seem to have labored in vain and to have spent Your strength for nought; but a coming day will show that a tremendous harvest will result from Your labors of love when You were down there unrecognized and misunderstood."

# WHY ISRAEL HAS BEEN SET ASIDE

*Isaiah 50:1-6*

Isaiah 50 shows why Israel has been set to one side during the present age. The question is raised in verse 1: "Where is the bill of your mother's divorcement?" In other words, why did God divorce His earthly bride? Israel is spoken of as the wife of Jehovah, but during the present age she is like a divorced wife. God no longer recognizes her as being in a covenant relationship. Why? On what grounds did God set her aside?

The answer comes in verses 2-6. What a wonderful passage! The answer begins with a question: "Wherefore, when I came, was there no man?" In other words, "When I came, there was no one to welcome Me." Ask any thoughtful Jew to consider this carefully; ask him who came. The rabbi must acknowledge that unquestionably it was Jehovah who visited Israel. The One who said, "I dry up the sea, I make the rivers a wilderness," was referring to the time when He dried up the waters of the Red Sea and later the waters of the Jordan so that Israel could go through. It is the eternal God speaking, the God of creation, the One who could say, "I clothe the heavens with blackness."

There is no change in person as He continues to tell how He humbled Himself and came down to earth, but we have an indication of the trinity in the statement, "The Lord God hath given me the tongue of the learned [the disciple]" (50:4). In other words, "I who clothe the heavens have come down to earth and taken the place of a disciple." The Lord Jesus Christ in infinite grace chose to

217

lay aside, as it were, His rightful claim to full deity. It is not that He laid aside His deity—He could not do that—but He refused to act in the power of His own omnipotence. He chose to learn while on earth from the Word of God and to be subject to the Holy Spirit. He "increased," we are told in Luke 2:52, "in wisdom and stature, and in favour with God and man."

Leeser's Jewish translation of Isaiah 50:4 reads, "The Lord hath given Me the power of the disciple, that I might learn how to comfort the weary with the Word." How well that statement fits in with the Savior's invitation: "Come unto me, all ye that labour and are heavy laden, and I will give you rest" (Matthew 11:28)! "We have not an high priest which cannot be touched with the feeling of our infirmities; but [one who] was in all points tempted like as we are" and "is able to succour them that are tempted" (Hebrews 4:15; 2:18). He came down to this earth and went through all human experience, except for sinning. Entering fully into our sorrows and troubles, He learned in a practical way how to comfort the weary with the Word.

And what treatment did He receive in return? He was delivered to Pilate and in his judgment hall He was handed over to the soldiers, who gathered about Him and in their ribaldry laughed at Him, struck Him, and exposed Him to all kinds of vulgarities and indecencies. That lowly man was God manifest in the flesh.

So Isaiah 50:1-6 tells us why Israel, the divorced state, has for the present been set to one side. They rejected their Messiah when He came in lowly grace.

## Isaiah 50:11

Who has ever suffered or known greater sorrows nationally than Israel? How our hearts should go out in yearning love and compassion to them! We once rejected Christ too, but through grace we have had our eyes opened so that we could receive Him as our Savior. Israel's eyes are still blinded. How we need to pray for them! Scripture says, "Pray for the peace of Jerusalem: they shall prosper that love thee" (Psalm 122:6). But we are so forgetful. When a Hebrew Christian spoke of his blinded brethren in our prayer meetings, we prayed earnestly for Israel, but when he was not there, we neglected to offer petitions for them. Prayer ascended for everything else, and everyone else, but no one ever voiced a request for Israel unless special attention had been called to the Jews.

As prophesied, Israel kindled her own fire when she rejected her Messiah. Although the Israelites have tried to walk in the light of the teachings of the rabbis, they have found sorrow upon sorrow. They will never be fully released from their "divorcement" until they look upon Him whom they pierced and mourn for Him "as one mourneth for his only son" and "as one that is in bitterness for his firstborn" (Zechariah 12:10).

## ISAIAH 51

# THE CALL TO
# AWAKE

In chapter 51 God stresses the disobedience of Israel and their suffering because of it and also emphasizes the coming day when Israel will recognize Messiah and be fully blessed.

God will fulfill every promise He has made. He told Israel to "look unto Abraham" because He had promised Abraham, "In thy seed shall all the nations of the earth be blessed" (Genesis 22:18). The children of Israel have failed to experience the benefits themselves, but the promise still stands. The day is coming when they will be fully blessed through the Son of Abraham and they will become like a nation of priests who will be used of God to bless all the Gentile nations.

The nations that once persecuted Israel will have to suffer. Those who are taken red-handed in opposition to God's Word will be destroyed. But after God has dealt with His enemies, the nations that have never been guilty of afflicting Israel will find the Lord as their Savior and enter into blessing in the millennial day.

In Isaiah 51:9, 51:17, and 52:1 we find three clear and definite calls to "awake." The first is the call of the people in their sorrow and trouble: "Awake, awake, put on strength, O arm of the Lord; awake, as in the ancient days, in the generations of old. Art thou not it that hath cut Rahab, and wounded the dragon?" (Rahab the dragon refers to Egypt.) Remembering how the "arm of the Lord" had acted on their behalf in ancient times, they cried out from the depths of their heart. In other words, they pleaded, "O God, do something to help us!"

As we will soon see in Isaiah 53, the "arm of the Lord" is a person. It is the Lord Jesus Christ Himself. So it was really He who was being addressed, though the people did not know it. They called on Him to rise for their deliverance and, thank God, in due time He will. But first a remnant of Israel will recognize their past failure and sin and turn back to the Lord. They will heed the words of 55:6-7: "Seek ye the Lord while he may be found, call ye upon him while he is near: Let the wicked forsake his way, and the unrighteous man his thoughts: and let him return unto the Lord, and He will have mercy upon him; and to our God, for He will abundantly pardon."

In response to the cry of the people in 51:9, God, through Isaiah, addressed Israel in her present broken condition (51:17). In this second call to "awake," the prophet wrote, "Awake, awake, stand up, O Jerusalem, which hast drunk at the hand of the Lord the cup of his fury." In effect God was saying to the people in their suffering and sorrow, "Arise from the dust; clothe yourself in your beautiful garments; turn from your iniquity, acknowledge your sin; confess your transgressions." When they do repent, then deliverance will come. In the Lord's own time He will bring them back to Zion. The ransomed ones will return "and everlasting joy shall be upon their head."

In the third call to "awake" (52:1), God addressed His people in their future blessed condition: "Awake, awake; put on thy strength, O Zion; put on the beautiful garments, O Jerusalem, the holy city."

# GOOD TIDINGS TO ALL

Isaiah 52 begins with the last of the three calls to "awake" (51:9; 51:17; 52:1). In this third call, God, through His prophet, addresses the restored people when they have at last repented. Now that they have turned back to Him, the day of their blessing has come. "Awake, awake; put on thy strength, O Zion," He says. "Put on thy beautiful garments, O Jerusalem." He wants them to "sing with gladness" (Jeremiah 31:7) as they come out of the lands of the Gentiles and enter their own land. The day is one of happy reconciliation with God and joyful subjection to the Savior whom He has provided.

The remnant company of the last days will go out over the mountains, out to the world, to proclaim the gospel of peace, "the gospel of the kingdom." It is not a different gospel from that which we preach today, for there is only one gospel. The apostle Paul said, "Though we, or an angel from heaven, preach any other gospel unto you than that which we have preached unto you, let him be accursed. As we said before, so say I now again, If any man preach any other gospel unto you than that ye have received, let him be accursed" (Galatians 1:8-9).

There is only one gospel, the gospel of God concerning His Son! But that gospel takes on different aspects at different times, according to God's dispensational dealings. John the Baptist proclaimed the gospel of the kingdom of God, but that doesn't mean that he did not tell sinners how to be saved. It was he who said, "Behold the Lamb of God, which taketh away the sin of the world" (John 1:29). But the emphasis of his message was the responsibility of Israel to receive the King, and so enter into the kingdom.

When the Lord Jesus began to preach, He went from city to city proclaiming the gospel of the kingdom and He sent His disciples out to preach it in all Israel. But when the kingdom was rejected, a new dispensation came in and now we preach the glorious gospel of the grace of God. The light of the knowledge of it shines in the face of Jesus Christ (2 Corinthians 4:6), for grace and truth came by Him. But does that mean that we have to be silent in regard to the King and His kingdom? Surely the answer is no, for during the forty days that Christ appeared on earth after His resurrection, He spoke to His disciples "of the things pertaining to the kingdom of God" and many years later Paul was still preaching the kingdom of God (Acts 1:3; 28:23,31). So we preach the gospel of the kingdom, but our emphasis is on God's grace for a lost, ruined world.

When this age has come to an end and the church has been taken home, God will call out a little company referred to in Daniel 12:3,10 as the *maskilim*, which means "the wise." They will go forth proclaiming the glad tidings that the time has drawn near when the Prince of Peace will return and that there will be blessing for all the world through Him. Isaiah was referring to such wise ones when he wrote, "How beautiful upon the mountains are the feet of him that bringeth good tidings, that publisheth peace; that bringeth good tidings of good, that publisheth salvation; that saith unto Zion, Thy God reigneth!" (52:7)

How fitting it is that these words should come here, just before Isaiah presents the greatest and most complete Messianic prophecy in all the Old Testament. In the prophecy, which begins in 52:13 and continues through chapter 53, we come to the very holy of holies.

# THE SUFFERING SAVIOR

Here the inspired writer gave us a graphic pen-portrait of the suffering Savior and told of the glorious work He was to undertake so that the sin question might be settled forever to the perfect satisfaction of God, the infinitely holy One. This great Messianic prophecy is referred to a number of times in the New Testament and in each instance is applied directly to our Lord Jesus Christ (for example Matthew 8:17; Acts 8:32-35; and 1 Peter 2:21-25).

Isaiah 52:13–53:12 presents Christ as the sinless substitute for sinful men—the One to whom our sins were imputed so that divine righteousness might be imputed to us who believe in Him. His lowly life, His rejection by His own people, His voluntary subjection to the suffering of the cross, His atoning sacrifice, His glorious resurrection, and the triumph of His gospel in the salvation of a great host of sinners are all foretold in a clear, concise way. No one but God Himself could have given us this remarkable delineation of the character and work of the Lord Jesus so long before He came into the world. God foreknew all that His Son was to endure, and some seven hundred years before Jesus was born in Bethlehem God gave the prophecy of the suffering Messiah to Isaiah to hand on to future generations.

The passage, by the way, is an example of Hebrew poetry, written in blank verse and divided into sections of three stanzas each. The first section is 52:13-15, and the other sections are in chapter 53.

*Isaiah 52:13–53:3*

This wonderful prophecy introduces the Servant of Jehovah, whose glory must be equal to the shame He endured. The passage begins, "Behold, my servant," and then continues to speak of Him as the suffering Savior.

Hebrew scholars tell us that the word "sprinkle" (52:15) is from the same root as that from which "astonied" (52:14) is derived, and the two verses really mean, "As many were astonished at Him, so shall He astonish many nations."

In Romans 10:16 Paul the apostle called our attention to the question in Isaiah 53:1—"Who hath believed our report?"—as evidence of the incredulity of Israel. The very people who for centuries had waited for the coming of their Messiah, fulfilled their own Scriptures by rejecting Him when He came. They failed to see in Jesus "the arm of the Lord" stretched forth for their salvation, and the great bulk of mankind today fail in the same way.

Christians often say that in their unconverted days the Lord was to them "as a root out of a dry ground" (53:2), but now they see Him as the "altogether lovely" One (Song of Solomon 5:16). However, the expression in Isaiah implies not lack of comeliness or beauty, but the fact that the Lord Jesus Christ grew up before God as a sprout, a root out of the dry ground of formalistic Israel. This man whose name is the Branch was the one lovely plant that Jehovah could gaze down on with such approval that He could open the heavens and announce, "This is my beloved Son, in whom I have found [all] my delight" (Darby's translation). To God, the blessed Lord was a tender plant, a plant of renown and beauty, growing out of the dry ground of Israel and of humanity in general. He was precious beyond words to God, but to unbelieving men He had "no form nor comeliness...no beauty." Men did not recognize the moral loveliness that He always exhibited.

Some Christian teachers have misunderstood the statement, "He hath no form nor comeliness," and have believed that the Lord Jesus Christ as man was so positively repulsive in appearance that no one would want to look at Him. But that view is not supported by other

Scripture passages. In Psalm 45:2 it is written of our blessed Lord, "Thou art fairer than the children of men," and we have every reason to believe that the Lord Jesus Christ, being the only sinless child that was ever born into the world, came here with a perfect human body that was spotlessly beautiful.

As He grew up and later matured, His appearance would have been splendid, but those who loved their sins were angered when they listened to His teaching and therefore saw no beauty in Him. Because of the sufferings He endured, His visage became "marred more than any man, and his form more than the sons of men." But as man here on earth, the Second Man, the last Adam, His human form, face, and features were absolutely perfect. Men looked on Him with scorn and disdain because His teaching interfered with the lives that they loved to live.

Isaiah prophesied that He would be "despised and rejected of men; a man of sorrows, and acquainted with grief" and this prophecy was fulfilled in the days of our Lord's ministry here on earth. There is no hint that before His ministry began He was despised and rejected; we are only told that "Jesus increased in wisdom and stature, and in favour with God and man" (Luke 2:52). He must have been accepted wherever He went, and He must have found favor in the eyes of His fellow townsmen because He was evidently a reader in the Nazareth synagogue; He went there and publicly began to read from this very book of Isaiah. It was when Christ went out on His great mission that men turned away from Him. "We hid as it were our faces from him…and we esteemed him not," even though He was suffering in our place. He endured patiently all the shame heaped upon Him.

### Isaiah 53:4-5

As Isaiah foresaw, it seemed as though God were angry with Christ. Men thought that His sufferings were deserved because of what He was in Himself. They said He had a devil, they called Him a Samaritan, and they considered Him to be a deceiver. People looked on the sorrows that He endured as divine judgments for His own sins, whereas He was bearing the griefs and the sorrows that sin had

brought on the human race. All through His lowly life Christ saw
the misery that sin had caused, and He suffered so that "with his
stripes" men might be healed. On the cross He endured vicariously
the judgment that our sins deserved. He was the great sin offering—and the peace offering too, making "peace through the blood
of his cross" (Colossians 1:20).

Surely Isaiah was speaking of substitutionary atonement. Sometimes people object to this interpretation because the word *substitution* is not found in the Bible, but when One is in the place of another, when One is taking the punishment that another deserves,
that is substitution. The prophetic statement is plain and definite:
"He hath borne our griefs....He was wounded for our transgressions, He was bruised for our iniquities." The chastisement whereby
our peace was made fell on Him.

### Isaiah 53:6

Here God, as it were, balances the books of the world with two
debit entries and one credit entry. The two debit entries are as follows: (1) "All we like sheep have gone astray"—in other words, the
whole fallen human race; and (2) "We have turned every one to his
own way"—in other words, each individual's own personal sin. The
credit entry reads, "The Lord [Jehovah] hath laid on him the iniquity of us all." That credit is sufficient to cancel all debits if men
would receive it.

These words of Isaiah epitomize the entire story of the Bible—
man's ruin both by nature and practice, and God's marvelous and
all-sufficient remedy. The verse begins with "all" and ends with
"all." One anxious soul, after being directed to this passage and
finding peace, said, "I bent low down and went in at the first 'all.' I
stood up straight and came out at the last." The first "all" is the
acknowledgment of our deep need; the second shows how fully that
need has been met in the cross of Christ. How blessed we are to be
numbered among those who have put in their claim and found salvation through the atoning work which there took place!

To me Isaiah 53:6 is the most wonderful text in the Bible. I have
been trying to preach on it for sixty years and it is the first portion

of Scripture I ever preached on. I started speaking on that verse when I was fourteen years old and out on the street with The Salvation Army in Los Angeles. I meant to preach for five minutes, but after half an hour the captain leaned over and said, "Boy, we should have been in the hall twenty minutes ago. You'll have to tell us the rest some other time." I have been trying to tell the rest all through the years, but I can never exhaust that text.

### Isaiah 53:7-8

In this passage Isaiah foretold the mock trials of the Lord. When the time came for the trials to be held, He was taken from one place to another so that His case could be heard, but there was no one to speak for Him. It was all contrary to law, yet God permitted it. Christ said nothing for Himself, and Pilate wondered greatly at His silence. Herod tried to make Him speak, but just as a lamb who is about to be slain and a sheep who is about to be shorn are dumb, He did not open His mouth. With no word of complaint He gave Himself into the hands of the wicked men who crucified Him because there was no other way whereby guilty sinners could be saved.

Through false evidence He was condemned to die as a felon, as if He were guilty of sedition against caesar, the head of imperial Rome. But God saw to it that His manner of life was fully declared, so that actually He was justified before His judges. For example Pilate's wife sent him the message, "Have thou nothing to do with that just man: for I have suffered many things this day in a dream because of him" (Matthew 27:19). Pilate himself "took water, and washed his hands before the multitude, saying, I am innocent of the blood of this just person" (27:24). Then as Christ hung on that cross, a thief by His side turned to his fellow and said, "Dost not thou fear God, seeing thou art in the same condemnation? And we indeed justly...but this man hath done nothing amiss" (Luke 23:40-41). God saw to it that the declaration of Christ's innocence was made.

Christ did "nothing amiss," yet He was allowed to suffer. Why? Because He was the great sin offering. "For the transgression of my people was he stricken," wrote Isaiah. The Lord Jesus was hurried from one judgment scene to another until at last He was nailed to the cross, there to endure all that our sins deserved.

### Isaiah 53:9-11

Man's intention was to cast out Christ's precious body along "with the wicked," to be devoured by vultures or jackals, or to be burned in the fires that destroyed the city's refuse in the valley of Hinnom. But God saw to it that He lay "with the rich in His death," as a testimony to His absolute holiness and perfection of spirit.

While the whole story of the life, death, mock trial, and condemnation of our Lord Jesus is reflected in Isaiah's wonderful Messianic prophecy, the four Gospel accounts of the crucifixion taken together give us the *full* meaning of the work of the cross. There Jesus is presented as enduring the awful shame and physical anguish caused by man without giving any evidence of perturbation of spirit during His first three hours on the cross. He was in perfect communion with the Father, showed tender concern for others, and spoke no word of self-pity for His own sufferings. But the last three hours were different, for Jesus was enduring the terrible ordeal of bearing the judgment our sins deserved. His cry of loneliness is the key to the deeper suffering of that period when God, the righteous Judge, had to abandon Him to the inward spiritual suffering of the Surety for sinners. It was then that His soul—not merely His body—was made an offering for sin.

Observe that it was Jehovah Himself who dealt with Christ in judgment when He hung on the tree. It was not only His physical sufferings that made propitiation for sin, but also what He suffered in His inmost being when His spotless soul became the great sin offering. In other words, it was not what man did to Him that made reconciliation for iniquity; it was what He endured at the hand of God. God's judgment led to Immanuel's orphaned cry, "My God, my God, why hast thou forsaken me?" He was forsaken that we might be received into divine favor.

But as also foretold, God raised up Jesus Christ from the dead and made Him the head of the new creation, which consists of all who are saved through the work He accomplished on the cross. Isaiah had prophesied that in resurrection He would "see his seed....He shall see of the travail of his soul, and shall be satisfied." The word "travail" refers to birth pangs, and Jesus travailed in His soul that millions might be born of the Word and Spirit of God and thus bring Him eternal joy and satisfaction. The gospel is based on what Christ endured on that cross, and the gospel message goes out to all who have ears to hear. Christ did not end His days by offering His body as a sin offering; instead He prolonged His days by coming back from the grave in resurrection life.

### Isaiah 53:12

How wonderful is the promise, "He shall divide the spoil with the strong"! Evidently here the phrase "the strong" refers to Satan, man's great enemy, for the Lord Jesus was referring to Satan when He said, "No man can enter into a strong man's house...except he will first bind the strong man" (Mark 3:27). The prospect of the Lord dividing the spoil with Satan should be a great encouragement to those who try to preach the gospel.

Many people have an idea that there will be far more people in Hell than in Heaven, but God's Word does not warrant that conclusion. The prophecy is that the spoil will be divided. When the disciples asked, "Are there few that be saved?" the Lord did not answer by saying, "Yes, only a few will be saved." He said, "Strive to enter in at the strait gate" (Luke 13:23-24). In other words, "Be in earnest about getting into the kingdom of God because many will strive to enter when it is too late."

The testimony of the Scriptures is that there will be far more people in Heaven than in Hell. We know that all the little ones will be in Heaven—all the millions who have died before coming to the age of accountability—because Jesus said, "It is not the will of your Father which is in heaven, that one of these little ones should perish" (Matthew 18:14). All those who have been mentally defective and never capable of accepting or rejecting Christ will be covered by His blood. In addition all those who have turned to Him in repentance and trusted in Him as Savior will be in Heaven.

Thus God will reward the Lord Jesus for what He accomplished on the cross. Men may think lightly of Christ's glorious work, but God does not.

# THE CALL TO SING

After all the darkness, the gloom, the suffering, and the sorrow of the cross in Isaiah 53, the first word of chapter 54 is "Sing"! Yes, after all that Jesus has done, we sing, but here the Spirit of God was directing His message to the remnant of Israel in the last days. He was calling on the once-unfruitful people to rejoice: "Sing, O barren, thou that didst not bear; break forth into singing, and cry aloud, thou that didst not travail with child."

Isaiah 54 pictures the remnant of Israel turning to the Lord in the last days and being used of God to bring a great multitude of Gentiles to Him, so that the desolate have more children than the married wife who had been set aside for so long. And all who are saved, both in millennial days and now, are saved through the glorious work of which Isaiah 53 speaks so clearly.

After the call to sing, come God's promises, and what wonderful promises they are! Note, however, that these promises are God's word to Israel. We Christians are such thieves—we steal so many things that belong to Israel and try to apply them to ourselves. This tendency was reflected in our old valued Bagster Bibles, where many of the chapters in Isaiah had headings such as "Curses on the Jews," "Punishment on the Jews," and "Judgment on the Jews," but "Blessings of the Church" and "Joys of the Church." All the judgment passages were definitely applied to the Jews, and all the glory passages to the church. But these headings were written by uninspired men who did not profess to insert them as the Word of God.

God promised to bring Israel back to Himself and bless them. He will not keep His fury forever, for He said, "This is as the waters of Noah unto me." Just as truly as He promised that the earth will never again be destroyed by a flood, He promised that the nation of

Israel will never be utterly destroyed, that someday a remnant will
be saved and become a great nation, and that Israel will blossom
and bud and fill the whole earth with goodness. "My kindness shall
not depart from thee," He said. "Great shall be the peace of thy
children."

# THE GREAT INVITATION

## *Isaiah 55:1-5*

If it were not for the truth set forth in Isaiah 53, the gracious invitation in Isaiah 55 could not possibly be extended. Chapter 55, you will remember, is included in the second section (chapters 49–57) of part three of the book of Isaiah. Throughout this section God is presenting His chosen Servant, our Lord Jesus Christ, as the Redeemer of Israel and of the world, whose rejection at His first coming was foreknown and plainly predicted, but whose propitiatory work was to open up the way for guilty sinners to find peace with God and pardon for all their transgressions. Because of His work God can send forth the gracious invitation for all men everywhere to partake of His salvation: "Ho, every one that thirsteth, come ye to the waters, and he that hath no money; come ye, buy, and eat; yea, come, buy wine and milk without money and without price."

Isaiah has been called the evangelical prophet and he well deserves the designation. Nowhere else in the Old Testament is the person and work of our Lord revealed as clearly and fully as in his wonderful book. Man is shown there to be utterly bankrupt spiritually, destitute of righteousness, and with no claim on God whatsoever; and Christ, Jehovah's sinless Servant, is presented as the great sin offering through whose infinite sacrifice all who come to Him in faith will be justified in His sight.

His salvation is based on righteousness. In the cross the sin question has been settled in a righteous way, and so God can now save all who come to Him in faith. It is hard for the natural man to appreciate the fullness of God's grace. It is so easy to think of God as a merchant with something to sell. But the truth is that God is too rich to seek to sell His salvation to anyone, and if He were to put a price on it, we would all be too poor to buy it.

In each dispensation salvation has been by grace alone. All who were saved in Old Testament times, in the various ages before the cross, owed everything to the work the Son of God eventually accomplished on Calvary. There were different degrees of light, and men were placed under various systems that stipulated their responsibilities to God in this world, but no man was ever saved by animal sacrifices (Hebrews 10:4), or "by the deeds of the law" (Romans 3:20).

So Isaiah, after having revealed so clearly the atoning death the Anointed of God was to die, called on all needy, troubled men to appropriate by faith the gracious provision he had depicted. The prophet's message to thirsty souls is identical to that proclaimed by the Lord Jesus at a later date (John 7:37), and the New Testament draws to a close with a similar proclamation (Revelation 22:17).

Isaiah not only emphasized the grace of God, which offers the water of life freely to all men, but also stressed the quickening and authoritative power of the Word of God, for it is through believing that Word that men receive divine life. The gospel message is the water of life, for the Holy Spirit uses the Word as living water to bring life to those dead in trespasses and sins and to refresh and satisfy thirsty souls who could never find true satisfaction in what this poor world has to offer. We may well be reminded of our Lord's words to the Samaritan woman: "Whosoever drinketh of the water that I shall give him shall never thirst; but [it] shall be in him a well [or fountain] of water springing up into everlasting life" (John 4:14).

Although not mentioned in Isaiah 55 by name, it is the Lord Jesus Himself to whom reference is made. He is God's "witness" who was sent into the world to be the Savior of sinners. For His advent Israel was taught to wait expectantly, but when He came in grace to save, they spurned and rejected His claims on them. Verse 5 clearly predicts the calling of the Gentiles in the wake of Israel's failure to recognize the Son of David in the person of the Lord Jesus Christ. Grace then went out to the nations who had hitherto been strangers to the covenants of promise (see Ephesians 2:12).

### Isaiah 55:6-13

Verse 6 says, "Seek ye the Lord while he may be found, call ye upon him while he is near." Men are responsible to turn to the Lord, and thus find Him as their deliverer. Scripture does not say "Seek" because He is hidden and has to be searched for, but because He calls for earnestness of purpose in turning to Him. Men must heed God's voice while He waits to be gracious, for if He is rejected too often, He may no longer strive with the hearts and consciences of those who harden themselves against Him.

"Let the wicked forsake his way," Isaiah said, by turning to God in true repentance and by acknowledging his utter helplessness. If he thus repudiates the thoughts of the natural heart, he may be assured that as he turns to the Lord, God waits to "abundantly pardon," for He delights to meet the trusting penitent in grace. How ready God is to take up those who turn to Him in confession of sin and who trust His love! Isaiah's own soul must have been stirred as he gave forth this proclamation.

What an encouragement it should be for every servant of Christ to remember that God has declared that His word will accomplish what He intended it to accomplish! Sometimes preachers become a little discouraged, feeling as if they were talking to a brazen wall, but God's Word will never return to Him void. So the prophetic Word will have a complete fulfillment in God's due time.

# ENCOURAGEMENT TO RIGHTEOUSNESS

C hapter 56 begins a portion of Isaiah that is of such an ex-
ceedingly practical nature that we may be inclined to look
over it carelessly and focus our attention on passages that
speak of great events that are to take place in the future and passages that record God's dealings with His people in the past. But
the great object of prophetic ministry is not simply to occupy God's
people with coming events, but also to impress their consciences so
that they will be motivated to live now in the light of the predicted
future. Such encouragement was needed in Israel of old and it is
needed just as much in this present church age.

Many people have an intellectual interest in prophecy and will
flock to hear a series of messages on the topic. Such messages are
very important, and fewer professed Christians would be lost to
orthodoxy if saved preachers gave more attention to the prophetic
Word. People are attracted to such systems as Seventh-Day Adventism and Jehovah's Witnesses because they are hungry to know
the future.

"The Voice of Prophecy" radio program appeals to so many because it attempts to open up the future. People are thrilled by the
messages they hear and then are swayed by announcers who suggest that listeners should take one of the sponsor's Bible-study
courses. The broadcasters never say over the air, "This is Seventh-
Day Adventist propaganda." They keep that fact hidden, and not
until the students are far along in their studies, do they see what the
subject really is. Thousands of people all over this country are swept
into Seventh-Day Adventism annually just because of their interest

in prophecy. If they had been properly instructed from the Scriptures earlier, they would not have been so susceptible.

Jehovah's Witnesses work on the same principle. They try to hide their real views while little by little they instruct listeners about their great program for the future. Knowledge of the truth concerning the second coming of the Lord, particularly in its two aspects, would preserve people from accepting the ridiculous teachings of the so-called Pastor Russell and Judge Rutherford. These early leaders of the Witnesses claimed that the Lord has already come, that He has been here since 1874, that He is showing Himself only to those of special spirituality, and that the millennium began in 1914 and we are already in it. Wonderful millennium, is it not? Who that has been well-instructed in clear Bible teaching would be carried away with such vagaries?

The need for clear teaching is evident. However, something of an intensely practical character should be incorporated with every prophetic message, lest its hearers be carried away with glowing pictures of the future and with the visions in Daniel and Revelation while being very careless and indifferent about their own lives.

Once when I was among several who were asked to give addresses on the second coming of the Lord, we were waiting for the meeting to begin and the speaker sitting beside me noticed someone entering the room. My colleague remarked, "There is one of the most godless men in our community and yet he is always on hand if anyone lectures on prophecy. He is so interested in finding out all about the future."

When I finished preaching, that godless man came up to me and said, "Brother, I'm glad to know that you hold the second coming. I hold that too."

I responded, "Do you? Does it hold you? It is one thing to hold the second coming; it is quite another thing to be held by it. The Word says, 'Every man that hath this hope in him purifieth himself, even as he is pure.' Does it have that effect on your heart and life?"

He said, "Who has been talking to you about me?"

Clearly something was wrong in that man's life. Many people are as guilty as he was. They want to know all about the horns of

Daniel and the beasts of Revelation, but they do not want anyone to probe their consciences.

In the book of Isaiah we find prophetic ministry in the proper proportion. Again and again after he gave pictures of the future, the prophet came down to the actual condition of the people at the time he was speaking. In chapter 56 he emphasized the importance of practical righteousness.

### Isaiah 56:1-5

Isaiah pointed out the importance of living in a godly way in the present and explained that in the future it will be as the nations learn to seek after righteousness that the blessing of the kingdom will be theirs. "Keep ye judgment, and do justice: for...salvation is near to come," he wrote. Because prophesied events are soon to take place, we should live *now* in the light of *then*.

Isaiah showed that no one will fail to receive the coming blessing if he is sincere in turning to God. Certain ones were prohibited from having any part in the services of the Lord in Old Testament times: a "eunuch" could not be a priest, and a "stranger" had no place in the congregation. But in the future, no matter what one's physical condition or nationality, if he earnestly desires to seek the Lord and do the will of God, his place in the kingdom will be the same as any other believer's. The kingdom will be open to everyone.

### Isaiah 56:6-7

Our Lord gave us the key to the practical application of this passage when He drove the money-changers out of the temple. "Is it not written," He asked, "My house shall be called of all nations the house of prayer? but ye have made it a den of thieves" (Mark 11:17). Isaiah 56:6-7 was God's word not only to Israel but also to the Gentiles: "Every one that keepeth the sabbath from polluting it, and taketh hold of my covenant; Even them will I bring to my holy mountain, and make them joyful in my house of prayer." God was assuring the Gentiles that they too would be blessed if they would seek His face and take hold of the Abrahamic covenant: "In thy seed shall all the nations of the earth be blessed" (Genesis 22:18). For Jews and Gentiles, as long as the Jewish dispensation lasted, the observance of the sabbath was an outward sign of allegiance to the Lord and recognition of His authority. The same will be true in the days of the great tribulation and on into the millennium.

Today we do not recognize the Jewish sabbath. Why? Because it was part of the law that was "done away" for us at Calvary. Christ "took [the law] out of the way, nailing it to his cross," and so the Word says, "Let no man therefore judge you in meat, or in drink, or in respect of an holyday...or of the sabbath days: Which are a shadow of things to come; but the body is of Christ" (Colossians 2:14-17). In Old Testament times the light of God was shining on Christ, and Christ cast His shadow before He came. One aspect of this shadow was the sabbath—rest at the end of a six-day period of labor. The Lord Jesus showed that He was the glorious fulfillment of that shadow when He said, "Come unto me, all ye that labour and are heavy laden, and I will give you rest" (Matthew 11:28).

Instead of the Jewish sabbath we now have the Lord's day. Some object to applying the term "the Lord's day" to the first day of the week and insist that in Revelation 1:10 ("I was in the Spirit on the Lord's day") "the Lord's day" means "the day of the Lord." We might take it for granted that the two expressions—"the day of the Lord" and "the Lord's day"—mean the same thing, and if the translation were exact, that might be so. But the term translated "Lord's" there is not in the possessive case; it is an adjective, so perhaps we should form an English adjective from the word "Lord," just as the adjective "Christian" was formed from the word "Christ." Then we would speak of the "Lordian" day just as we speak of a Christian spirit, a Christian church, a Christian atmosphere.

If we were looking at the furniture in the White House and the guard said either, "That is the president's chair," or "That is the chair of the president," the words would mean the same thing. But if the guard spoke of the "presidential chair," his words would mean something altogether different.

The adjective in Revelation 1:10 has been translated "lordly" by some people, but that term does not convey the same thought—a lordly day would be a day that is superior to other days. The first day of the week is "Lordian" because it reminds us of the resurrection of our blessed Lord from the dead.

The early Christians, who understood better than we do what some of the cryptic expressions in the book of Revelation mean, recognized Sunday as the "Lordian" day. Whether they used the Greek term *Kuriakos* or the Latin *Dominical*, they meant the same thing.

Down through the centuries the Christian church has voluntarily kept the "Lordian" day—and mark the word *voluntarily*—in memory of the resurrection of our Lord Jesus Christ. Its very voluntariness gives the observance value in the sight of the Lord. If a loving friend gives you a birthday present, its special value is that it shows his kindly thought. If you had written to say, "I am going to have a birthday and will expect a present from you," it would lose all its value. So when Seventh-day Adventists challenge us, "Show us a commandment in the New Testament telling us to observe the first day of the week," we say, "There is no commandment. We are under grace, not law." When they ask, "Then why do you observe it?" we answer, "Because of the gratitude in our hearts to the Lord Jesus, who rose from the dead on the first day of the week."

The first day of the week has been given a special place in the book of the Acts and in 1 Corinthians. That special place has been marked from the beginning of Christianity to the present time. Just as Israel of old showed their love for Jehovah and their reverence for His name by their recognition of the sabbath, we show our love and reverence for Christ by our observance of the Lord's day. Christians should be very careful about the use of the Lord's day and never allow themselves to treat it as a common day or to be indifferent to its claims.

Suppose the Lord's day were taken away from us. Suppose this country were to become like communist Russia, where every day was a secular day and no special privileges were allowed. How we would miss those privileges! And if we had neglected to observe the Lord's day in the past, how bitterly we would rue the memory of our carelessness!

For Israel of old, sabbath-keeping was absolutely legal, but we are told "that the righteousness of the law [is] fulfilled in us, who walk not after the flesh, but after the Spirit." In the body of Christ we are "dead to the law," yet every righteous requirement of the law will be met in us as we walk in the power of the Holy Spirit (Romans 8:4; 7:4).

# THE GOD OF THE AGES

### *Isaiah 57:1-2*

Chapter 57 begins with special comfort for those who, while seeking to be faithful to the Lord, suffer at the hands of others, even unto death. Isaiah wrote that such righteous ones "shall enter into peace."

There is always the danger of thinking that those who die before the fulfillment of promises have lost the promised blessings. The Thessalonians thought along those lines, for they were concerned about some of their number who had died before the second coming of Christ. To comfort them Paul wrote, "I would not have you to be ignorant, brethren, concerning them which are asleep, that ye sorrow not, even as others which have no hope" (1 Thessalonians 4:13). He went on to show that those who had died would have their part in the rapture and would share in the glory when the Lord Jesus Christ descended to take the kingdom.

In Israel in Isaiah's day some feared that their fellow believers who had died would not benefit from future blessings, that those who were put to death in times of persecution would miss so much and would not be here for the kingdom at all. People forgot that "the righteous is taken away from the evil to come" and that though he is taken away from here, God has provided something for him. Everyone will rest "in his uprightness" before God—he will have his place of blessing. There is no need to grieve for those who have gone before, for they are in the care of the blessed Lord; they have gone home to be with Him.

After offering comfort in 57:1-2, Isaiah went on to stress again
the importance of godliness.

### Isaiah 57:15

This is the only place in the King James version where the English word "eternity" occurs. The Hebrew word there so rendered is
found in many other places, but it is translated differently. For example Psalm 90:2 might have been rendered, "From eternity to eternity, Thou art God," but it reads, "From everlasting to everlasting,
thou art God." In Isaiah 57:15 the word "eternity" stands out clearly
and definitely.

"The high and lofty One that inhabiteth eternity" inhabits the
ages. God dwells in all the ages, for that is what eternity is: a succession of ages. Sometimes in trying to explain eternity, preachers
speak of it as an unchanging period, and in one sense that is true.
They quote Revelation 10:6, which says, "There should be time no
longer," and think of time as embracing the ages through which
mankind passes on earth. But according to this view, when men
leave this world or when the ages of time expire, suddenly there
will be no more ages—and that is not true. There were ages in the
past before this world came into existence, and there will be ages
and ages throughout the great day of God, the eternal day of God.

Throughout eternity one great age after another unfolds, revealing ever more wonderful things in connection with the wisdom,
grace, love, and power of our God, who inhabits all the ages. He is
the God of eternity, yet He says that He dwells in the heart of the
one "that is of a contrite and humble spirit" and "trembleth" at His
Word (Isaiah 57:15; 66:2).

Because prophetic truth is one thing that often makes men tremble,
it should be driven home to their consciences. Prophecy ought to
make people examine themselves before God, and the truth of the
coming of the Lord for His church surely ought to make every Christian heart ask, "Am I so living that I would be glad and ready to
welcome the Lord Jesus at any moment?" Many of us make plans
and have associations of which we would be ashamed if the Lord
should suddenly come.

Years ago, before World War I, Professor Stroeter, a well-known German teacher of prophecy, used to travel through the country to give lectures during which he used charts to unfold the dispensations. His lectures attracted the attention of the German emperor Kaiser Wilhelm, who in spite of his many idiosyncrasies was quite a Bible student and used to preach in the palace chapel on many occasions. The curious kaiser invited Professor Stroeter to his palace. The professor was taken into the library where he spread out his charts on the table, and the kaiser followed him as he pointed out various events in the dispensations until the second coming of the Lord. After a lengthy conversation on that subject, the kaiser said, "Do I understand you aright? Do you mean to say that Jesus Christ is coming back literally and that when He returns, all the kingdoms of the world are going to be destroyed and He will set up His kingdom on the ruins of them all?"

Professor Stroeter said, "Exactly, Your Majesty, exactly."

"Oh, no," said the kaiser, "I can't have that! Why that would interfere with all my plans!"

The kaiser's plans were interfered with anyway, but there are many others who, if honest, would also have to say, "The coming of the Lord would interfere with all my plans." However, if we are walking with God as we should be, if our hearts are contrite and we tremble at the Word, we will welcome the return of the blessed Lord. Isaiah impressed on the people of his day the importance of this spirit of waiting and readiness.

The chapter, and the section on the rejection of the Messiah (Isaiah 49–57), end as has previously been noted by repeating, "There is no peace, saith my God, to the wicked."

# ISAIAH 58

# FASTS AND SABBATHS PLEASING TO GOD

This chapter begins the last section of the last part of the book of Isaiah. In this section (chapters 58–66), which consists mostly of visions of the coming glory, the prophet told us the wonderful things that will take place at the coming of the Lord. But since God was still concerned with practical things, Isaiah also called the nation to heed His voice and get right with God so that judgment might be averted and blessing ensured.

### Isaiah 58:1-12

Isaiah 58 commences with the words, "Cry aloud, spare not....Shew my people their transgression," and then goes on to emphasize the sins of Israel. The great sin that the prophet stressed was their reliance on mere formal observance of ritual and ceremony when their hearts were far from God.

Isaiah dealt particularly with the question of fasting. There was a definite fast required in Leviticus 23, but in addition to this the Jews punctiliously observed a great number of other fasts. They boasted of their abstention from food and drink at certain hours and on certain days, and took it for granted that this pleased God. But He commended those who fasted from far different motives; He was pleased with those who fasted so that their minds, taken away from other things, might be able to give attention to the things of the Spirit. So there is reproof, not praise, for merely formal fasts.

The Jews used the fast to cover up other offenses, just as some today say, "If I give some money to charity, that makes up for other things." These people are misusing the text that says, "Charity shall cover the multitude of sins" (1 Peter 4:8). That is not what the Lord meant at all.

Israel fasted "for strife and debate," but in His fasts God called on the Jews to recognize the importance of self-judgment. The fasts gave them opportunity to come before Him, to meditate on His dealings with them, to meditate on their own failures and sins, to confess them, and then to demonstrate the compassion of God by giving practical assistance to those who were needy. In other words, what God had in mind was not simply that they should deny themselves a little food, but that they should be constantly living lives of self-denial, dividing what God gave them with others, and sharing with the poor.

The Lord Jesus is in full harmony with Isaiah; the same Spirit spoke through both. The Lord Jesus said, "Moreover when ye fast, be not...of a sad countenance...that thou appear not unto men to fast" (Matthew 6:16-18). In the case of the fasting Jews of Isaiah's day, people would look at any one of them and say, "That's a godly man—he hasn't eaten anything since three o'clock yesterday afternoon." But the Lord said in effect, "When you fast, keep it a secret between you and God, and be cheerful among the people." The Lord promised, both through Isaiah and Matthew, that if there is real self-judgment and self-denial, He will reward those who fast. And what a reward there is!

### Isaiah 58:13-14

Here Isaiah returned to the subject of the sabbath. As has already been noted, the Christian voluntarily observes the first day of the week instead of the sabbath. The sabbath was a covenant sign for the Jew, but the blessing attending their appointed day may be ours abundantly.

It is all-important to realize that men mean more to God than forms and ceremonies, even those of His own devising. "The sabbath was made for man, and not man for the sabbath" (Mark 2:27).

He who is "Lord...of the sabbath" is pleased when we use His holy day to bless and help those in trouble and to relieve the afflicted as far as we are able to do so. Truly to keep the first day of the week holy to the Lord is to use it for rest, worship, and ministry to others. To think only of relaxation and spend this day in pleasure-seeking is to fail to use it for the purpose God had in mind in preserving its privileges for us. One Christian said, "I get so weary with all the burdens of business throughout the week that I must have rest and exercise on Sunday. So I use the Lord's day afternoons for visiting in the hospital and seeking to comfort and help the friendless." He returned to work on Monday refreshed and ready for another six days of toil.

Let us cherish our privileges and neither despise them, nor hedge them about with legal enactments for which there is no Biblical authorization.

# ADDERS' EGGS AND SPIDERS' WEBS

I saiah 59 is a very solemn passage in which God calls the people to repentance, but then gives wonderful promises of blessings that are to be bestowed under Messiah's reign.

### Isaiah 59:1-8

When the people sought the Lord, He did not seem to answer or hear because there was unjudged sin that needed to be dealt with. The psalmist had written long before, "If I regard iniquity in my heart, the Lord will not hear me" (Psalm 66:18), and now Isaiah was saying to the people, "Your iniquities have separated between you and your God, and your sins have hid his face from you, that he will not hear." They were covering up their sins and hoping to please God by observance of outward form and attendance to ritual, but He said of them, "They hatch cockatrice' [the adder's] eggs, and weave the spider's web....Their feet run to evil." Part of this portion of Scripture is taken up in Romans 3, where Paul wrote, "Their feet are swift to shed blood" (3:15).

The Isaiah passage pictures a people who professedly were the Lord's. They went along with all the outward forms of religion—attending the services of the temple, offering their sacrifices, fasting before men—and hoped thus to provide a righteousness that would be satisfactory to God. But He said that their preaching and teaching were false and therefore poisonous, so that "he that eateth of their eggs dieth." The false teaching brought eternal ruin to those who accepted it.

Such pretenders, Scripture says, "weave the spider's web," but "their webs shall not become garments, neither shall they cover themselves with their works." The spider's web is beautiful, but it is just foam. It proceeds from the spider itself, and many preachers, like spiders, spin webs out of their own heads instead of bringing messages from the Word of God. And people who try to clothe themselves with their own righteousness are like those who might try to make garments out of spiders' webs. It has been tried, but found impossible.

What a contrast there is between a spider's web and a silkworm's cocoon, though both come out of the creature itself! The cocoon furnishes the material that makes beautiful and lasting clothing for kings and princes while the web is a bit of fluff that soon disappears.

Some years ago there came to Los Angeles a so-called human fly. It was announced that on a given day he would climb up the facade of one of the tall department stores in that great metropolis, and long before the appointed time thousands of eager spectators gathered to watch him perform the seemingly impossible feat. Slowly and carefully he mounted the building, now clinging to a window ledge, later to a jutting brick, then to a cornice. Higher and higher he went, against apparently insurmountable difficulties. When at last he was nearing the top, he felt around to right and left and above his head for something firm enough to support his weight so that he could go further up, and soon he seemed to spy what looked like a gray bit of stone or discolored brick protruding from the smooth wall. He reached for the gray object, but it was just beyond him, so he ventured all on a spring-like movement, grasped the protrusion and, before the horrified eyes of the spectators, fell to the ground and was broken to pieces. In his dead hand was found a spider's web! What he evidently mistook for solid stone or brick turned out to be nothing but dried froth.

How sad it is that many are trying to climb to Heaven by their own efforts and will find at last that they have ventured all on a spider's web and so are lost forever! Christ, and Christ alone, can save. His gospel is unfailing and peace-giving. It is neither an adder's egg nor a spider's web, but the "power of God unto salvation to every one that believeth" (Romans 1:16).

"The garments of salvation," "the best robe," "the robe of right-eousness" are provided by God Himself, through the death of His Son, to all who admit their guilt and trust His grace. "He gives the garment of praise for the spirit of heaviness" (Isaiah 61:3,10; Luke 15:22). How futile are human efforts to fit the ungodly for the di-vine Presence! Spiders' webs will not avail to cover the moral na-kedness of Christ-rejecting sinners.

Think again of the difference between a web and the cocoon of a silkworm. This marvelous little being spins a thread of such strength that it is readily woven into cloth of the utmost beauty and made up into garments of glory. But the silkworm must die so that the floss may be woven. Is it too much to say that here we have in nature more than a hint of Him who in the depth of His humiliation could exclaim, "I am a worm and no man" (Psalm 22:6), and who gave His life that we might be clothed in glory?

### Isaiah 59:16-21

In this passage we find a prophecy of the omniscient One giving deliverance. Yes, "the Redeemer shall come"! All hope for guilty man, for Israel, and for the Gentile nations is in the Man at God's right hand. It is the Lord Jesus Christ who was spoken of here. There was no intercessor, no deliverer, so "his [own] arm brought salva-tion." He came in grace the first time to settle the sin question on the cross and He is coming again to bring in the glory. It is for His coming the people wait.

# GOD GLORIFIED IN THE REMNANT

A rise, shine; for thy light is come, and the glory of the Lord is risen upon thee." Thus the chapter begins and after that call the prophet goes on to show why the light is needed. The reason is the darkness.

"Darkness shall cover the earth," but restored Israel will be brought to the forefront of God's plan and blessing for the whole earth. The kings of the earth will bow down to them; the nations that once persecuted Israel will come and acknowledge that God is with them and will seek to enter into fellowship and communion with them. This prophecy is to be taken literally. God will deal thus with His people Israel and will bring the nations that once antagonized and persecuted them into blessed harmony with them in the last days.

Verse 20 assures the remnant, "The Lord shall be thine everlasting light, and the days of thy mourning shall be ended." What a day that will be for Israel after the long centuries of suffering! This promise applies throughout the millennial glory and on into the eternal state, for God will never give up this people. They will always have a separate place in His mind, as the church will always have hers. God has various groups, each with its own place in His plans, but all alike are redeemed by the precious blood of the Lord Jesus Christ.

# ISAIAH 61

# THE ANOINTED
# SERVANT

In chapter 61 we find the passage to which the Lord Jesus turned when He stood up to read in the synagogue in Nazareth (see Luke 4).

The Gospel of Luke tells us that after Christ was baptized in the Jordan and tempted in the wilderness, He traveled through Judea to Galilee and entered the city of Nazareth, where He had been brought up. Then "as his custom was, he went into the synagogue on the sabbath day" (4:16), and that is very significant.

As already remarked, we have little information about the early life of the Lord Jesus Christ, and men have tried to imagine what might have taken place between His childhood and His thirtieth year, when John baptized Him and He consecrated Himself to His great work. For example some years ago a Russian author indulged his vain imagination and wrote a book purporting to be a translation of a record (supposedly found in a Lama monastery in Tibet) of the journeys of Issah, who was to be identified with Jesus. The book said that Issah came from Palestine through India to Tibet, where among the lamas he learned secrets that enabled him to perform miracles; eventually, according to the narrative, Issah went back to Palestine to begin his work, but was suspected by the Jewish leaders of trying to subvert their teaching and at last was crucified. At first many readers hailed the record found in the monastery as a wonderful discovery that might add to our knowledge of Jesus, but finally the author confessed that the record was a fabrication and that the book was not a translation but a story written by himself.

Whereas people try to imagine what Jesus did during those early years, Scripture says that when some of His townspeople came to hear Him, they said, "Is not this the carpenter?" (Mark 6:3) They had known Him as a carpenter and, according to Luke, as a man whose custom it was to go to the synagogue on the sabbath day. The fact that the Lord attended the synagogue services shows that He submitted Himself not only to the laws divinely given, but also to the ordinary regulations of the rabbis. Apparently He also took part in the services, for the rabbis evidently recognized His right to go up to the dais and read from the Holy Scriptures.

### *Isaiah 61:1-3*

In that synagogue at Nazareth the book of the prophet Isaiah was handed to Him and He read 61:1-2a:

> The Spirit of the Lord God is upon me; because the Lord hath anointed me to preach good tidings unto the meek; he hath sent me to bind up the brokenhearted, to proclaim liberty to the captives, and the opening of the prison to them that are bound; To proclaim the acceptable year of the Lord, . . .

He read to the middle of the sentence and then closed the book. Why did He not go on with Isaiah's words about "the day of vengeance"? The reason is that His first and second comings are intimately linked together in Isaiah 61, and Christ only wanted to read the part that tells what He came to do at His first coming. He stopped at what we would call a comma and put the whole dispensation in which you and I live into that comma, for it is still "the acceptable year of the Lord." As Paul wrote, "Now is the accepted time;...now is the day of salvation" (2 Corinthians 6:2).

We have not moved one iota beyond that point where Jesus closed the book. The rest of the sentence carries us on into the day of the Lord after this present age has come to an end. Speaking metaphorically, when He comes again, He will open that book once more, and the rest of the passage will all be fulfilled to the letter. Christ came the first time "to proclaim the acceptable year of the Lord," and He is coming again to declare "the day of vengeance of our

God." When God destroys those who are in red-handed opposition to Himself and those who are the enemies of His people Israel, it will be the time of the Lord's vengeance.

Then our Lord will bring consolation and blessing to those who have suffered so much; He will "comfort all that mourn." This glorious prophecy will be fulfilled literally for all Israel after the judgments of the day of the Lord have been poured out on the wicked. He will give them "beauty for ashes, the oil of joy for mourning, the garment of praise for the spirit of heaviness." The figurative language here suggests a funeral and a wedding, for at funeral services Jews put ashes on their heads and mourn and lament, and at weddings they wear bridal wreaths and beautiful garments. When Israel's long centuries of mourning are over, she will enter into the joyousness of her marriage to Jehovah and all the blessings attendant to it.

In the meantime each individual soul who trusts in Christ may enjoy the blessings here enumerated. Christ gives the wedding garments of praise in place of the funereal attire of the mourner. Those who have sought in vain for peace and satisfaction in the world and whose fondest hopes have failed may find fullness of joy and satisfaction in Christ, who is glorified in all His saints and who finds His joy in their eternal blessing.

Our English word "comfort" is from two Latin roots, *con,* "to be with," and *fortis,* "strong." Literally "comfort" means "to strengthen by companionship." A child facing a long walk on a dark night may be filled with fear, but if his father goes with him and takes his hand as they walk together through the gloom of the night, all fear is gone. Likewise God would have us realize the blessed reality of His presence with us as we face the trials and griefs to which all are exposed while passing through the changing scenes of time and sense. It is His presence that will keep the heart in peace and free the spirit from fear. Nothing but what His love allows can come into the lives of those who know the Lord; and what He allows, He will use for our blessing as we go through it all in subjection to His holy will and in implicit dependence on Himself.

The world is now in the parenthesis between the sixty-ninth and seventieth weeks of Daniel—that is, between the beginning of "the acceptable year of the Lord" and "the day of vengeance of our God"

(Isaiah 61:2; Luke 4:19). Other passages contain the same thought—that "the day of vengeance" has not yet come. First Peter 3:10-12 is an example. The apostle, quoting Psalm 34:12-16, said that those who would "see good days" should "seek peace" because "the face of the Lord is against them that do evil"—but he stopped there; he did not go on to speak of retribution because "the day of salvation" is not over. The psalmist, looking beyond this age of grace, had said that those who desire to "see good" should "seek peace" because "the face of the Lord is against them that do evil, *to cut off the remembrance of them from the earth*" (italics added).

Today God is against wickedness and corruption, but the time has not yet come when He will cut off the memory of evil-doers from the earth. We can still preach the gospel of the grace of God to the worst sinners, for God is still offering His salvation to the vilest of them.

### *Isaiah 61:6,10-11*

We are living in this period between the first coming of Christ and His second coming. The first coming had to do with the fulfillment of the early prophecies, and the second coming has to do with the fulfillment of the later prophecies, which are linked up with the restoration of Israel and the blessing of the whole Gentile world. When restored, Israel will be a nation of priests who will go into God's presence on behalf of all the other peoples of the earth. Israel will also be God's messengers to them.

How much the wonderful promises in Isaiah 61 should mean to God's earthly people, and how interested we should be in them! While our blessings are heavenly and theirs, to a great extent, will be earthly, their salvation is the same as ours. "He hath clothed me," they will be able to sing in that day, "with the garments of salvation, he hath covered me with the robe of [His] righteousness." Can we not say the same today? At one time we were trying to piece together a covering for ourselves with the filthy rags of our own unrighteousness, but we have cast that to one side, for God has provided a robe of righteousness for men and women who have no righteousness of their own. In that coming day Israel will learn this precious truth and they will rejoice in the righteousness of God that will be bestowed on them.

In reference to that future day, the prophet Jeremiah said, "This is his name whereby he shall be called, [*Jehovah-tsidkenu*] the Lord our righteousness." And then a little further on in his prophecy, speaking of Jerusalem and her restoration, he said, "This is the name wherewith she shall be called, [*Jehovah-tsidkenu*] the Lord our righteousness" (23:6; 33:16). The day will come when Jerusalem will recognize that she has no righteousness of her own, and the people of Israel will find their righteousness in the Lord God Himself. What a blessed thing it is to learn that lesson even now!

So many people have never learned it. Years ago I met a man who had been a pastor of a church for thirteen years, but didn't know how sinners were saved. Then he attended some lectures on Romans 1–3 that made him realize that he had no righteousness of his own and that God had a righteousness for men who had none of their own. He said, "Oh, I can't tell you what that meant to me! I found out that if I just trusted the Lord Jesus Christ, I was made the righteousness of God in Him."

Many people try to build up a righteousness of their own—and poor Israel is still doing that. The apostle Paul said, "They being ignorant of God's righteousness, and going about to establish their own righteousness, have not submitted themselves unto the righteousness of God" (Romans 10:3). In that coming day everything will be changed. Their eyes will be opened and, seeing in Christ their Redeemer, they will be able to sing with gladness, "He hath clothed me with the garments of salvation, he hath covered me with the robe of righteousness."

# PROCLAMATION TO THE REMNANT

How precious the proclamation is! "Behold, the Lord hath proclaimed unto the end of the world, Say ye to the daughter of Zion, Behold, thy salvation cometh; behold, his reward is with him, and his work before him. And they shall call them, The holy people, The redeemed of the Lord: and thou shalt be called, Sought out, A city not forsaken." These words, even today, would naturally comfort the heart of every redeemed Hebrew as he thinks of his people still wandering in the darkness of unbelief and as he prays for the peace of Jerusalem and looks forward to the day when the Gentiles will see the righteousness of Israel.

Isaiah prophesied that one day Jerusalem would be "a crown of glory in the hand of the Lord." At the very beginning of the tribulation period a remnant will be called out to carry this message to all their brethren and to intercede for them. The remnant will look to God to hasten the day when Jerusalem will be "a royal diadem," for the prophet wrote, "Ye that make mention of the Lord, keep not silence, And give him no rest, till he establish, and till he make Jerusalem a praise in the earth."

The Lord in His grace will restore Israel to Himself and bring them into all the blessing of the Abrahamic covenant. The day will come when all this will be fulfilled. The prophet's words hardly need comment—they are so clear, so plain.

# THE WARRIOR FROM EDOM

### Isaiah 63:1-6

In this majestic passage we are given a glimpse of Israel's Redeemer with His garments red from the blood of their enemies. He is coming from the east, from whence Israel's enemies generally came; Syria was pressing on Israel at the time Isaiah was writing, and Assyria would come through the lands of Moab and Edom.

Looking ahead to the last days and the time of Israel's great trial during the tribulation period, Isaiah gave us this wonderful picture of the Lord coming toward the land as a conqueror driving His foes before Him and taking vengeance on Israel's adversaries in order to redeem His chosen people. It is He who will be Israel's final deliverer from their foes, just as He came Himself to die for their sins on the cross. "I looked, and there was none to help," He said. "Therefore mine own arm brought salvation."

We need to remember that the salvation that is the subject of 63:1-6 is from Israel's enemies, and that the deliverance from every power that has oppressed them brings Israel into blessing in their land. Verse 3 has often been misapplied in that the words "I have trodden the winepress alone" have been used in connection with the agony that our blessed Lord went through in Gethsemane's garden. There is a sense in which one might think of Him as "treading the winepress" in Gethsemane, but the context in Isaiah concerns judgment on the foes of Israel. The whole passage links with Revelation 14:15-20; in the scene depicted there the vine of the earth is fully ripe and is cast into the great wine press of the wrath of God.

In the East when the grapes were gathered and thrown into the wine press, the young men would take off some of their garments, step barefoot into the winefat, tread on the fruit, and become spattered with the red blood of the grapes. It was always a time of great rejoicing and the Greeks observed it as a festival in honor of the god Dionysus (the Roman Bacchus). Among the Hebrews too there was an annual treading of the grapes, so they would understand the symbolism of God putting into the wine press all who had sought to destroy His chosen people, then looking for someone to tread that wine press, and finding no one to help, treading the wine press alone.

In Revelation 19 we read of a wonderful vision of the Lord descending from Heaven. He is pictured as a mighty warrior astride a great white charger and He is "clothed with a vesture dipped in blood" (19:13). That blood, His own precious blood which would naturally have stained His vesture as it poured from the wound in His side, is the symbol of His love for His people. But in Isaiah 63 His garments are stained with the blood of His enemies, for the prophet was speaking of "the day of vengeance of our God" (61:2). When that day comes, all those who are found to be in opposition to God will be destroyed.

If you look carefully into the prophetic Word and the book of Revelation, you will see that there are two different kinds of judgment on the world at the time of the Lord's second advent: the warrior judgment and what might be called the sessional judgment. These two aspects of one judgment may be distinguished, but not separated.

The warrior judgment is represented by the treading of the wine press. The nations will gather together and the Lord will descend in power from Heaven and destroy all found in definite, open opposition to God and His people. "The Lord Jesus shall be revealed...in flaming fire taking vengeance on them that know not God, and that obey not the gospel" (2 Thessalonians 1:7-8)—that is, those who have had every opportunity to be saved and have turned away and taken the place of enemies of God and His people.

The sessional judgment is described in Matthew 25:31-32: "When the Son of man shall come in his glory, and all the holy angels with him, then shall he sit upon the throne of his glory: And before him shall be gathered all nations: and he shall separate them one from another, as a shepherd divideth his sheep from the goats." There He is not dealing with the nations that have been maintaining a vicious attitude toward God and His people; He is judging nations according to their attitude toward the messengers of Israel who have gone through the world proclaiming the coming of the King.

Many of those nations have never before heard the gospel. They are judged according to their reception of those who have at last brought them the good news, but their salvation depends on whether or not they now have faith in Christ. The "sheep" in Matthew 25 are not saved because of what they have done for the Lord's people, and the others are not lost because of their bad treatment of them. But if there is real faith, it has been revealed by good treatment of the Lord's messengers; and where there is no faith, the lack has been evidenced by indifference to those witnesses.

Judgment is always according to works and so Christ speaks of the nations' treatment of those who have carried the message: "Inasmuch as ye have done it unto one of the least of these my brethren, ye have done it unto me....Inasmuch as ye did it not to one of the least of these [my brethren], ye did it not to me" (Matthew 25:40,45).

## Isaiah 63:7-9

This precious portion applies to God's care for all His people in any dispensation. Isaiah was primarily dealing with the suffering saints of the last days as well as those who might be suffering for the truth's sake in his own day, but the passage may be taken to heart by God's afflicted people in any time because He is always concerned about His children. One beautiful translation of 1 Peter 5:7 reads, "Casting all your care upon Him, for it matters to God about you." Isaiah's prophecy agrees, for it says, "In all their affliction he was afflicted, and the angel of his presence saved them."

God is not an unmoved spectator as He gazes on the sufferings of His saints, for His heart of compassion goes out to every one of them. If He permits the suffering to go on, He is waiting like a refiner of silver to purge His people from all dross so that His own countenance may be fully disclosed in them. What a comfort a passage like Isaiah 63:7-9 will be to the remnant of Israel in the last days when they are being tormented by the beast and the false prophet. The King for whom those Israelites are waiting will come, their sufferings will end, and they will enter into all the blessings that He has predicted.

# THE HEART-CRY OF THE REMNANT

In chapter 64 we find what might be called the heart-cry of the remnant in the last days. While the prayer is suitable for any of God's people who feel the need of divine intervention at a time of trial or affliction, in actual prophetic application the prayer reveals the hearts of the people of Israel as they will be when they are suffering under the beast and the antichrist. They cry to the Lord, "Oh that thou wouldest rend the heavens, that thou wouldest come down"!

Not knowing "what [God] hath prepared for him that waiteth for him" (64:4), they pray for Him to intervene. The apostle Paul quoted the Septuagint version of this verse in 1 Corinthians 2:9: "Eye hath not seen, nor ear heard...the things which God hath prepared for them that love him." Then he immediately added in verse 10, "But God hath revealed them unto us by his Spirit"—a revelation of which Isaiah knew nothing, for God had reserved it for a future day. Disregarding the added revelation, people often quote verse 9 as if the words stand today as they did in Isaiah's time. They forget that Paul went on to say, "But God hath revealed them unto us by his Spirit....But we have the mind of Christ" (2:10,16).

How fitting will be the cry for help on the lips and from the hearts of the desperate remnant of Israel in the last days. Seeing no help in man, they will call on God to intervene as the nations are gathering together as prophesied in Zechariah 14:2; there we read that God said, "I will gather all nations against Jerusalem to battle." The remnant will see that ominous assemblage and cry out in effect, "O God, will You not deal with these nations Yourself? Will You not give the deliverance for which our hearts crave?"

Realizing that if God is to act on their behalf they must take their rightful place in His presence, the remnant will take that place of confession, self-judgment, and repentance. Since they know that God has so often shown patience to Israel, they will not indulge in self-justification. Isaiah foresaw that rather than asking God to intervene because of their merits or their faithfulness, they will say, "Our iniquities, like the wind, have taken us away." In other words, "We understand why we and our fathers have been suffering throughout the centuries."

"We are all as an unclean thing," they will confess, "and all our righteousnesses are as filthy rags." The reference is not merely to filth resulting from dragging garments in the streets, but also to contamination from within. The remnant will acknowledge that they are unclean because of the corruption of their hearts, but they will turn to God because He has specifically promised, "He that covereth his sins shall not prosper: but whoso confesseth and forsaketh them shall have mercy" (Proverbs 28:13).

David cried out in Psalm 25:11, "O Lord, pardon mine iniquity; for it is *great*" (italics added). If he had been like some of us, he might have said, "O Lord, pardon mine iniquity, for after all it is not very great. I didn't really mean to do wrong. I failed, but I am sorry. I did not mean to be bad." That is the way people talk today, but David said his iniquity was "great." Only a great God can pardon great iniquity.

The remnant are similarly depicted in Isaiah 64 as not trying to justify themselves or cover up their sins, but making full and frank confession of their sin and iniquity and acknowledging that they have no righteousness of their own to plead. All their own imagined righteousnesses are but contaminated rags in the sight of a holy God. When we take this attitude, we too may count on God to answer our heart-cries with blessing.

# NEW HEAVENS AND A NEW EARTH

*Isaiah 65:1-7*

Here God explained—if I may use the word, since God does not have to explain—why judgments had fallen on the people. Meeting the remnant in grace, He made clear to them that He had punished Israel because of the sins—some open, some hidden—the people had committed. They had set aside His own holy law and had brought in the practices of the heathen round about them. Dwelling "among the graves" for an Israelite was an unclean thing and it illustrates for us the uncleanness into which the people had lapsed. Because of all this, God's face was averted; He could not deal with them as He would otherwise have desired.

Today the Lord still calls His people to separation from the evils around them. "Come out from among them, and be ye separate, saith the Lord, and touch not the unclean thing" (2 Corinthians 6:17). "Be ye not unequally yoked together with unbelievers: for what fellowship...hath light with darkness? And what concord hath Christ with Belial? or what part hath he that believeth with an infidel?" (6:14-15) His call is to complete separation from fellowship with those who are walking in avowed disobedience to His Word. To those who heed His call, the Lord almighty immediately says, "And I will be a Father unto you" (6:18).

Surely God is the Father of all His people, but He is not always free to be a Father "unto" us in the way He desires. Just as any loving father delights to give his children one demonstration after another of his loving interest in them, God our Father wants to show his concern for us. That is implied in being a Father "unto" us. He is the Father of every one of us, but if we walk in disobedience, the holiness of His own nature hinders Him from doing the things that His heart yearns to do.

Israel of old had become contaminated by their association with the heathen nations around them, for "evil communications corrupt good manners" (1 Corinthians 15:33). And the reason that God calls on His people to come out from the world and be separate today is that they cannot go on with the world and maintain their Christian testimony.

People who think that the way to win the world is to be "hail-fellow-well-met" with them, are like the young boys who caught two baby linnets and meant to teach them to sing. The boys had a canary who sang very beautifully and they thought that the linnets, never having heard other linnets chirping, would learn to sing by listening to the canary's sweet notes. So the youngsters made little cages for the linnets and put one on each side of the canary's cage. For some time there were no results and then one day the boys said, "Oh, listen. Our canary is cheeping like a linnet!" Instead of the linnets' learning the canary's long-cherished lovely song, the canary learned to chirp like the linnets. The results are similar when God's people have fellowship with the ungodly. Instead of the unbelievers' learning the ways of Christ, the children of God soon follow the ways of the ungodly.

The principle of separation certainly applies to the marriage relationship, for Scripture has made it very clear that a child of God and an unsaved person should not contemplate marriage. An old Puritan quaintly said, "If you are a child of God and you marry a child of the devil, you can expect to have trouble with your father-in-law."

Then too, many a Christian hoping to make more money has gone into partnership with an unsaved man in some business venture and has soon found that he has put himself under an unequal yoke. The unsaved man may feel perfectly free to do things that a conscientious Christian cannot do. The Christian either has to take a stand against his partner or go along with him, and if he does the latter, he will lose his Christian testimony.

The results are the same when Christians associate themselves with all kinds of secret societies. Two Scripture verses should keep us out of them all. The first is John 18:20, where it is recorded that Jesus said, "In secret have I said nothing." We can conclude from this that He could not have been a member of any secret society or lodge. The second verse, already referred to, is 2 Corinthians 6:14, where Paul said, "Be ye not unequally yoked together with unbelievers." The apostle was alluding to the Old Testament directive that stated, "Thou shalt not plow with an ox and an ass [yoked] together" (Deuteronomy 22:10). The ox was a clean beast and could be offered to God as a sacrifice, but the ass was looked on as ceremonially unclean; the two were not to be yoked together. In secret orders there are both saved and unsaved people, and if we want to have a bright testimony for Christ, we must walk apart from that unequal yoke.

When Israel in disobedience mingled with the Gentile nations and began to participate in their evil practices, God had to pour out His judgment. But when His people turned back to Him and confessed their sins, God in His infinite grace was ready to give deliverance.

### Isaiah 65:8-16

God compared His people to the one large cluster of grapes left in a vineyard. This cluster might seem to be good for nothing, yet God said, "Destroy it not; for a blessing is in it." He will not destroy His people completely, for He will take out of them a nucleus for the coming restored nation of the last days.

He will make "the valley of Achor" a means of blessing to them. That valley was the place where Achan and his family were stoned to death because of their sin when the people first entered the land. The word *Achor* ("trouble") speaks to us of the troubles that we bring on ourselves by our own willfulness. God can work in grace to make those very sorrows an eventual means of blessing for us, just as God will use all of Israel's past waywardness to correct and bless them. As Jeremiah said, "Thine own wickedness shall correct thee, and thy backslidings shall reprove thee" (2:19). God overrules even the failures of His people when they turn their hearts to Him and thus learn lessons that can be of help and blessing to them in the days to come.

### *Isaiah 65:17-25*

There are promises for the obedient in the land, and Isaiah foresaw the fulfillment of those promises. We are given only a glimpse of the new heavens and the new earth, for God gave no description or instruction as to what will take place at the time of fulfillment. He simply said, "I create new heavens and a new earth," and then He added, "I create Jerusalem a rejoicing." Just as surely as He will bring in new heavens and a new earth, He will fulfill every promise made to Israel and make Jerusalem a center of joy and blessing to the whole world.

There is also a warning for the rebellious, because when God called they did not answer and when He spoke they did not hear. In contrast, God's promise regarding His people in millennial days is, "Before they call, I will answer; and while they are yet speaking, I will hear" (65:12,24). This is a promise that abides. God's people can claim it today because it has to do with that which is spiritual. Blessed "with all spiritual blessings in heavenly places in Christ" (Ephesians 1:3), we can appropriate and act on everything spiritual in the Old Testament, but we are not at liberty to claim the promises that have to do simply with temporal things.

The last three chapters of Isaiah are intimately linked together. Chapter 64 presents the prayer of the remnant and chapter 65 gives the Lord's answer. His indignation had been aroused against many because of their idolatry, their hypocrisy, and the abominations they had committed, but He assured the faithful remnant, those who had truly turned to Him, that He was about to intervene on their behalf. Chapter 66 again brings before us the rebellious part of the nation and the sins that had moved God's heart and caused Him to turn His people over to the power of the enemy; and again for those who had trusted in Him there is assurance that not one of His promises would fail. He would bring the remnant into fullness of blessing.

We have compared the Old Testament prophets to a man looking at a mountain range. At first he sees one great peak and then the clouds rise and he sees a higher peak beyond. In Isaiah 65–66 the prophet lifts his telescope a little higher and, looking beyond that second great peak, gets a momentary glimpse of what God has in store for His people for all eternity: the new heavens and the new earth.

Referring to these two chapters, the apostle Peter spoke of the passing of the day of the Lord and the bringing in of the day of God, when everything that man has been building up through the years will collapse and the heavens and the earth will melt with fervent heat. "Nevertheless," the apostle said, "we, according to his promise, look for new heavens and a new earth, wherein dwelleth righteousness" (2 Peter 3:12-13). That promise was given through Isaiah in chapters 65 and 66 and nowhere else.

In the book of Revelation we read of John's vision in which he also looked beyond the millennial glory and said, "I saw a new heaven and a new earth...and there was no more sea...for the former things are passed away" (21:1-4). He foresaw the absolute perfection of the new creation and described the blessedness of the redeemed in the eternal state.

We are not told in so many words that the eternal abode of the redeemed of Israel who have been with the Lord in millennial glory will be on the new earth, but as we consider what is said in Isaiah 65–66, we naturally come to that conclusion. The church, the body of Christ, with all the Old Testament saints and those who will have died down through the centuries right up to the beginning of the millennium, will have their place in the new heavens. Scripture seems to suggest the distinction: the church as the bride and the friends of the bridegroom will be the heavenly saints with Christ above, while renewed Israel will be with Christ here on the new earth. There will be a wonderful intimate link between the two groups; heaven and earth will, as it were, be as one.

When that day comes, we may all find that we have had very imperfect conceptions of things. We have the guidance of the Spirit of God in the direct statements He has given us, but we are prone to misunderstand. If before the Lord came the first time, a scholar had tried to get clearly in mind the succession of events in connection with that advent, perhaps he would have been much perplexed and confused and probably he would have come to very wrong conclusions. But when the Lord actually came and one event after another took place as predicted, it was seen that the prophets had foretold all these things, though they might have misunderstood the order of their occurrence. The prophets themselves, we are told, searched their own writings for "what, or what manner of time the Spirit of Christ which was in them did signify, when it testified beforehand the sufferings of Christ, and the glory that should follow" (1 Peter 1:11).

While studying Isaiah the prophet, did you ever think that Isaiah studied Isaiah the prophet? After he had written what God gave him by divine inspiration, he sat down, pondered over his own scrolls, and studied carefully what God had inspired him to write. He was trying to see clearly the succession of events, the order in which things would take place, and then it was revealed to him, as to the other prophets, that it was not yet the time for a full understanding, that much of the fulfillment was reserved for a future day. "It was revealed, that not unto themselves, but unto us they did minister." Not unto themselves, but unto us they made these things known. And now their prophecies are opened up by "the Holy Ghost sent down from heaven" (1 Peter 1:10-12). So of those things which are still unfulfilled, still in the future, we should not speak too dogmatically.

# THE LORD WORSHIPED

I n this last chapter of Isaiah God again stressed the failures of His people, and then closed by telling them of the wonderful conditions that will prevail in the days of the kingdom and giving them another glimpse of the new heavens and the new earth. "It shall come to pass that from one new moon to another, and from one sabbath to another, shall all flesh come to worship before me, saith the Lord."

As we read Isaiah 66, we will see that it gathers together the threads of God's ways of holiness and grace.

## *Isaiah 66:1-12*

Once more Isaiah emphasized that He who fills Heaven and earth cannot be confined to any house here, yet He deigns to dwell in the hearts of the lowly and the contrite. "Thus saith the Lord," the prophet wrote, "The heaven is my throne, and the earth is my footstool....But to this man will I look, even to him that is poor and of a contrite spirit, and trembleth at my word" (66:1-2; also see 57:15). Those who walk carefully, fearing lest they might act contrary to the Word of God, and those who tremble at the Word may have the assurance that He will take care of them. God is looking not for great ability or wonderful eloquence on the part of His servants, but for hearts subject to His truth, and when He finds that, He will intervene on behalf of His people.

Those who are merely formalists, who do not know the realities of spiritual things, will look down on the contrite ones, think of them with contempt, perhaps call them fanatics, and accuse them of all kinds of folly. Therefore the Lord said to the humble, "Your brethren that hated you, that cast you out for my name's sake, said, Let the Lord be glorified: but he shall appear to your joy, and they shall be ashamed." Note that God said it was for His name's sake. Although the remnant of Israel will be despised by those who do not take their place of repentance before God, the Lord will appear to the glory of that remnant and their enemies will be ashamed.

The offerings of those who have only a facade of pleasing God are an offense. "They have chosen their own ways," but God will do His choosing too and "bring their fears upon them" because when He called and spoke, they did not answer or hear. Instead they did evil and chose what did not please Him (66:3-4; also see 65:12). Those who heard His voice heard the promise, "Before they call, I will answer; and while they are yet speaking, I will hear" (65:24).

Jehovah said to His people that He would give them peace "like a river" (66:12), and speaking as God the Creator, He said there would be "peace to him that is far off, and to him that is near" (57:19). But He also expressed twice the solemn certainty that "there is no peace...unto the wicked" (48:22; 57:21).

### Isaiah 66:13-24

In 66:13 we read that the Lord promised His people, "As one whom his mother comforteth, so will I comfort you; and ye shall be comforted in Jerusalem." Other verses such as 40:1 and 61:2 also speak of comfort (compare chapters 40 and 61 for God's plan and design for His people). The Hebrew word translated "comfort" in 66:13 is derived from a root meaning "to sigh." Thus the verse might be rendered, "As one whom his mother sighs with, so will I sigh with you." We know how a loving mother shares the sufferings of her child; taking the little one in her arms, she sighs with him as he sobs out his grief on her bosom.

In a similar way God sympathizes with us in our trials. When the Israelites were in bondage in Egypt He said, "I have surely seen the affliction of my people....I know their sorrows; And I am come down to deliver them" (Exodus 3:7-8), and He is ever the same in His concern for His afflicted children. His great heart of love is moved with compassion as He beholds the ravages that sin has made and the sufferings that it has caused for all mankind. Yet we often think of Him as a stern Judge rather than a tender, loving Father and thus are slow to refer our troubles to Him.

Although the Lord will comfort His servants, Isaiah said that He will show "his indignation toward his enemies" and rebuke them "with flames of fire." The whole book of Revelation bears witness to this. Isaiah added that "the slain of the Lord shall be many" and those who are in the place of blessing will from time to time see the dead bodies of the slain, "for their worm shall not die, neither shall their fire be quenched." The Lord Jesus quoted the words from 66:24 again and again when referring to the final state of the eternally lost: "Their worm dieth not, and the fire is not quenched" (Mark 9:43-48).

So death and the curse will be present in the millennium, but Scripture seems to indicate that death will come only to those who definitely rebel against the King, who sin against Him. In Isaiah 65:20-22 we read of the longevity of the people in the millennium: "As the days of a tree are the days of my people." If a man dies at one hundred years of age, he will be counted as a child. However, the transgressors will be "consumed."

And so the book of Isaiah ends with God's holiness and glory revealed and magnified as well as His divine compassions.

> Here Thy bright character is known,
>     Nor dare a creature guess
> Which of His glories brightest shone—
>     The justice or the grace.

Someday all of Isaiah's prophecies will be fulfilled. Meanwhile it is as true for us as for God's ancient people that

> Upon the wings of every hour
> We read Thy patience still.

"Blessing, and honour, and glory, and power, be unto him that sitteth upon the throne, and unto the Lamb for ever and ever" (Revelation 5:13).

# AUTHOR BIOGRAPHY

HENRY ALLAN IRONSIDE, one of this century's greatest preachers, was born in Toronto, Canada, on October 14, 1876. He lived his life by faith; his needs at crucial moments were met in the most remarkable ways.

Though his classes stopped with grammar school, his fondness for reading and an incredibly retentive memory put learning to use. His scholarship was well recognized in academic circles with Wheaton College awarding an honorary Litt.D. in 1930 and Bob Jones University an honorary D.D. in 1942. Dr. Ironside was also appointed to the boards of numerous Bible institutes, seminaries, and Christian organizations.

"HAI" lived to preach and he did so widely throughout the United States and abroad. E. Schuyler English, in his biography of Ironside, revealed that during 1948, the year HAI was 72, and in spite of failing eyesight, he "gave 569 addresses, besides participating in many other ways." In his eighteen years at Chicago's Moody Memorial Church, his only pastorate, every Sunday but two had at least one profession of faith in Christ.

H. A. Ironside went to be with the Lord on January 15, 1951. Throughout his ministry, he authored expositions on 51 books of the Bible and through the great clarity of his messages led hundreds of thousands, worldwide, to a knowledge of God's Word. His words are as fresh and meaningful today as when first preached.

The official biography of Dr. Ironside, *H. A. Ironside: Ordained of the Lord*, is available from the publisher.

# THE WRITTEN MINISTRY OF H. A. IRONSIDE

## *Expositions*

Joshua
Ezra
Nehemiah
Esther
Psalms (1-41 only)
Proverbs
Song of Solomon
Isaiah
Jeremiah
Lamentations
Ezekiel
Daniel
The Minor Prophets
Matthew
Mark
Luke
John

Acts
Romans
1 & 2 Corinthians
Galatians
Ephesians
Philippians
Colossians
1 & 2 Thessalonians
1 & 2 Timothy
Titus
Philemon
Hebrews
James
1 & 2 Peter
1,2, & 3 John
Jude
Revelation

## *Doctrinal Works*

Baptism
Death and Afterward
Eternal Security of the Believer
Holiness: The False and
   the True
The Holy Trinity

Letters to a Roman Catholic
   Priest
The Levitical Offerings
Not Wrath But Rapture
Wrongly Dividing the Word
   of Truth

## *Historical Works*

The Four Hundred Silent Years
A Historical Sketch of the Brethren Movement

Other works by the author are brought back into print from time to time. All of this material is available from your local Christian bookstore or from the publisher.

# LOIZEAUX

### A Heritage of Ministry . . .

Paul and Timothy Loizeaux began their printing and publishing activities in the farming community of Vinton, Iowa, in 1876. Their tools were rudimentary: a hand press, several fonts of loose type, ink, and a small supply of paper. There was certainly no dream of a thriving commercial enterprise. It was merely the means of supplying the literature needs for their own ministries, with the hope that the Lord would grant a wider circulation. It wasn't a business; it was a ministry.

### Our Foundation Is the Word of God

We stand without embarrassment on the great fundamentals of the faith: the inspiration and authority of Scripture, the deity and spotless humanity of our Lord Jesus Christ, His atoning sacrifice and resurrection, the indwelling of the Holy Spirit, the unity of the church, the second coming of the Lord, and the eternal destinies of the saved and lost.

### Our Mission Is to Help People Understand God's Word

We are not in the entertainment business. We only publish books and computer software we believe will be of genuine help to God's people, both through the faithful exposition of Scripture and practical application of its principles to contemporary need.

Faithfulness to the Word and consistency in what we publish have been hallmarks of Loizeaux through four generations. And that means when you see the name Loizeaux on the outside, you can trust what is on the inside. That is our promise to the Lord...and to you.

If Paul and Timothy were to visit us today they would still recognize the work they began in 1876. Because some very important ings haven't changed at all...this is still a ministry.